# EPISTEMOLOGY
## Theory of Knowledge

by Archie J. Bahm

ISBN: 0-911714-21-9
LCN : 94-90614

To

Elisa

Books by the Author

Ethics: The Science of Oughtness

Ethics as a Behavioral Science

What Makes Acts Right?

Why Be Moral?

Philosophy: An Introduction

Metaphysics: An Introduction

The World's Living Religions

Comparative Philosophy

The Philosopher's World Model

# CONTENTS

page

# CONTENTS

# INTRODUCTION

Although to be a person is to know, and thus nothing is more common to persons than knowing, the nature of knowledge is so complex that few persons, that is, few knowers, know much about it. Inquiry into the nature of knowledge, commonly called "Theory of Knowledge" or "Epistemology," is a science originating in the question, "What is knowledge?" It involves many other questions, such as "What is truth?" "What is certainty?" and their opposites, such as "What is ignorance?" "What is falsity?" "What is doubt?" Each of these questions involves still others, such as "What is consciousness?" "What is awareness?" "What is intuition?" "What is inference?" "What are sensation, perception, conception, memory, imagination, anticipation, thinking, mind, desire, frustration, satisfaction, questioning, problem-solving, feeling, emotion, interest, purpose, language, communication, agreement, dreaming, idealizing, liking, disliking, wanting, hoping, fearing, contentment, and apathy?" As inquiry proceeds more deeply into the foregoing questions, other questions occur. Not only does each new specialty in science and technology tend to uncover problems concerning its own specialized knowing, but persons specializing in inquiring into the foregoing questions often develop, or overlap with, other inquiries such as philosophy of science, philosophy of language, philosophy of values, philosophy of education (learning, or acquiring knowledge), psychology, and logic.

Knowing does not occur in isolation from its causes and conditions, so a full inquiry into the nature of knowledge should include inquiry into all of the conditions and causes of knowledge, including varieties of causes of different kinds of knowledge. Thus sciences concerned with the nature of mind, the nervous system, the human body, and all of the conditions for these things become involved. Epistemology is indebted to not only psychology, physiology, biology, chemistry, and physics as providing some understanding of the conditions of knowing, but also to astronomy, geology, ecology, economics, history, anthropology, sociology, political science, ethics, philosophy of religion, and their many subsciences for information about details essential to a full understanding of the nature of knowledge.

Not all of the questions involved in understanding the nature of knowledge can be explored here. Selection is necessary. Some that seem most basic are examined. Since this work is designed as a companion work to my *Metaphysics: An Introduction*, questions about the nature of existence are not focal points of our inquiry, even though they cannot be avoided entirely. My experience with teaching courses in metaphysics and epistemology, and with many textbooks designed for such courses, has been that, when inquiring into the nature of existence, persons often want to solve problems about the nature of knowledge first, and when inquiring into the nature of knowledge, want to solve problems about the nature of existence first. My annoyance with such misdirected textbooks has led me to try to keep attention focused on questions concerning the nature of existence in my *Metaphysics: An Introduction* and on questions concerning the nature of experience in the present work. Since experience exists, all that exists in experience is also a subject for metaphysical inquiry. Since the only existence that a metaphysician can know is existence as experienced, all existence that is experienced is also a subject for epistemological inquiry. Epistemology and metaphysics interdepend because the subjects of their inquiry interdepend.

Choosing the most appropriate term for our inquiry is complicated by conflicting traditions of emphases. Although we keep the traditional terms, "epistemology" and "theory of knowledge," as appropriate, the word "experience," which has a more inclusive connotation, is chosen as even more appropriate and adequate for our purposes. "Experience" includes both knowledge and ignorance, consciousness, subconsciousness and unconsciousness, and many known and as-yet-unknown conditions (and perhaps some unknowable conditions) essential to the nature of knowing. How much neuro-chemical processes in a brain function as part of a person's experience, how much socio-economic-political influences on a person function as part of one's experience, and how much one's hereditary, foetal, natal, and infantile conditionings continue to participate in constituting one's current experiences, are questions relevant to, even basic to, fuller understanding of the nature of knowledge. The importance of diet, drugs, changes in atmospheric pressure, X-rays and all other rays passing through a body, environmental pollution, nervous tension, and aging need to be recognized as factors influencing knowing.

Experience involves both structure and process. Too often theories of knowledge emphasize the nature of knowledge as primarily structural. But knowing is a part of living and living is essentially processual. To ignore either the structural or processual aspects of knowledge is to be seriously deficient. Despite my intention to give equal emphasis to structure and process in what follows, I expect to find structural aspects of experience easier to describe and fear that processual aspects will lack adequate treatment.[1]

# One
# INTUITION

## A. WHAT IS INTUITION?

Intuition is immediacy of apprehension. Whenever awareness of appearance occurs and nothing intervenes between the awareness and what appears in awareness, that awareness intuits that appearance. Intuition is the name we give to the way awareness apprehends when awareness apprehends appearance directly. No intuiting exists apart from awareness. No awareness exists without intuiting.

Despite its simplicity, something more can be said about intuiting. Six characteristics of its nature may be distinguished: immediacy of apprehension, transparency, omnipresence, kinds, variability, and limits.

**1. Immediacy of apprehension.** Four factors in immediacy of apprehension may be differentiated: apprehension, immediacy, appearance, and intuiter.

**a. Apprehension.** To apprehend is to grasp. Intuition apprehends, not as a hand grasps a glass, but in the sense that what is apprehended occurs in awareness all at once. When two or more objects are intuited, apprehending comprehends them together. When they are apprehended all at once, they exist together in that apprehension. When only one object appears, such as a sky cloudless from horizon to horizon, unity is present without togetherness unless the object is so extended that the extension implies plurality. Apprehending thus involves objective unity, whether the object itself appears unified or whether many objects are unified.

Intuition may apprehend more than one object, with or without pattern, more than one event, with or without pattern, more than one quality, with or without pattern, more than one dimension, more than one feeling, more than one idea, more than one distinction, etc. Intuition may apprehend, and thus unite, not only formal, spatial, temporal, processual, sensory, emotional, paradoxical and frustrating kinds of pluralities but may also unify them in a single gestalt. As a unity, an intuition functions as a simple, nonrelational, nondimensional whole. As a unity of pluralities, an intuition may be not only relational and dimensional but also multi-relational and multidimensional. Since all knowledge, no matter how complex and variegated, presupposes apprehension by intuition, intuition must be capable of apprehending all of the complexity that can be grasped in any single act of attention. If the mind can intuitively unify successive acts of attention, then the apprehensive capacity of intuition extends to include them.

**b. Immediacy.** Immediacy involves an additional kind of unity, namely, the unity of awareness and appearance, or the unity of apprehending and of what is being apprehended. Since nothing separates awareness and appearance, we must recognize a unity, if not identity. Immediacy is not mediacy, or the apprehension of appearance through or by means of something else. The fact that intuiting involves immediacy does not prevent it, including awareness, appearance and immediacy of apprehension, from being caused or mediated. Experience is caused, and consciousness is conditioned, and intuition occurs as a result of its causes and conditions. Such mediating factors in the production of intuition do not destroy its immediacy but contribute causally to it.

**c. Appearance.** What intuition apprehends is appearance. Without appearance there is no intuition. Without intuition there is no appearance. Appearance is a kind of being, even if very temporary. The being of the appearance is apprehended in intuition. Intuition exists both as an act of apprehending and as apprehending the being of the appearing which is intuited.[1]

What appears has been called a "datum." A datum is something "given." But apprehending, in grasping, also "takes." So intuiting involves both something being given and something being taken. What appears is given; but if there is any incapacity of an intuiter to apprehend what is given, then less than what is given is taken, or if an intuiter always brings some contribution of his own to the way in which he apprehends, then he adds something to what is taken. When what is given is modified by the way in which it is taken, the appearance is a product of both factors causing what is given and what is taken.

d. **Intuiter.** Intuiting is not self-acting but is an action of an actor or intuiter. Although a fully adequate epistemology will involve also a fully adequate understanding of the nature of persons as agents, including as intuiters, no theory of the nature of an intuiter will be developed in this chapter. How a person functions as an agent, whether through one's body, through one's brain, through one's mind, or through one's self, calls for further explanation. But that intuiting involves an intuiting agency seems beyond doubt.[2]

**2. Transparency.** Intuiting objects does not normally call attention to itself as intuition. Just as we see through glasses or through our eyes without seeing the glasses or our eyes, so we intuit objects without intuiting our intuiting of objects. Although intuitive self-reflection is possible, the intuiting of an intuition has its own transparency. Transparency, in this sense, seems to be a universal characteristic of intuiting.

**3. Omnipresence.** All knowing involves intuition. When any knowledge is mediated, it can be known actually only when such mediation terminates in some moment of immediacy. As long as potential knowledge fails to reach awareness in which its appearance is being intuited, it remains potential and not actual. When a person infers, that person does not escape intuiting but engages in a more complex intuition, usually in a series of intuitings.

**4. Kinds.** Although all intuitings are alike in consisting in the immediacy with which awareness apprehends appearance, the many kinds of appearances constitute many kinds of intuitings. Since intuition is an ingredient in all knowing, it exists in as many kinds as there are kinds of knowing. The Library of Congress system of classification, or any complete classification of kinds of knowledge that develops, is also a classification of the kinds of intuition in the sense that intuition is present in all such kinds. Kinds of intuition will be examined further below when kinds of inference are explored.

5. **Variability.** Not only does intuition vary enough to participate as an essential condition of all kinds of actual knowing, but also relative to the four factors mentioned above, when immediacy of apprehension was examined.

a. **Apprehension.** Intuitions vary in complexity, in magnitude and in intensity depending on the simplicity or complexity of their contents, on the length or shortness of pulses of attention, and on the vitality or debility of the intuiter while intuiting.

b. **Immediacy.** Although in one sense immediacy is immediacy and there are no degrees of it, in another sense intuiting apprehends appearances and appearances often embody apparent mediacies. Most of our waking, or at least working, life is occupied with beliefs about apparently real things. When a person is aware that that person's knowledge is caused or mediated, intuiting such knowledge embodies both immediacy and mediacy. An intuition does not cease to be constituted by its immediacy when it becomes constituted also by awareness of mediacy. Apparent mediacy itself is immediately apprehended.

Some intuitings are primarily contemplative and exist without awareness of mediacy. Some intuitings are primarily practical and fully occupied with mediacy. When a person is overwhelmed by fear or motivated by zeal, one's intuitings are suffused with mediacy.

c. **Appearance.** In addition to seemingly endless varieties of appearance, appearances vary relative to how much of what is apprehended is "given" and how much is "taken." Some kinds of apprehendings are primarily received in the sense that they accept passively what is given to be grasped. Some kinds of apprehendings are primarily restrictive, or constructive, in the sense that they accept only what the apprehender is willing, or able, to accept. Experiences differ regarding the differing amounts of contributions from memory, creative imagination, subconscious fears or manias, bodily health, disabilities or tensions, and conscious or unconscious purposes in influencing what is apprehended. A person cannot intuit when capacity to intuit is lacking, since capacities are constant conditions of what and how what is taken is given. Variations in environmental and physiological causes of what is given in appearance also condition intuitions. A person cannot intuit as given what the causes of what is given do not supply.[3]

d. **Intuiter.** The agency and power employed in acts of intuiting depends upon and varies with the health, vitality, tonicity, alertness, and interest of the intuiter. These vary from moment to moment, day to day, and during different stages in life, in each person, as well as varying in these ways in different persons. Past experiences, habits and skills, and development of differing degrees of facility (exemplified in speedy typewriting, auto racing, or mental calculation) all influence the ways intuiters intuit.

6. **Limits.** Acts of intuition have limits of many kinds. Not only are they limited by limits in what can be caused to appear and in capacities to apprehend, but also by limits in the nature of acts of attending. Although persons awake from morning until night may seem to be conscious continuously, evidence from eye jerks, for example, indicate that awareness is interrupted repeatedly. Persons are not aware that they are not aware when they are not aware, so they are not aware of such interruptions. How long does awareness endure between interruptions? The length varies, but within limits. When a person is alert, present awareness tends to endure longer than when the person is drowsy. Some indication of length may be observed by watching another person read. Although to the reader a line appears continuous and awareness of it appears uninterrupted as reading continues, one can observe that another person's eyes stop, then move, then stop, then move, etc., as long as the reading continues. Each stop suggests an act of apprehension. Each move, of which a person is unaware, suggests an instant of unawareness. If intuiting occurs

only during an act of attentive apprehending involving only a few seconds' awareness, it does not last long. If so, and if there can be no knowledge without awareness and intuiting, then all knowledge itself exists actually only during instants lasting only a few seconds at a time.

The roles of brain and mind in maintaining thought processes over long periods of time and how they function relative to actualizing knowledge during acts of attention require more intensive study. Is one's ability to intuit limited to each such act of attending or can a mind retain a consciousness intuiting more than one act of attention? We know that more than one object or event can be intuited in a single act of attention. Normal acts include two or three, and with effort, a person can attend to four or five lines or tones. Attentive geniuses attain seven distinct objects of attention in a single act. But our problem has to do not merely with limits within an act but with how many acts, if more than one, can be apprehended in a single intuition. I do not know the answer. But knowledge appears to involve some continuity of consciousness provided by mind and brain over and above that occurring recurrently in moments of attentive awareness. Not all acts of thought are tied to eye jerks or to visual perception; but all acts of thought seem to occur in successive acts of attending nevertheless. What are the durational limits of intuitings I am unable to say; but that intuitings have durational limits of variably short lengths seems probable.[4]


# B. PRESENCE

Each act of intuiting apprehends a moment of consciousness here called "presence." The term "presence" is chosen because it connotes (or is intended to connote) both what is present in awareness and the present being of what is in awareness. Presence consists of what is being apprehended as present, not of what is absent, and presence consists of what is being apprehended as temporally present, not of what is before or after the intuited present. All that is apprehended in an act of intuition, whether spatial or temporal, complex or simple, formed or formless, static or flowing, value or valueless, is intuited in presence, or in "a presence" when one act of intuiting is distinguished from another or others.

Efforts to understand the nature of presence encounter the question: "How long is the present?" The intuited present is not "a specious present," as claimed by those inferring that "the present," mathematically conceived, is an infinitesimal duration, or a temporal instant without duration, somehow dividing past from future. External guestimates of how long in clock time an act of intuition lasts suggest lengths equal to the pauses between eye jerks when one is reading. Such pauses can be observed to varying length, especially when physiological conditions are conductive to alertness or drowsiness, although maximum observed lengths are measured in fractions of seconds. External evidences of gaps between moments of awareness exist, and these convince us that consciousness is actually discontinuousness in the sense that gaps of unawareness intervene between pulses of awareness. But, since we are not aware of what we are not aware, such awareness itself does not appear in presence. Yet, evidently each presence endures for a very short time and for only a very short time. The duration of each such presence is a genuinely present duration and is intuited as such. Whether a presence is occupied by apparently continuous duration or by apparently rapidly occurring events or by both is a matter of particular observation.

The present section is devoted to examining some additional characteristics of presence. I do not propose that each of these characteristics is self-evidently obvious in each presence, since the universal characteristics of consciousness normally tend to function transparently. I am proposing that, if and when a person stops to examine each moment of awareness, these characteristics can be observed to be present. Each will appear as present to an observer only if and when attention is focused upon it. But each is presumed to exist as a characteristic (either an inherent condition or a normally recurring characteristic) constantly. Each proposed characteristic is presented as an hypothesis for further testing. Readers may test each hypothesis for themselves.

1. **Universal conditions of presence.** In addition to the characteristics of intuition outlined in Section A, the following eight characteristics, or pairs of characteristics, are proposed as universal conditions of presence.

a. **Awareness-appearance.** Awareness and appearance interdepend. Awareness is awareness of appearance. Appearance is appearance in awareness. Without awareness there is no appearance. Without appearance there is no awareness. Awareness and appearance are equally essential ingredients in consciousness. In functioning as complementary opposites they constitute a polarity with a range of variations such that at times consciousness may be experienced as more fully constituted by awareness and at other times by appearance. When a person is alert with expectation, awareness may be experienced as awaiting appearance; when one feels impressed by appearance, it may be experienced as overwhelming.

b. **Subject-object.** What appears is always an object of awareness. Appearance is always objective. All objects appear or are apparent. Awareness, i.e., awaring, involves an awarer (intuiter). An awarer, or agency that is aware, is called a "subject." Awareness is always subjective. All subjects are aware. (Persons, which are more than subjects, function as subjects whenever they are aware of objects actually.) Just as awareness and appearance involve each other, so subjects and objects involve each other. All objects are objects for subjects and all subjects are aware of objects. Like other polarities universally characterizing consciousness, this one also occurs in variations ranging from consciousness occupied primarily with objects to consciousness occupied primarily with a subject.

c. **Clarity and vagueness.** Appearance may be clear or vague, distinct or indistinct. When appearance is clear and distinct, awareness is clear and distinct. When appearance is vague or indistinct, awareness is vague or indistinct. The vagueness-clarity polarity omnipresently characterizes experience either transparently or by calling attention to itself during sudden shifts from more to less (as with zoom lenses) or when desire for more of one or the other has been aroused.

d. **Objectivity-objects.** What appears as object may be, and tends to be, both a field containing all of the objects and all of the objects contained therein. The field as a whole is continuous; the particular objects appear within the continuum, and two or more of them may appear to form a pattern. The whole of a moment of awareness is continuous both spatially and temporally, so much so that there may be no explicit awareness of (attention to) the continuity as such. The objects are contents of awareness, but so is the continuity, the wholeness, the unity. Failing to find a better word for such continuity, I choose the generalized word "objectivity." All that appears is objective, both the continuity and the objects contained therein, and any apparent relations or forms or patterns, etc., of objects, which are also objects.

There is a kind of polarity between objectivity and objects, for the parts (objects) are not the whole (objectivity), and vice versa, and yet each interdepends with the other, the parts (objects) participating in the objectivity (whole) and objectivity inclusive of all of its parts, even at times consisting entirely of parts apparently (i.e., at times may be filled with objects). At times, consciousness may be occupied by a single object. The bothness of objects and objectivity is intuited (or at least intuitable). Again, we may observe the complementary oppositeness of objectivity-objects as constituting a universal characteristic of conscious experience, and the principle of polarity basic[5] to organic epistemology as observably present in the foundations of experience.

e. **Attention-inattention.** What appears as object is attended to when we are aware of it. Awareness involves attention, either particularized, i.e., of some object or objects, or generalized, as when contemplating objectivity or the whole field of appearance. When attention is focused on a particular object, other objects, and objectivity, receive less attention or even no attention. Some speak of objects receiving less attention or little attention as constituting a "fringe" of consciousness. Since attention may shift from one object to another, or from an object to objectivity, what appears without being focused upon may then become focused upon. Sometimes attention is alert and rapidly shifting to many objects; sometimes it is relaxed and indifferently attentive. At times, especially when one is drowsy or sleepy, attention may diminish to barest awareness, to inattention, and cease altogether (terminating awareness). Variations in attentiveness and inattentiveness range to extremes, and exist together as focus and fringe, inderdependently as complementary opposites.

f. **Intention-unintended.** Attention involves intention. To attend is to intend. To attend is to intend to attend. To attend is to be aware of apparent objects. To attend is to be aware of apparent objects as they are, i.e., as they appear. To attend involves a willingness to be aware of apparent objects as they are, i.e., as they appear; this means a willingness to be objective. Attention involves an intention to apprehend objectively. "Objectivity," now meaning a willingness to be aware of things as they are, is itself a subjective attitude inherent in intention to attend. Objectivity, in this sense, is a natural universal characteristic of consciousness. Explanation of how such a natural universal becomes modified or substituted by prejudicial willfulness will be postponed here.

Just as some of many apparent objects remain unattended, so inattention is accompanied by unintention or absence of intention to attend to them. When both attended and unattended objects appear in awareness, then both intentional attention and unintentional inattention occur together, and ranges of variations from intense intention to complete unintending exemplify their complementary oppositeness as constituting another polar category of presence. As one of the variations, a person may intend to be inattentive, either to a particular object, to a fringe, or even to all objects when opting contemplative attention to objectivity. A person may intend to be unattending when trying to fall asleep.

g. **Present-absent**. Appearance appears as present. Absence of appearance does not appear; appearance of absence does. Appearance of absence is not a universal characteristic of presence, but absence does appear at times, and a person may focus attention on such apparent absence. Appearance of absence is observed in processing when something not appearing appears and when something appearing ceases to appear. Appearance of absence involves awareness of absence, but absence of appearance does not.

When absence appears in any presence, what appears as absent and what appears as present appear together in an intuition. Although opposites, appearances of what is present and of what is absent complement each other in completing the appearances apprehended together in an act of intuition. Although presence is normally more fully occupied by awareness of what appears as present, variations range from awareness involving no appearance of absence to awareness involving appearance of complete absence. Visual awareness of sudden darkness when lights go out may be intuited as total absence. A yogin may achieve awareness of total absence momentarily, but achievement of complete absence of appearance (the ultimate aim of yoga is awareness without appearance) is unlikely until *mukti*, death.

h. **Present-passing**. All that appears appears as present. Awareness apprehends appearance intuitively, so all that awareness apprehends is apprehended as present. Sometimes what appears appears as passing. Such apparent passing appears as present. Thus, such apparent passing appears as both passing and present. What is present remains the same from beginning to end of such present because, as intuited, it is intuited all at once, or all together, with any beginning and ending in that togetherness. The present, as present, does not appear as passing. But any awareness of passing, in any moment of awareness, is apprehended as all-at-once in that present. Passing involves a before, an occurrence, and an after. When passing is apprehended, such before, occurrence and after, are intuited together in a present. The presence of apparent passing within an apparently unpassing present involves a unity of opposites complementing each other in constituting the appearances apprehended.

Contemplative attention to present appearance as present, without awareness of apparent passage, seems common enough (in my experience) so that I do not claim that awareness of apparent passing is a universal characteristic of presence, even though passing does seem to be present as a transparent universal characteristic. Consciousness conceived as awareness extending beyond single pulses of awareness tends to include, if not passing within a pulse, at least passing from pulse to pulse, although even awareness of this passing may be suspended for some time. But, sooner or later, awareness of passing occurs. Awareness of passing is a normal characteristic of consciousness. Maximums of duration of awareness without appearance of passing doubtless will be determined, although again, like world records broken by athletes, such maximums may then be extended.

An additional reason why awareness of the presentness of what appears is a universal condition of presence and awareness of passing is less common is that the awarer, or subject of awareness, also remains the same during each intuition. The intuiter does not pass during an intuition, and functions in awareness of appearance, even if only vaguely, as present and not as passing. Hence there is a present subject-object polarity contributing stability to presence.

Sometimes presence is much more fully occupied with awareness of passing than at others. Doubtless, some people experience awareness of passing more often (and more vividly) than others. I suspect that increased physiological activity (more common in youth than in the aged) with stronger or more rapid cardiac pulsation may produce increased awareness of rhythmic passage as a fringe appearance, although such increased activity is often accompanied also by increased alertness and longer attention span.

2. **Recurrent contents of presence:** Other contents of consciousness that appear in presence either universally (as some claim) or recurrently may be noted:

a. **Feeling:** some claim that feeling tone, positive (enjoyed), negative (suffered), or neutral, is omnipresent even when transparent.

b. **Attitude:** like-dislike, approve-disapprove, accept-reject.

c. **Desire:** and satisfaction-frustration, enthusiasm-apathy, contentment-disturbance.

d. **Will:** willfulness, willingness, will-lessness.

e. **Sensation:** single, multiple, multisensory; pain and pleasure, hunger and thirst, etc.

f. **Forms:** patterns, relations (same-different, simple-complex, spaces, times).

g. **Concepts:** kinds, universals: pure, mixed with sensations, feelings, desires, etc.

h. **Emotion:** fear, hope, sorrow, elation, love, pride.

i. **Inference:** immediate and mediated of many kinds.

j. **All other:** All other ingredients in experience and kinds of knowledge appear in presence, including questions, doubts, commitments, and convictions. My view is that the ways in which these occur in presence are so interinvolved with physical, biological, physiological, psychological, and social conditions of consciousness and with inferences about them that examination of their nature and contributions to knowledge should be postponed until the nature of their causal conditions have been examined.

3. **Two dimensions of presence:** Two dimensions, appearing as pairs of polar opposites, past-future and subject-object, constitute four additional characteristics not only recurring constantly but almost universally present. They normally involve inferences also and are mentioned here in preparation for more detailed treatment later.

a. **Past.** Awareness of what appears as past, immediate or remote, is a natural constituent of presence. Such appearance participates in after-images, awareness of passing, memory, knowledge of what has passed and is past, and some generalizations about continuing beings and processes.

**b. Future.** Awareness of what appears as future is a natural ingredient in presence. Such appearance participates in anticipation, hope, expectation, planning, problem-solving efforts, and in some generalizations about continuing beings and processes.

**c. Subject.** Awareness of what appears as subject is a universal characteristic of presence, as previously indicated. Awareness of self, which not only functions as subject, intuiter, apprehender, but also as intender, willer, agent, as a presence-transcending continuant, as a rememberer, knower, anticipator, and as judge and enjoyer and sufferer, is a recurringly common characteristic of presence, often including awareness of past and future as opposing directions of a past-future dimension.

**d. Objects.** Awareness of what appears as objective, or objects, is a universal characteristic of presence, as previously noted. Awareness of objects, not merely as appearances, or as apparent objects, but as apparently real objects is a normally recurrent characteristic of presence. The apparently real existence of many objects, perhaps of most objects, involves appearing as having an existence and nature that is independent, either wholly or partly, of their being apprehended. Most of our beliefs and knowledge are about apparently real objects, including those constituting our environment, natural and artificial, momentary and enduring, near and far, and other persons, our bodies, and our minds when we seek to examine them. Although the subject-object dimension is essential to intuition and presence, apparent extensions of its directions to include self and the world constitute a self-world dimension as a normally recurring characteristic of presence.

The foregoing four directions are directions which inferences take in expanding and transcending presence. The four directions may be used in classifying kinds of knowledge. But when we learn that intricately interdependent, dialectically developing, multidisciplinary kinds of knowledge are needed for adequate understanding of existence as experienced, such a classification must be considered elementary.

## C. EXPANDING PRESENCE

Although each act of intuition apprehends a presence, absence of awareness of any gaps between such acts yields an appearance (awareness-appearance) of continuity of two or more presences. Although attention to objects is inherent in the awareness constituting a presence, absence of awareness of gaps results in apparent continuity of attention during more than one presence. Such an extension of attention is included in what is called "attention span." This problem of apparent continuity of supposedly different intuitions raises the question of whether or not intuition itself somehow undergoes expansion and consequently whether or not presence itself, supposedly constituted of a single act of intuition, expands to include several acts of intuition which somehow appear as continuous and hence, in some sense, also as an enlarged single, or unified, act of intuiting.

How long may such apparent continuity extend as conscious continuity of awareness-appearance? The question is important for epistemology because, if the ultimate locus of certainty is the self-evidential apparent so-ness of what is apprehended in intuition, then any extension of such intuition results in an extension of the ultimate locus of certainty. In itself, a particular act of intuition need not be experienced in terms of a certainty-uncertainty problem, for what is involved in immediacy of apprehension is both a willingness to be objective (to apprehend objects which appear as they appear) and absence of doubt about what is apprehended. This does not constitute certainty after doubt, but merely the kind of ultimate locus of the immediacy of apprehension in terms of which any settlement of doubt may seem justified. Certainty involves intuition. How much claim to certainty is warranted depends in part upon how long a duration of presence, or how long a duration of attention span, can be included in either a single act of intuition or in a unified, or unbroken unity of, intuitive apprehension.

Since, at some time at least, we are unaware of gaps in awareness from waking to sleeping, the seeming certainty attributed to naive realistic attitudes may seem justified by this kind of reasoning about presence. Yet evidence for limitations of attention spans must also be recognized as casting doubt about the reliability of intuition when intuitive apprehension seems to extend beyond such limitations. As long as awareness of appearance continues apparently without gaps or discontinuity, no evidence, or reason for doubting such continuity, appears. Any claim, or theory claiming, that discontinuity occurs actually even though without appearing, must itself be justified by appealing to some theory involving just the kind of intuition now being questioned. That is, a theory claiming that expanded continuity of presence is dubious even though no doubt arises within the intuited expansion (i.e., no evidence appears during the intuited expansion) seems to be claiming either that it is founded on a more reliable theory of intuition (and presence), or that we must infer that even the most intuitively certain apprehensions (apprehensions in which no doubt occurs) are unreliable, or that some other source of certainty (such as theoretical formal coherence) or of reliable probability (such as empirical or pragmatic persisting successes) is available.

The issue here is of utmost significance because, if intuited awareness of appearance cannot be trusted, there seems to be nothing else to trust. If temporal limitations of an act of intuition do exist, but do not appear within the act itself, then any temporally continuing intuitive action that does not detect such limits must be regarded either as actually expanding the temporal range of its intuitive (whole-grasping) power or as apprehending as if continuous what is not actually continuous in whatever sense gaps of any relevant kind exist.

If intuition apprehends as continuous what is, at least partly, temporally discontinuous, recognition of such a fact properly raises doubt about its reliability. If such doubt is to be eliminated or reduced, then some relevant attempt must be made to do so. If what is intuitively apprehended as continuous is, at least partly, discontinuous, then recognition (or theoretical speculation) that the complex of conditions within which an intuition occurs may provide conditions of stability and continuity in addition to, and over and above, those enabling the act of intuition to apprehend integratingly, to which the intuiting agency has, by nature, become accustomed, then the doubt-raising significance of the unapparent discontinuities may diminish or disappear. Such conclusion involves an acceptable theory of the complex of conditions.

If by apprehending as continuous what is known to be conditioned by gaps in the causes of appearance, an intuiter actually apprehends together in a temporally expanded appearance (expanded presence), then such act of intuiting may be regarded as integrative actualization -- a creative act interpretable as part of a larger creative process. This interpretation again involves a theory of the conditions of intuiting. But it also can serve as a basis for a theory about still higher levels and larger wholes of temporal integration, mentally as well as physically, and of more complex kinds of conceptual unification that have their own kinds of intuitive obviousness for those who participate in them.[6]

# D. TRANSCENDING PRESENCE

Another way of expanding awareness is through inference. Some inferences about apparently real objects involve inferences about the real nature of those apparently real objects. In whatever way an object appears as real, i.e., as independent of its being apprehended, something more (i.e., whatever constitutes it as independent) than its appearing is intended. Such an inference, occurring within a presence, infers or postulates the being of something more than occurs within that presence. To the extent that this something more is more than what occurs within a presence, such presence is apparently projectively transcended.

Each such inference is intuited. The appearance of the apparently real object is intuited. The apparent realness of the apparently real object is intuited. So any apparent transcendence of presence inherent in inferring that the apparent realness of the apparently real object involves something more than occurs within presence may be interpreted as some transcendence of presence.

A person may infer, and intuit inferring, without being aware of inference as inference. That is, inference may also be transparent in the sense that we infer without having our attention called to the fact that we are inferring. Naively realistic inferences seem to be a recurrently common characteristic of presence. Additional kinds of realistic inferences may be demonstrated as additional ways of expanding awareness. Chapter 2, "Inference," and the remainder of this work, pertain to ways of expanding and transcending presence.

# Two
# INFERENCE

## A. WHAT IS INFERENCE?

An inference is an act of intuiting in which the intuiter is aware of an appearance that appears both to be what it is as it appears and to involve something more than what it is as it first appears. Inferences vary both regarding the kinds of "more than" ("more than what it is as it appears") and regarding how "how much more" ("how much more it is than it appears") appears or does not appear. Variations range from complete absence of attention to any "more" as more to clear attention to any "more" and concern about its nature.

Inference, as defined here, is defined in terms of intuition and as a kind of intuition. The nature of intuition (see Chapter 1) is presupposed here.

Relative to presence, inferences are of two kinds: those occurring entirely within presence and those involving transcendence of presence. Examples of inferences occurring entirely within presence: When awareness of an apparent feeling or object appearing twice generates expectation that it will appear again, such expectation involves an inference that it will appear again. "This person is a husband; therefore he is a man." "Two plus two equals four." "I want, therefore I lack." Examination of the kinds of inferences occurring entirely within presence can be a major undertaking in itself. It can be complicated by ways, if any, of expanding presence. But such examination will not detain us here. My primary concern in Chapter 2, and in most of the remainder of this work, is with presence-transcending inferences.

Presence-transcending inferences are classified into the following three kinds. Although principles for distinguishing these kinds can be stated clearly, clear assignment of some inferences to these classes may not be possible. These three kinds are named "immediate inference," "intermediate inference," and "mediate(d)" inference."

# B. IMMEDIATE INFERENCE

Although, as indicated above, many immediate inferences occur entirely within presence, attention here is devoted to presence-transcending inferences. By "immediate inference" here is meant a presence-transcending inference in which awareness of transcending presence is absent. The inferred object appears as present in awareness without awareness of anything intermediating between its appearance and the awareness of it. The inferred object appears also as real in the sense that it does not appear to depend for its being upon its being in awareness. The objects of such immediate inferences are intuited not merely as apparent but as apparently real. Since a willingness to be objective, i.e., to be aware of apparent objects as they appear, is essential to the nature of intuition, intuition of apparently real objects involves a willingness to be aware of them as apparently real. Since intuition involves apprehending (being aware of) appearances as they appear, apprehending apparently real objects involves trusting them to be as real as they appear to be. The attitude typical of immediate inferences is often referred to as "naively realistic."

Naively realistic awareness involves inference about the reality of the apparently real object without awareness of the inferential nature of the inference. Awareness intuits appearance, and immediacy involves no awareness of any mediating factors, including any inferential factors, so intuiting immediate inference involves extending intuition from merely apparent objects to apparently real objects. Immediate inference is transparent in the sense that one apprehends intuitively through it without being aware of its inferential nature.

Examples of the kinds of immediate inference will be examined (1) in relation to the four kinds of appearances discussed in Chapter 1, Section B, part 3 ("Two Dimensions of Presence"), interpreted as constituting four directions of transcendence (apparent past, apparent future, apparent self-as-subject, and apparent objects), and then (2) larger, more comprehensive kinds, often inclusive of one or more of the four directions but also extending beyond them in various ways.

## FOUR DIRECTIONS OF TRANSCENDENCE

**1. Past.** When what was a present appearance has disappeared from presence and reappears as past, its appearance as past is a present appearance. Naively realistic immediate inference intuits what appears as past as actually past. Through immediate inference a person seems to be apprehending a past appearance and apprehending the past appearance as it appeared previously. Absence of intermediating factors constitutes the inference of apparently real pastness an immediate inference.

Since the problem of error does not normally arise with immediate inference, the fact that the previous appearance no longer exists as such is ignored. Naively realistic immediate inferences about past appearances involve error that remains unnoticed. The present appearance of the previous appearance as past is intuited in a present awareness. The apparently real pastness is trusted as intuitively obvious. When so, we find intuition, which we must trust, combined with inference, which may not be, and in this case is not, completely trustworthy. The present appearance of a past appearance is intuited. In such intuition one is aware of what appears. The inference that the apparently past appearance is as it was and that it is as real as it appears may be false. But immediate inference does not normally involve awareness of falsity. Naive realistic awareness of what appears as past remains assured of the reliability of its appearances.

**2. Future.** Anticipation of future experience is a most common characteristic of consciousness. When turning the pages of a book one expects that a next page will appear. When driving a car one may anticipate the experience that will occur when going over a bump observed on the road. When observing food on one's plate, one may anticipate how it will taste. Before a future experience occurs actually, its apparent reality as an apparent future experience may be apparent in a presence. To the extent that a present apprehension intuits an anticipated apparently real future appearance without awareness of any intermediating factors, the inference is immediate.

Inferences regarding future appearances differ from inferences regarding past appearances in one respect: the possibilities of anticipated future appearances appearing differently than anticipated seem to be greater than the possibilities that remembered past experiences will appear different than originally experienced, unless one's memory has become very unreliable. Hence, the problem of error, and of truth, becomes somewhat more important relative to inferences about future experiences than to inferences about past experiences. However, as long as the inference remains immediate, the problem of error does not normally arise.

**3. Self.** A self-as-subject-aware-of-objects, functioning in a subject-object polarity, universally conditioning presence even if transparently, may become aware of itself, and thus function as an object for itself as subject. When it does so and is conscious of its functioning substantially by continuing to be a subject during many presences and as transcending many presences, it normally infers that it exists also as real. By "real" here is meant that, although appearing in presence as subject, it exists also as something more than appears in any one presence and so exists in such a way that its existence does not depend completely on its functioning as a subject in any one presence.

A naive realistic immediate inference that a self exists and functions substantially seems to be a normal kind of immediate inference and one that normally continues or recurs in conscious experience. When and because a self observes itself functioning in many ways in addition to being merely a subject aware of objects (such as acting as an agent of willingness or willfulness, as a rememberer, as an anticipator, as a generalizer, and any other of the functions acquired and observed), it automatically and naively conceives itself as really embodying these functions within itself.

**4. Objects.** Although immediate inferences regarding apparently real past objects, future objects, and self as object have been discussed already, emphasis is needed also regarding the roles not only (a) of objects of perception, (b) of objects of conceptual generalization, (c) of contributions of creative imagination to objects, (d) of language, and (e) of other persons as objects, but also (f) of knowledge of objects as itself as an object of knowledge.

**a. Perception.** Immediate inference naive realistically apprehends apparently real objects intuitively, that is, willingly accepts their apparent realness just as it appears. Tables and trees, wind and rain, heat and cold, lightning and thunder, persons and dogs, food and drink, music and flowers, all appear as realities observed. Although visual perception is most common, auditory, tactile, kinesthetic, olfactory, and gustatory perception are also normal, and unconscious blending of multisensory apprehension occurs often. Sensory mediation of perceived objects does not normally call attention to itself except when some deficiency, obstacle, or specifically sensory feature (for example, chewing to taste) also appears. Sensory end organs normally function transparently in making their contributions to naive realistic perceptions of apparently real objects.

**b. Conceptual generalization.** Apparently real samenesses of apparently real objects are observed, and each such observed apparently real sameness is a concept (universal, kind) naive-realistically inferred to exist as a property common to two or more apparently real objects. Naive observers do not normally become aware of concepts as concepts but attribute observed samenesses to the objects observed. That is, concepts function transparently in perception of apparently real objects. But observed samenesses and differences are accepted as really existing in the objects as observed.

Although further investigation will reveal limitations on the kinds of generalizations available to immediate inference, immediate inference does not present itself as involving limitations, except when they appear in specific situations ("I cannot distinguish them in the dark"). That is, conceptual generalizations about whether objects are permanent or changing, simple or complex, larger or smaller, spatial or temporal, rigid or flexible, alive or dead, causers or caused, dangerous or safe, useful or useless, beautiful or ugly, near or distant, independent or dependent, etc., may, and often do, function in naive realistic apprehensions of apparently real objects. Doubtless, observations of more frequently recurring samenesses and differences contribute to habits of conceptual generalization and to the transparency with which they are inferred to exist as present in apparently real objects.

c. **Creative imagination.** Contributions of brain and mind to the way objects appear may produce a result in which such contributions determine in large measure how the objects appear. Children fearfully report seeing animals or ghosts under their beds. Desired objects are inferred to be good, to really embody something that makes them desired. Ink blot tests give evidence that persons see shapes, flowers, faces, etc., as a result of observed suggestion. The point emphasized here is that, although creative imagination often contributes much to the way objects appear, naive realistic inferences normally apprehend such apparently real objects as being as real as they appear. Contributions of creative imagination to how objects appear are transparent in uncritical intuition.

d. **Language.** Although naming and language are not essential to immediate inferences of many kinds, when names do appear as names of apparently real objects, they may also appear as real and even as real as the objects named. Not only concepts, but also words, when apprehended as apparently real objects, tend to be accepted as having the reality that appears. The media conveying words, such as printed letters or spoken sounds, also tend to be inferred as having apparent reality. Printed words tend to appear to really embody the meanings attributed to them. Language itself may appear as an apparently real complex of objects existing independently of the reader or listener. One skilled in language usage tends to use language transparently in referring to objects.

e. **Other persons.** An infant naturally develops a naively realistic attitude toward its mother. People tend to have naively realistic attitudes regarding other persons, including their bodily size and shape, vigor or lethargy, ways of behaving actively or passively, interests, habits, attitudes and whether friendly or dangerous. The problem of other minds is dealt with naively also: other persons have minds, conscious experiences, awareness of objects the same as we do, unless some evidence of difference appears. When efforts to communicate produce satisfactory responses, the naive realistic conclusion is that other persons really understand what is intended.

f. **Knowledge.** Immediate inferences occur not only relative to the foregoing kinds of objects but also relative to all other kinds of objects. Conceptual generalizations become "ideas," and sometimes "ideals." A proposed "theory" may become useful as a "working hypothesis" and eventually be regarded as a "law." Beliefs to which one is committed may be regarded as a "doctrine." Knowledge accumulated as the various "sciences," knowledge of specialists skilled in trades or professions, knowledge believed stored in libraries, knowledge taught in educational curricula, and knowledge embedded in the cultural heritage of a civilization, all may be regarded as having some objective reality.

Except when attending to mediating or intermediating factors or to apparent errors (or to doubts and uncertainties), one tends to retain a naive attitude toward all apparently real objects. In fact, even the most complicated mediating theory tends to be treated by theorists as itself something immediately present in awareness as well as really true in its unapparent detail. Any final test of the truth of a theory will require intuitive assent that it really explains as it claims to do. Whether or not affirmation of a conclusion after doubt has arisen can be considered naive, such affirmation will be considered certain only if apparent fulfillment of its claims is intuited.

## LARGER, MORE COMPREHENSIVE, KINDS OF INFERENCE

1. **Participation.** "Participation" means that something that exists functions as part of a larger whole. "Participation" connotes involving both a whole and its parts, the parts being parts of the whole, and the whole including all of its parts within itself as a whole of such parts. Immediate inference (and all inferences) involves participation in the sense that an inference involves two or more parts which function as parts of the inference as a whole.[1]

"Inference" involves awareness of appearance which both appears to be what it is as it appears and to involve something more than what it is as it appears. (See Chapter 1, Section A.) Both the "what it is" and the "something more than what it is" participate in inference. Each act of inferring involves the participation in an intuition of both something that appears to be what it is and something that appears to be more than what the first appearance is and some kind or degree of unity or continuity of both. Each act of inference is intuited as having some kind of wholeness about it. Such wholeness, continuity, unity or identity serves as a basis for certainty (or rather absence of uncertainty, since certainty seems to be characteristic only of inferences made after questions of uncertainty have arisen and infect the way awareness apprehends appearances).

Since, in "immediate inferences," there is no awareness of intermediating factors, the continuity present in the mutual participation of "what it is" and the "something more than what it is" as parts of the inference as a whole and the embodiment in the whole of both as parts function as constituents in a mental entity (even if existing for only an instant) which has a kind of being basic to consciousness, knowledge, experience, and science.[2]

Presence-transcending immediate inference involves awareness of both something that appears within presence and something more that appears as if existing (even if only instantaneously) as more than presence. Such inference involves awareness of both what appears within presence and also something that appears as if transcending presence or even as apart from presence and awareness of both of these together within, that is, as participating in, the inference as a whole. [A person does not normally pay attention to (that is, stand outside of one's immediate inferences to be aware of them and their functioning as whole embodying such participating parts) the wholeness of such inferences or to their whole-parts natures. Yet our present analysis seems to require interpreting immediate inference in this way.] The unity or continuity of the two parts of an immediate inference within the whole of the inference constitute something ultimate in the way of consciousness, experience, knowledge, and science. One major purpose of the present chapter is to emphasize such ultimacy and to emphasize the importance of recognizing it as foundational to theory of knowledge.

Analysis of the nature of inference, here focusing on the nature of immediate inference, is intended also as preparatory to extending such analysis to the natures of intermediate and mediate inferences. Questions about how much less certainty (or absence of uncertainty) is possible when mediating and intermediating factors appear in inferences remain to be investigated. Problems of uncertainty become aggravated when persons adopt habits of inferring regarding mediate appearances in ways in which they regard their inferences as immediate. When the tentativity which we advocate as needed is ignored (that is, forgotten, or willfully rejected), then tendencies to infer dogmatically (that is, with conviction) may not only be experienced but, too often, enjoyed -- as if enjoying feelings of certainty.

Part of the problem, of trying to locate some (even momentary) ultimate basis of certainty (absence of uncertainty) in presence-transcending immediate inferences is that the "more than" appearing as transcendent tends to have some character or nature of its own that may involve a complexity preventing it from being incorporated (embodied) completely within the continuity of the inference as a whole. The transition, in our study, from immediate to intermediated inferences may be regarded as a gradual one, with some only minimal additional factors disturbing the completeness of the unity or wholeness of the immediate inference. Does examination of some minimal disturbance of completeness of the unitary character of an immediate inference deserve attention to some principle implicitly vitiating the momentary absence of uncertainty? When and how does any minute element of uncertainty vitiate the seemingly complete absence of uncertainty in an immediate inference? [This question may be irrelevant here, if *any* degree of uncertainty depends upon some prior encounter with doubt such that doubt then continues to infect any feelings of certainty (absence of uncertainty). The influence of such doubt upon an immediate inference would, seemingly, occur only relative to immediate inferences occurring after such doubt and being influenced by it.]

Since the ways in which different kinds of inference merge into each other in ordinary experience, especially in mature persons, involve many ways in which inferences involve such complicating implications, this kind of problem needs to be dealt with more generally. So these initial efforts may be regarded as preparatory to later generalizations which, hopefully, can be made with some reliability.

This problem of trying to explore merely immediate inferences which transcend presence by citing examples of larger and more comprehensive kinds of transcendence tends to border on, or to extend over the border of, such desire to retain the discussion as a discussion of immediate inference. The following examples of larger, more comprehensive, presence-transcending inferences invite extensions and so an attempt will be made to restrain the treatment in ways that may seem unduly undeveloped.

**2. Mind.** Intuition involves an intuiter. Inference involves an inferer. Inference involves intuition. Inferer thus involves intuiter.

Although a single intuition or a single immediate inference may not, merely by itself, appear with awareness that a subject, or a self-as-subject, is implicit within it, experience is such that many intuitions or immediate inferences occur, one after another, in ways implying, even when awareness of such implication remains unclear or absent, that such subjectivity persists and continues, or continually recurs, in some way transcending such particular presence. Such subjectivity does not, merely as such, imply the existence of mind. But any attempt to understand, and apprehend, what is involved in such continuing transcendence seems to require an inference that something that conditions and somehow retains and, where memory is involved, contains, many, even all, such inferences, and that which transcends them in some continuous way, exists.

How mind is first presented in awareness in an infant can only be guessed. Awareness of some continuity of self as agency of intuition and inference (including memory and anticipation) seems probable. The nature and extensiveness of mind seems likely to be very vague at first. I do not have a theory of the stages in the development of awareness of mind in infants. I do not even have an adequate theory of how mind is understood by adults normally. But it does seem that each person tends to infer the existence of some part of one's person that serves as an organism somehow containing, and thus in some way uniting, the numerous intuitions and inferences experienced in awareness, even if also being involved in forgetting some of them.

Such organism, here interpreted as mind, not only extends beyond each presence. It also extends beyond all of them, and tends to be interpreted as having potentiality for including additional future intuitions and inferences, perhaps without limit. Interpreted in this way, mind is understood as a whole of parts, a whole in which the intuitions, inferences, etc., participate as parts, and as a whole

inclusive of, and embodying, all of these parts. Again, I judge that
awareness of such whole and parts (mind and ideas [intuitions,
inferences]) mutually involve each other in such a way that they share
some unity, identity, wholeness, or continuity of being while at the
same time existing as distinguishably different parts and whole.
There is something ultimate about the continuity between a mind and
its ideas (intuitions, inferences) which serves as a basis for assurance
about the reliability available in some knowledge.

A mind and its ideas grow together. We do not first have a mind
and then ideas, even though ideas which are acquired later do enter a
mind having prior existence. Biological processes (to be considered
later) provide the conditions involving potentialities for the
emergence of intuitions and inferences and their participation in a
mind which must somehow be present, potentially at least, in order
for a second intuition (intuition in a second presence) to join a first
one (intuition in a previous presence). How all such developments
take place before birth remains a mystery, at least to me now. But
that some such development does occur seems plausible. It is one
way of accounting for the emergence of mind as a presence-
transcending agent and, in the present context of inquiry, something
that is larger and more comprehensive than a single presence and the
four directions of intuiting and inferring observable therein.

(Problems regarding relating mind and self, although relevant here,
are postponed. Doubtless we sometimes regard mind as part of self,
and sometimes self as part of mind. How much we regard mind and
self as identical and how much we are able to distinguish some
difference remains an interesting question. When self is regarded as
part of mind interpreted as transcending presence more
comprehensively, then self is also involved in being interpreted as
transcending presence more comprehensively. The roles of self, and
mind, are more fully developed relative to intermediating and
mediated inferences.)

**3. Environment:** What more that transcends presence should be included here? Two kinds of things, named "body" and "surroundings," will serve as samples:

a. **Body.** (Biologically, body is already a precondition of mind, intuition, and inference. Mind depends on brain. All this will be discussed later. Solution to the mind-body problem is a prerequisite to an adequate theory of knowledge. No such solution is in sight. Yet we do know many facts that must be taken into consideration in forming the most adequate theory of knowledge that we can formulate. Body and mind evolve together; they did historically [we now infer], and they do in each person, from foetus to birth, surely. There is some kind of unifying process involved in the uniting of ovum and sperm that provides for all of the additional kinds of emerging unity embodied within a person. Or perhaps there is some kind of organizing process involved in uniting sperm and ovum that provides for the potentialities of all other processes producing whole-part organic unity emerging within a person, to say nothing of capacities for uniting interactively with the environment, in ways that are also organic or are involving both whole and parts interdependingly, in multileveled ways.)

Whether physical scientists can trace the origins of such organizing capacities of beings to subatomic particles or to astronomical supergalaxies, I do not know. But evidences are growing that biologists, at least, are discovering more of them, and more intricate kinds of organization, which function as essential conditions of the kinds of organizing (part-whole) entities appearing as acts of intuition, as acts of inference, as presence, as minds, as persons (mind-body, etc., beings), as well as groups, societies, and man-machine organisms.

My task here is to examine the role of presence-transcending immediate inferences as exemplified in more comprehensive kinds of transcendence. The human body seems to be a proper candidate for such examination. The importance of the body becomes immediately obvious when we consider that many immediate inferences involve sensation and thus the bodily organs of sensation and perception. Although feelings of identity of self with body are often so intimate that body does not appear as transcendent, any inference regarding it seems to involve transcending presence.

Although single inferences, if and when such occur, may not involve awareness of body as extending beyond presence, any awareness of continuingly recurring inferences seems likely to involve awareness of body unless one has somehow yogically (for example, as in hyperventilation) isolated what appears in awareness from any awareness of body. The common recurrence of seeing, hearing, touching, smelling, tasting, lifting, bending, walking, etc., all involve awareness of the body. Although particular inferences may refer to particular parts of the body, or to a particular sensory end organ, rather than to something interpreted as surrounding (in an environmental way) the inference, experience normally involves persons in interpreting, and in being aware of, their body as something more extensive than presence. Problems of how the body is inferred to function as a unit have their own time for inquiry. Explanations are likely to involve primarily mediate inferences, although some persons may prefer "mystical" apprehensions of bodily unity, or even unity of personality with something transcending mind-body, etc.

Sensation and perception involve intuition and inference, and they too may function transparently in the sense that a person who is inferring regarding what is perceived may not be aware of the role and function of sensory and perceptive organs. We do not see our eyes when we are seeing an apple. This transparency has a role to play regarding the unifying power of an intuition involved in an immediate inference regarding a presence-transcending object involving use of a bodily sensory end organ (and brain, etc., which also functions transparently; and yet is involved in, and contributes mightily to, the unifying, organizing processes involved in knowing).

**b. Surroundings.** How and to what extent do naive realistic immediate inferences apprehend participation of the intuiter (inferer; realist) in larger wholes that appear to surround him?

Consider a room in which a person is aware of his being in the room. Although the room is outside of his body, for example, a person aware of being in a room, that is, of participating in the being of the room including him, is involved in some kind of awareness of identity of himself, his body, and the room as some kind of being or entity. As he experiences continuity temporally of his being in the room, a unity involving such temporal continuity is also involved. How is all this intuited in a naive realistic inference, which involves giving his own body, mind, self, and presence a participatory role in the being of the room and in being in the room?

Here again some term ("gestalt" may be used, although I hesitate to use it because of the peculiarities of the conditions in which its formalized meaning were developed; there is more than "form," more than "visual form," to the present problem) is needed to describe the kind of organic unity in which a person finds himself partially identified with a room that surrounds him, while at the same time retaining his own individuality as a person, and having his own constituents as parts of himself as he participates in the room.

There is some kind of continuity, organic unity, between a person's awareness of himself as an integrated entity and the surrounding room which has its own unified nature as remaining the same in structure and in surrounding him completely. This unity, continuity, seems "gathered up," or rather emerges as such, as the person apprehends his participation in the room. The inference is naively realistic to the extent that he accepts the room as it appears as real, and as real as it appears, and himself as real (in whatever ways he and his body exist as real beings within the real room), and seems to do this all unreflectively. Persons usually have no feelings of uncertainty regarding their presence in, and participating in, a room. Exceptions occur, of course, and feelings of opposition of a person to his surroundings, including a room, are often interpreted as imprisoning him, temporarily or even permanently.

When feelings of opposition to a room occur, then a person may be involved in a naively realistic inference about the existence of such opposition, and of its role in his surroundings. But even when so inferring, some kind of unity, encompassing himself, the room, and apparent opposition between the two, seems involved in his inferring. As naively realistic, a person may respond spontaneously with fear of imprisonment when discovering that a door is locked. Some kind of unity, that is, organic unity, seems involved here and serves as a basis for absence of uncertainty regarding one's temporarily imprisoned condition (as participant).

How shall the absence of uncertainty experienced in the presence of such feelings of opposition be considered in trying to generalize about the nature of certainty, or absence of uncertainty? When uncertainty does exist, after doubt, or after experienced unreliability of any sort, it needs to be recognized as a condition of such knowing. Generalizations about doubts, kinds of doubt, degrees of doubt, etc., need to be developed and tested. But, here, attention is being called to how extensively does an epistemologist need to base conclusions about absence of uncertainty (e.g., here in naively realistic situations)? Are all of the kinds of unity mentioned in the foregoing of equal significance as bases for such generalizations? Or does each additional step involve some weakening of the evidence because the kind of unity, organic unity, may not be as clearly an example of an intuition in which uncertainty is absent?

Consider the surroundings beyond a room (a house inclusive of a room, perhaps). How far may naive realistic inferences extend? To the trees, mountains, clouds, sky, sun, stars, horizon, etc.?

Surely all things that can be seen, heard, or otherwise sensed may be objects of naive realistic inference. To what extent can a person naive realistically apprehend participation in a field enclosed by trees, a valley bounded by mountains, a sky covered with clouds, lighted up by lightning, a sky filled with stars at night? All these seem commonplace. To what extent is absence of uncertainty in such inferences evidence regarding the nature of inference involving absence of uncertainty?

Are there any limits to the extensiveness of the surroundings to which naively realistic inferences can extend? Part of the problem here has to do with the role of creative imagination in naively realistic inferences. The problem becomes acute in examining the nature of dreams, where inferences tend to appear as genuinely naively realistic as when one is awake. If we observe absence of uncertainty in the naively realistic inferences of dreamers, to what extent is this evidence of the nature of the absence of uncertainty? And when we (mediatingly, or at least intermediatingly) become aware of the unreliability of dreams relative to the reliability of waking inferences, we find (mediatingly) that the evidence available in such dreams seems quite unreliable (at least regarding waking reliability).

If the same organic unity functions as a basis for apparent absence of uncertainty in dreams as in waking naively realistic inferences, then some doubt seems to be cast upon relying upon such same kind of basis in waking life. Here is evidence that the quest for certainty must end in failure, at least partial failure. This does not end the quest, since the importance of certainty, or as much certainty as is possible, is important for feelings of confidence in understanding and for hope for continuing survival.

Of course, since the processes of biological evolution have been so self-sufficient (that is, is not depending on developing epistemology as a science) in producing human beings with all of their capacities, we may be able to rely upon what it has provided even if we are not able to understand it fully. "Muddling through" has been occurring for a long time, and people tend to survive in spite of their many erroneous judgments. So, it may be that only in the final chapters of our work will we come to some explanation of the bases for reliable judgments, that is, in the nature of the physiological (brain-functioning) and the biochemical bases of such processes. The biological conditions of human knowing are essentials for such knowing, and our investigation into the nature of knowledge cannot be completed adequately until we understand their roles as essential conditions. How such conditions provide seeming certainty (or absence of uncertainty) remains to be investigated. It may be that absence of uncertainty is a normal condition, and the occurrence of doubt, and even of continuing uncertainties based on the evidences for such doubts, may be aberrations in a system wherein absence of uncertainty is more normal, natural, and to be expected when the causes of doubt do not occur.

What kind of conclusion (tentative hypothesis) is warranted at the end of a section on "immediate inference?" We have not yet discussed the nature, basis for, and kinds of doubt. So with "immediate inference" we remain in a realm of theory where experience is occupied by inferences from which feelings of uncertainty are absent.

Hence, we are still exploring a realm of certainty in the sense that uncertainty is absent, even though no distinct feelings of certainty after doubt occur. How reliable are inferences from which feelings of uncertainty are absent? Actually we do rely on them. We have no lack of confidence in them while we are experiencing them. We do accept them, regard them with confidence, and continue to depend on them. Roy Wood Sellars uses the name "Natural Realism" as a synonym for "Naive Realism."[3] There is something natural, and normal, about most of our naive realistic inferences. They exist, in some fundamental sense, as foundational to theory of knowledge. Even after we become sophisticated in our understandings, structured by mediated theories of great complexity and intricate demonstration, and professionally tested, we continue to function as naive realists in most of our inferences. After all of the doubts we are about to, and will yet, raise regarding any inadequacies of naively realistic immediate inferences, we will find ourselves continuing to rely on them naturally most of the time.

It is true that intermediating and mediated factors enter into our mental conditioning in ways that these function in naively realistic inferences, and such factors complicate our evaluation of the nature and reliability of such inferences. Questions can be raised about the degrees and ways in which mediating conceptions participate in immediate inferences and to what extent these make them more reliable, or less reliable, or variable in their reliability.

My conclusion (tentative hypothesis) is that we cannot abandon reliance on naively realistic immediate inferences entirely no matter how much evidence we find giving rise to doubts. The absence of uncertainty observed in intuition (awareness of appearance), in inferences entirely within presence, in presence-transcending immediate inferences, serves as something basic in theory of knowledge.

Given this tentative conclusion to this section on "Immediate Inference," I am ready to examine the problems of error, doubt, uncertainty, and what, if anything, can be done to overcome, or minimize, their roles in developing reliable knowledge.

# C. INTERMEDIATE INFERENCE

By "intermediate inference" here is meant a presence-transcending inference in which what appears appears as having a real as well as an apparent nature. A distinction between apparent and real is inherent in intermediate inferences, even when the distinction does not receive focal attention. The distinction between apparent and real results from awareness of error. Error appears whenever what appears to be appears also to be not what it appears to be. Apparent inconsistency between appearing to be, that is, to be in some way, and appearing not what it appears to be, that is, in that way, generates distrust of such appearance. Distrust of appearance disturbs the willingness to be objective (i.e., to accept appearances as they appear) inherent in normal intuition. Distrust of appearances generates an attitude of uncertainty about them. So intermediate inferences tend to be characterized by some uncertainty about how much what is apparently real actually reveals about the nature of the real. When intermediate inferences are characterized by uncertainty, the willingness with which appearances are apprehended tends to be tinged with an attitude of venturesomeness and of tentativity regarding accepting appearances as they appear.

How much each apprehender is disturbed varies considerably. Some apparent errors disturb little. Some persons seem less disturbed by apparent errors than others. Persons seem less disturbed by apparent errors at some times than at others. Some apparent errors are very disturbing. When apparent error disturbs apprehenders greatly, because lack of confidence in the reliability of inferences inhibits belief and action, explanation of why error appears is desired. This desire is the source of motivation for efforts to develop a theory of knowledge (and of error, truth, and certainty) generally, and of all of the sciences dealing with particular kinds of apparently real objects.

The attitude typical of intermediate inference is more critical and less naive than that of immediate inferences. One might call it a "Critical Realism," but I prefer to call it a "tentative realism," where the word "tentative" means both critical (uncertain) and venturesome, both holding on and holding loosely enough to be willing to let go in light of further evidence (appearance).

"Intermediate inferences" are intermediate between "immediate" and "mediated" inferences in the sense that, like immediate inference, intermediate inference involves some trust of appearances, including appearances of what appears as real (even if that trust is mixed with distrust as a result of awareness of error) and, like mediate inference, intermediate inference seeks explanation of apparent error in terms of some theory about the real nature of things (except that its trust of such theory is also mixed with distrust to the extent that the intuited apparently real objects are denied ultimacy). Intermediate inferences do not infer that apparently real objects appear as completely illusory, as "mediate" inferences do. Intermediate inferences retain the appearance of the apparently real objects as genuine evidence, that is, as having a contribution to make to knowledge, and not as something to be explained away completely. Erroneous aspects of apparently real objects are recognized and interpreted when possible, but the apparently real objects are accepted as genuinely real appearances. Explanations of error may claim that some other kind of reality, either some kind explained in terms of other apparently real objects or of some kind explained in terms of supposedly real things that cannot appear except indirectly in terms postulated by some theory, is needed to account for error. Intermediate inference has the task of accounting for both how apparently real objects do appear and how apparent error appears.

Examples of kinds of intermediate inferences will be examined comparatively with the kinds of inferences considered in the previous section, that is, (1) the four kinds of inferences exemplifying the four kinds of transcendence of presence (i.e., about past, future, self, and objects, including objects of perception, conception, language, creative imagination, other persons, and knowledge), and (2) larger, more comprehensive, kinds of knowledge (about participation, mind, and environment, including body and surroundings).

## FOUR DIRECTIONS OF TRANSCENDENCE

Four kinds of intermediate inference are distinguished based on the four directions of presence-transcending immediate inferences discussed in the previous section: those pertaining to what appears as past, future, self-as-subject, and objects of several kinds.

**1. Past.** When a previous appearance is remembered or recalled, awareness may occur that some passage of time has intervened and that other conditions may be involved in such remembering or recalling. Intermediate inferences range from those approximating immediate inferences to those approximating mediated inferences. Although no attention need be focused on any passage of time or upon any other conditions involved in remembering, awareness of the recalled appearances as really past and that lapse(s) in awareness between such past appearance and its present recall seems minimal for "intermediate inference" about what is past.

Although one may retain a naive attitude toward the completeness or accuracy of recall, intermediate inferences about past experiences tend to be characterized by some doubt (little or much). Experiences with forgetting and even erroneous recall tend to condition intermediate inferences with some feeling of uncertainty. Distrust of memory often increases with illness, fatigue, and aging. Does all forgetting, when one is aware of forgetting, involve awareness of error, or awareness of possible error? When we are aware that we have forgotten something, are we not aware that we once knew something which we now know that we do not know?

Examples of error in an immediate past: (a) This morning when I deliberately stepped on what appeared to be a small black bug crawling on my bathroom floor, the black appearance persisted. Then I realized that the black appearance was a floater in the center of my vision, and that my inference and action were mistaken because I erroneously mistook the floater for a bug. (b) I have just returned from a grocery store where I left my wife waiting for a butcher to cut a roast and I wandered to a distant aisle in search of another item. When I returned to the meat counter, my wife had disappeared. I erroneously expected to find her where I had left her, and realized my error when observing her absence and her impatiently waiting for me to bring more money to the checkout stand. Awareness of error regarding these immediately past experiences (bug on floor; wife at meat counter) occurred amid numerous immediate (naive realistic) inferences and it was apprehended as an immediate (naively realistic) inference. That is, my awareness of error involved an inference that I was really mistaken (i.e., that the error of which I was aware did actually occur in the real immediate past).

During much of the year I wear ski goggles to prevent or reduce allergic reactions to quantities of pollen floating in the air. Three days ago I left them somewhere, and then I tried and failed to locate them in several different places during the past three days. This search involved me in a multiplicity of errors, since I became aware of my error each time I failed to locate the goggles in a particular place. I even inferred that I had not left them in the place where I finally found them, thus being involved in an additional kind of error regarding my past experience. These experiences, although involving greater awareness of lapses of time, all involved primarily immediate (naively realistic) inferences, and each awareness of error (that the goggles were not in the place investigated) was interpreted as (inferred to be) real error.

In interpreting the apprehension of error here as realistic, and thus in a sense as naive realistic, I am raising the question of how, when immediate (naive realistic) inferences remain free from error, can one immediately (naive realistically) infer that one is apprehending real error? The act of inferring is itself naive but the object observed involves awareness of a contradiction, thereby terminating the naivete. Answers to questions about how to explain the error are not always obvious, even if the above examples may provide sufficient evidence. When persons are only slightly disturbed by awareness of error, they tend to dismiss the problem as unimportant. But when persons feel more deeply concerned about the reliability of their inferences, they then tend to develop concern for how to avoid errors, and often adopt an attitude of uncertainty when making some inferences, thus transcending a completely naive attitude. When inferences are infected with feelings of uncertainty, they may be interpreted as being no longer completely naive.

An example of error in a more distant past concerning the date of my birth has disturbed me recurringly. The date of my birth stated by my mother, and confirmed by early family records, is August 21, 1907. I have always used this date on all kinds of records and expect to continue to use it thus in the future, with two exceptions. When applying for life insurance policies and passports, a required birth certificate reported my birth as August 29, 1907. My two kinds of certification remain contradictory, and efforts to resolve the contradiction have failed. Here the error involves more than my own personal recollections. It involves the testimony of my mother and any others who have known me from birth and legal records presumably accurately recorded and transcribed. Efforts to rectify confusing handwritten scripts of 1 and 9 failed. Suspicion that the rural physician recorded a menstrual due date of August 29 and failed to remember the birth as a few days premature (now speculated at eight) remains merely a speculated suspicion. Inferences about this error are no longer naive. Yet they are judged to be quite realistic in the sense that I must continue to recognize the error existing whether I am aware of it or not. Although reliable information about my birth date may be missing, reliable information that an error exists is recurringly presented and duly apprehended.

**2. Future.** Anticipated future experiences may embody errors in many ways, some involving more immediate inferences, some more intermediate inferences, and some almost completely mediated inferences.

Simple examples of errors in inference about future experiences include: One may infer that a liquid about to be drunk will be sweet, but it tastes sour. One may flip a switch expecting a light to go on, but none does. One may step on a board, expecting it to remain stable, but it does not. One may believe that one's body has a certain weight, but stepping on a scale proves differently.

More complicated examples of errors may be illustrated by my recent experience, when I volunteered to house-sit for my son and family while they went on a vacation trip, expecting to operate his computerized lawn sprinkling system as I had done previously. But on arrival, I realized that I had forgotten the formula for its operation. This example involves both error regarding inference about the past (that I could remember the formula) as well as about the future (that I could operate the system).

Errors in inferences about the future often involve implications, even if not actual inferences, about other directions within and transcending presence. They may also involve some kinds of truth.

For example, when I promised to exchange the humidifier on my wife's oxygen tank today (a promise I failed to keep, thereby involving error), I also stated, "I know that I will forget to do that," thereby making a true statement (intending that the statement would be false even while expecting it to become true).

The more we become aware of and concerned about preventing error, the more our anticipation of future experiences tends to become suffused with doubt and uncertainty about what will appear. Such inferences are treated here as "intermediate" in the sense that, although one does experience some present appearance of what is expected to appear in the future, just how it will appear remains somewhat uncertain. That is, one has some trust that what will appear will be at least somewhat like it is expected to be. (Even a complete failure to appear becomes experienced as an appearing to fail to appear.)

These anticipated future experiences now appear as real in the sense that they appear to be future and not already present, and do not depend for their being in the future upon their being already present. But present appearances of future appearances are presently intuited and intuited as if the future appearances are not yet present. When awareness of error occurs, then one tends to seek to understand and explain why it appears. Although particular explanations may be wild and various, we shall offer some seemingly plausible suggestions in the following pages and chapters.

Yet, in spite of awareness of errors, even repeated kind of errors, we also experience repeated success in carrying out some intentions, including habits of success regarding many of them, and retain confidence that an inference involved in such intentions will succeed as intended and avoid awareness of error. Habits of walking, eating, sleeping, speaking, seeing, especially when exercised in environments ordered with dependable regularities of surface, sky, mountains, buildings, plants, animals, and persons, appear to be dependable and tend to justify making inferences about future experiences. Although awareness of error tends to produce caution, it does not necessarily eliminate confidence that we can know, even feel certain, when making some inferences about future experiences.

But after the problem of error has arisen in ways causing concern about such inferences, then a quest for truth and certainty tends to become a recurrent, if not a continuing, concern. Theories of truth tend to be explored more often by dealing with inferences about objects than with inferences about past and future experiences. They will be examined below under "a. Perception."

**3. Self.** Since the nature of self, and errors involving inferences about it, are so intimately and complexly interrelated with a self's inferences about objects, including self-as-object, problems concerning errors, truth, and certainty about them will be more fully explored, and more fruitfully explored, after we have examined immediate inferences about objects in some detail.

**4. Objects.** Experience seems most fully occupied with awareness of objects, usually present objects, but also with present appearances of past, future, absent, imagined, and continuing objects. Objects are of so many kinds, having differing natures, that exploration of intermediate inferences about objects needs to be divided for convenience. Kinds of objects selected for examination here will be treated under the following titles: a. Perception. b. Conception. c. Imagination. d. Language. e. Other persons. f. Knowledge.

**a. Perception.** Perception involves sensation, and since persons normally have some fifteen or more different kinds of sensory end organs, they can have that many different kinds of single-sensory perception as well as many kinds of multi-sensory perception. Examination of only one of these, visual perception, will serve our purpose here.

Error in visual perception has been exemplified traditionally by a stick or pencil half-submerged in water in a way producing a visual appearance of the stick as bent or broken while extending one's hand along the stick results in sensing an unbent and unbroken appearance. Explanation is usually offered in terms of mediated factors such as differences in refraction of light waves due to differing density of air and liquid. Acceptance of such explanation requires some understanding of, and willingness to make inferences about, the (mediated) nature of light waves, air, liquid density, etc. Confidence in such explanation requires additional confidence in mediate inferences (which, as we shall see, are involved in their own kinds of uncertainties), unless one can be satisfied with relatively naive realistic inferences about such refracting and differing liquid densities. By repeatedly immersing the stick again and again, and repeatedly viewing the stick as appearing both bent and straight, one may become habituated to experiencing the error and accept it as a rather queer but recurringly present objectively real error.

Exploration of the problem of visual error can be pursued conveniently by recalling John Locke's distinction between "primary, secondary, and tertiary ideas." He accepted a naive realistic view of the nature of objects as embodying such characteristics or qualities as size, shape, length, solidity, and motion, and postulated the theory that appearances of these characteristics in awareness should be interpreted as "primary ideas" in the sense that they copy or reproduce in awareness the real qualities of the real things. But appearances of color, sound, taste, and odor, which vary from person to person and from time to time, do not exist in real things even though they are caused to appear in awareness by "secondary qualities" in the real things. These appearances, which he called "secondary ideas," do not copy or resemble real characteristics of the real thing, so a person makes an erroneous inference whenever he does apprehend the apparent color of a thing as if it were a real color. He may make such an inference naive realistically, but his inference is in error, even though he is unaware of his error. Locke adds "tertiary ideas": such as good and bad, and beautiful and ugly, to his list of ideas, describing them as not even sense-dependent and as even more unlike characteristics of the real thing than color, for example. One may naive realistically infer that the cake is good as well as soft and sweet, but such inference is inherently erroneous. Locke's interpretation, usually called "Representative Realism," is intended to warn us of the unreliability of many of our sensory inferences, and that perception, upon which we depend so completely and constantly, is naturally fraught with error and thus is unreliable much of the time.

Locke's theory of knowledge permits errors of judgment about primary ideas also, although they occur less frequently. It also states, quite clearly, even if not very adequately, a theory of truth. "Primary ideas" are true when they "resemble," or copy, "primary qualities." This is sometimes known as "the copy theory of truth." When asked to provide a test for the truth of an idea, Locke cannot do so, at least not directly. Such a test would involve having both the primary idea and the primary quality in awareness so that awareness of comparison could be made. But this is impossible because primary qualities never appear in awareness except as represented by primary ideas. How, then, can one have any assurance that one's primary ideas are true? One cannot. What one can do, Locke the empiricist proposes, is to trace the ideas back to their original sensations upon which they were based. But this too is impossible, because those past sensations no longer exist, and one cannot reenact one's past sensations. At best one may be able to remember some of them, but such recall is subject to deficiencies normal to memory. Locke's theory of truth thus involves a kind of agnosticism in the sense of having no copy test for his copy theory of truth. His predicament influenced David Hume to adopt a seemingly thorough-going skepticism. And Hume's influence upon epistemology has been quite devastating in its effects on many students of philosophy.

Fortunately, British empiricism has been surpassed by American Pragmatism, especially in the philosophies of William James and John Dewey. Pragmatists do not presuppose a copy theory, but test the truth of ideas by trying them out in practice and then those which "work," that is, appear to perform ("behave") as expected, are judged to be true. The test of the truth of an idea lies in its future, not in past sensations, and depends upon its fulfilling its function as predicted. Of course, we must have sufficient faith or confidence in an idea to try it out in practice. Thus truth has a subjective aspect that James called "a will to believe." But we do have ideas about real things, and "This notion of a reality independent of either of us . . . lies at the basis of the pragmatist definition of truth."[4] "The belief that there are real things is one that works so well that we could hardly get along without it."[5]

Locke's copy theory and James' workability theory are only two of many theories forming the background for The Organicist Theory of Truth, first formulated as "The Generic Theory of Truth"[6]: "Truth is a property of a belief when what is believed to be is, when what is believed to be not, is not, when what is believed to be so, is so, or when what is believed to be not so, is not so." This theory was conceived as a genus of which other theories are species, after an inductive study of many theories of truth. "When a realist believes that his idea corresponds to some independent reality, if his idea does so correspond, then his belief is true. But his belief is true, not because all beliefs are claims of correspondence of ideas with independent reality, but because what he judges to be so is so."

"When an idealist believes that his idea is consistent with the whole system of ideas, if his idea is consistent with the whole system of ideas, then his belief is true. But his belief is true, not because all beliefs are claims of consistency of ideas with the whole system of ideas, but because what he judges to be so is so. When a pragmatist believes that his idea is useful, if his idea is useful, then his belief is true. But his belief is true, not because all beliefs are claims of usefulness, but because what he judges to be so is so. . . .When an authoritarian believes that his idea is in accord with the authority, then his belief is true. . . .When an intuitionist believes that his idea is self-evident, if his idea is self-evident, then his belief is true. . . .When a traditionalist believes that his idea is customarily believed, if his idea is customarily believed, then his belief is true. . . .But [in each case] his belief is true not because it is [in accord with authority, self-evidence, customarily believed], but because what is believed to be so is so."

"The generic theory is intended to comprehend all of the variations in specifications that can occur in thinking. The truth of each judgment depends upon whether there are whatever specifications that are judged to be." Final formulation of "The Organicist Theory of Truth" involved realization that a formulation by Aristotle, at first assumed to be identical in intent with that of the generic theory, actually involved an opposing emphasis, interpretable as a complementary opposite. For Aristotle, "To say of what is that it is not, or of what is not that it is, is false, while to say of what is that it is and of what is not that it is not, is true."[7] His statement seems to treat "what is" as basic and truth as "saying what is." The generic theory treated "what is believed to be" as basic and as true when based on "what is." The Organicist theory finds both of the foregoing as needed in stating part of its theory as a whole. *What is believed (or said) to be* and *what is* are both essential. But sometimes we intend that *what is* is basic (as when I press a table top to assure myself of its solidity) and sometimes we *intend* that *what is believed to be* is basic (as when I believe that I have enough energy to climb a stairs). "Sometimes our intentions are more pliable and sometimes more rigorous relative to both the definiteness of our beliefs and to how close an approximation, in either direction, is required for truth to exist."[8]

The Organicist Theory of Truth, which is intended to serve universally as a theory of truth, extends beyond true and false perception, but is not, in itself, a theory of perception.[9] An adequate theory of perception will include consideration of what is there called the "intraorganic and extraorganic conditions of perception," including items yet to be considered below in the following section, "Mediated Inference." Organicism as a theory intends acceptance of tested and approved scientific conclusions of physiologists and psychologists regarding the nature of perception, and these will not be stated here.

One often-overlooked kind of condition and possible error has been emphasized by Roy Wood Sellars in his *Critical Realism*.[10] The apparently real nature of an apparently real thing may be different from how it actually exists. For example, a diamond may appear as glass, or glass as a diamond (a difference testable by a local jeweler). Also, one may reach for a pen with black ink and later discover that it has blue ink, or mistake one distant mountain peak for another and discover a mistake by consulting a map. Awareness of such errors tends to produce additional doubt about the reliability of intermediate inferences.

But persons normally do develop habits of perceiving upon which they can and do rely and the intermediating factors do participate in such habitual inferences in ways usually experienced with the confidence normally apprehended in immediate inferences. Perception of novelties may be experienced with more uncertainty, but the kinds or degrees of uncertainty tend to diminish when a person is motivated to become a novelty seeker.

b. **Conception.** Whenever one is aware that what appears as two or more appearances ("things") also appear alike in any way, that appearing alike is "a concept." Such "appearing alike" embodies a likeness. Such likeness is called "a universal" in the sense that it is common to all of the (two or more) appearances ("things"). In this sense, all "concepts" are "universals."

Such awareness of two or more appearances appearing alike in some way is a "concrete universal," to use a traditional term which seems not best suited for our purposes. The purpose here is to distinguish a "concrete universal" from an "abstract universal," in which what is common to the two or more appearances is attended to as something in itself and in this way is abstracted from its concrete context. What is abstracted appears as an abstract object in the sense that its nature as a kind of commonness, or universal, becomes the primary object of attention. How much such commonness which is abstracted may be apprehended as appearing as something in itself needs consideration. Some abstractions abstract very little, in the sense that the appearances from which they are abstracted remain either as background, fringe, or implicit (either vaguely or clearly) continuingly. Some abstractions may become very abstract in the sense that the appearances from which they are abstracted seem to have disappeared entirely (even from memory). The range of degrees and kinds of abstraction needs recognition and exploration and further observation (but, then, most of the rest of this work, and other works, are involved in doing just this).

Concepts may be concepts of mere appearances, or of apparent realities, or of combinations of mere appearances and apparent realities. Concepts may be very simple, as in our initial example, or very complex, as when comparing sciences or civilizations. They may pertain to past, future, self, objects, and to larger wholes within which the experiencer is participating. They may be conceptions of negation, absence, and nothing, as well as of time and timelessness, desires and desirelessness, distinctions and indistinctness, of change, process, dialectic, polarity, and organicity.[11] They may be concepts of errors, of truth, of uncertainty, of certainty, as well as of good and bad, right and wrong, beauty and ugliness, hope and fear, urgency and apathy, emotion and inertness, life and death.

Although concepts originate in an infant's experience by "empirical" means, that is, by observations involving awareness of similarities and differences, they may also become associated as abstractions in the imaginative construction of new concepts. Such constructed imaginative concepts also vary regarding the role of "concrete" features in which they appear embedded. They may also vary regarding the apparent reality attributed to them by the apprehending constructor or imaginer. As people grow older, and richer in experiences contributing to what is remembered and to what is imagined, the roles of apparently concrete features tend to vary, become more complex, even more fluid, as is obvious in dreams. Doubtless eventually the imaginative construction of concepts becomes much more contributive to actual awareness than additional empirical factors. This occurs constantly in dreams. When waking from a dream, people tend to regard dream experiences as unrealistic and unreliable. But dreams too vary in reliability and occasionally contribute to waking solutions.

Constructed concepts receiving common approval become embedded in culture and come to be experienced as having a realistic character that culture provides. Although I idealize science as being primarily empirical, (that is, based on inferences about apparently real concrete objects), actually some constructed abstractions do occur and become accepted means for further pursuits of solving mediated problems of understanding the nature of apparently real existence.

The problem of the extent to which concepts, having been abstracted from particular appearances and purified in the sense that the concepts abstracted appear to be completely free from (now independent of) any empirical sources, may be inferred to be real, even to exist in some temporal or even nontemporal way independently of their entering into awareness, has become one of great significance for both metaphysics and epistemology. The assumption that such concepts not only can and do have being independent of experience but also that they have a timeless reality prior to awareness and even constitute a necessary precondition of their appearance in awareness seems to be a common one, and one expressed early by Plato. This view has been continued by "logical realists" and by those who interpreted such concepts as real "essences" (including A.N. Whitehead's "eternal objects"). This view has the convenience of assuming that, since the concepts themselves are really eternal, one can rely on them. They then appear to serve as a basis for perfect reliability, as long as one's apprehensions and inferences conform strictly to their natures.

The primary difficulty with this view is that its assumptions are assumed rather than proved by the empirical means from which they were derived. It is true that use of such assumptions has proved useful in solving some problems, and such usefulness must be taken into consideration in any final evaluation of such assumptions. But the appearance of contradictions in their use must also be recognized and considered in any evaluation. Failure to recognize the empirical origin of such concepts, the uncertainties involved in making the immediate, intermediate, and mediated inferences, contribute to persisting uncertainties about their reliability.  The confidence in using mathematics in dealing with practical affairs, especially nuclear physics and galactic astronomy, needs to be challenged constantly in terms of the empirical origins and subjective contributions to concept construction.

Concepts consist not only in likeness, or sameness, of two or more things.  They also involve differences, since the two or more things that are alike must also be two or more different things.   The sameness unifies, or is observed as a unity of, the two or more different things.  Thus a concept involves a unity or wholeness of two or more parts.  In this sense, each concept is, or involves, an organic unity.  Organic unity is not something mysterious or occult, but is present as an observable ingredient characteristic (embodied nature) of every concept.  In this way, organic unity is a most foundational feature of knowing and a basic, or first principle, of epistemology.

When concepts are observed as embedded in particulars (as "concrete universals"), the role of the parts, and differences between the parts, appears more obvious.  But when concepts are abstracted from their empirical sources, what happens to the differences and to organic unity?  The unity of the concept remains more clearly, and may even attain greater clarity.  But the nature of the meaning inherent in the concept involves its unity being a unity of differences and a whole of parts, if not explicitly, then implicitly (or "tacitly"). I suggest that one of the reasons why concepts interpreted by some thinkers as eternal forms is that forms require more than mere sameness but involve some wholeness of a form having formal parts. The idea of organic unity is retained in such abstracting (and reifying) and serves as a basis for regarding such forms as entitive.

Confidence in the reliability of inferences based in concepts may be supported by awareness of the obvious organic unity (interdependence, interpenetration, interexistence) of the whole and parts of each concept.  Simple concepts tend to be apprehended without feelings of uncertainty. They tend to appear as obvious (or as obviously "so"). They are what they are. They appear to be what they appear as, whether as merely apparent or as apparently real. They have a nature which is entitive in the sense of having the being which they appear to have. Intuition of such being is experienced normally (at least in simple concepts) without uncertainty. Absence of uncertainty enables inference to proceed with confidence.

Whether confidence can be maintained as concepts become more complex, or become concepts of concepts, requires additional consideration. Uncertainties may be granted by some ways of relating concepts. But deductive inferences (and perhaps all deductive logics) depend for their validity upon a series of intuitions conceptually interrelating other intuited concepts. It is the intuition of conceptual relations between other concepts that provides feelings of certainty, or confidence, in deductive reasoning. The conceptual relations between, or the concepts relating, other conceptions themselves embody their own organic unity uniting the concepts involved in serial deduction. When examining deductively implications of complex concepts, further questions about the reliability of inferences arise. More complex concepts may be discovered to involve inconsistencies, even contradictions, that generate doubts needing further attention.

Understanding the nature of concepts is further complicated by the fact that they not only originate in "concrete" appearances but also contribute to and participate in perceptions and imaginations. Although one may intuit a sensation without conceptual ingredients, most, if not all, percepts do involve conceptual ingredients, even if not clearly as such. The organic unity of concepts ingredient in percepts contributes to the organic unity of the percept. Part of the confidence with which we function as Naive Realists is due to the organic unity present in the conceptual ingredients in percepts. This confidence also often pervades our faith in the desirability of realizing imaginatively constructed ideals.

Some concepts are more rigid and some more flexible. Each of these kinds has its own contribution to make to confidence in knowing because each has its own kind of organic unity. The rigidity of rigid concepts may provide feelings of reliability in the sense that they are experienced as embodying stable continuity. A more rigid concept may remain a continuing whole with exactly the same parts. A less rigid concept may remain a continuing whole with the same number of parts or with parts of the same kind even though some parts become exchanged for other equivalent parts. The flexibility of flexible concepts may provide feelings of reliability in the sense that they retain a functional unity while integrating additional parts or eliminating some parts or both. A more flexible concept may unite characteristics embodied in more differing kinds of objects or may unite more different kinds of characteristics in a few objects. A less flexible concept may unite characteristics in fewer kinds of objects or may unite fewer kinds of characteristics.

More rigidity in a concept is exemplified in the idea of an abstract triangle, or in the idea of a house that retains its structure (and functions) for many years. Less rigidity in a concept is exemplified when one observes triangularity in drawn, printed, painted, sawed, carved, or welded triangles, or in the idea of a house owned by, or rented to, several different families successively, or to a family increasing its number of children, which also varies in other ways including functions concerned with feeding, health, recreation, business, religion, education, etc.

The organic unity of a concept depends on its ability to unify its different parts, old or new, in ways consistent with its nature. When either more rigid or more flexible concepts cannot retain essential parts or incorporate changes appropriately relevant to their natures, then additional concepts tend to emerge. When these are similar in nature, some kind or degree of unity continues, which may support continuing or recurrent confidence. When these additional concepts are different, then whether confidence appears or disappears will depend on its acceptability as relevant to the kind of problem that the concepts are intended to serve. Where there is desire for novelty, then recurrence of novelty itself involves a kind of recurrence that serves confidence.

c. **Imagination.** By "imagination" here we mean appearances in awareness that have constituents that are either partly or wholly contributed by the mind. For example, a stone may appear in awareness as a tan surface. Awareness of color and extension do involve subjective (including bodily) factors in making perception possible (for awareness of color involves the whole visual apparatus of the nervous system and body and the projection of apparent color as an apparent object). Although mind is also involved in such awareness of the color of a stone, we tend to regard sensory awareness as involving little or no contributions to be called "imaginary." "The imaginary" seems intended to refer to contributions of the mind made in addition to contributions made by the body. They are caused primarily by the nature, structure, and functioning of the mind, including its constitution as caused by previous experiences beginning at birth.

Mind has the ability to reconstruct and to newly construct concepts (and images, if "concepts" fails to connote perceptual ingredients) which only distantly resemble perceptual experiences. Devotion to dreaming, including day-dreaming, tends to permit and encourage novelty of construction, and results often in fantastic images. Most of our experiences, and probably all experiences of adults, involve mentally-provided contributions. As persons age, habits of perceiving, conceiving, and imagining tend both toward greater rigidity in the ways objects appear and consequently toward lesser abilities to grasp novelties contributed by real things. The more uniform and habitual that the ways of imagining become in a person, the more confidence one tends to have regarding them, unless one has developed habits of being uncertain about some kinds of appearances.

A central problem regarding imagining, and regarding all knowledge, is the relative amounts sometimes referred to as "given" and "taken." The more an appearance is constituted by contributions from real things, or by the causal processes and conditions existing outside of a person, the more it is said to be "given." The more an appearance is constituted by contributions from the mind, the more it is said to be "taken." Whether and how much the contributions of the body, including the brain, are regarded as serving as contributions to what is given or to how what is given is taken is a matter for further consideration, depending on what these contributions are. The mutual dependence of mind and brain makes problems of distinguishing here very difficult at present. The structure and functioning of the brain, etc., do limit and condition the way what appears is "taken." Such limiting conditions function as factors in the way what appears is "taken," and thus have their constant effects upon how what is given appears.

A general principle regarding the roles of "given" and "taken" to imagination, and knowledge (including science, philosophy, religion, art, government, etc.) is that both givenness and takenness are essential conditions. Ranges in variations in the relative contributions of each seem endless. On the one hand, an infant's awareness of sensory givens probably has minimal contribution in the process of taking except those provided by its inherited physiology and foetal and earlier infantile conditionings. Contributions from its relatively undeveloped mind are minimal at first, but they increase rapidly as it responds, positively or negatively, to stimuli and to feelings of satisfaction regarding its needs and desires.

Adults occasionally may be shocked by sufficiently new sensory or comprehensive experiences in ways such that the givenness of what appears is primary, even if only momentarily. Minds naturally respond by trying to interpret (that is, to provide contributions to the way what appears is taken) what appears to have occurred or to exist. In dreams, especially in fantastic dreams, contributions by the mind to what appears seem to be total. Yet most of the images are tinged with remnants of previous experiences, including those having perceptual origins. The very limitations on the way what appears can be taken tend to function as limitations in what can be imagined when contributions are made primarily by the mind. Some persons enjoy and encourage appearances of fantastic images. Some deliberately seek to extend completely abstracted structures in constructing imaginary worlds (such as a fourth or fifth dimension, and "star wars"). Some engage in artistic experiments aiming to reify images admired by their minds, as in fiction.

How is the problem of certainty (desired in science, philosophy business, government, and religion) or of lack of uncertainty (confidence) conditioned by the nature and kinds of imagination? On the one hand, contributions made to our experiences as naive realists tend not to shake our confidence. Also, when awareness is occupied by mere dreaming, where anxieties about solving life's problems are missing, absence of uncertainty usually prevails. However, many dreams do have contributions from the mind projecting both problems and frustrations as well as solutions, often contributing fears, and pains, and disasters that fill awareness with uncertainty. Children commonly fear ghosts, bears, or snakes under their beds. Thus the mind itself can contribute uncertainties to many dream experiences. It may do the same when a person is awake and is speculating on how problems being faced will develop.

People differ regarding how much, and in what ways, feelings of uncertainty are contributed by their minds. Depth psychology has become an important science aimed at understanding the roles of different "layers" of experience (genetically hereditary, foetal, infantile, maternal affection, family friendliness, environmental security, formal education, accidents, thefts, riots, war, etc.) which may continue to function in making contributions to images recurrently presented in awareness. Contributions to uncertainty may have many sources, especially those uncertainties firmly embedded in a mind as phobias, whether pertaining primarily to fixed kinds of problems or to feelings of inability to face problems of any kind. Uncertainties contributed by minds to the knowledge upon which we rely constitute a continuing major area of investigation by epistemologists trying to understand the quest for certainty.

Imagination plays an important role in religion, since concern for understanding, seeking to achieve, and efforts to secure and maintain, the inferred values of one's life as a whole normally involve large amounts of imaginative contributions to shaping one's ideals. Although we cannot review the history of self-help (nontheistic) and other-help (theistic) religions here, we can call attention to the numerous varieties of differing conceptions constituting the history of theology, where the needs of peoples of different times required imagining a deity with abilities appropriate to dealing with them. Totems, shamen, Hindu deities, and ethical monotheisms all exemplify intermediated inferences. God is inferred to be something like a person in Hebraic, Christian and Islamic traditions. Yet in spite of the ninety-nine names of Allah, the Islamic prohibition implies a nature different from anything visibly knowable and thus seems to involve some mediated inference. Although in idealizing God as perfect, Thomas Aquinas' inference seems intermediate; but when he defines God as "pure act," the inference seems mediated; there is nothing like it in personal experience.

Ideas of heaven require large measures of imagination, some persons inferring it to be like a happy family and some inferring that persons will be so fully entranced with the beatific vision of the perfect goodness and beauty of God that no attention will be paid to the imperfect goodness of family loved ones. When technically-conceived theisms require intricate mediated inferences (such as, Alfred Whitehead's "primordial nature of God"), questions arise about whether they are "religiously available." Simpler conceptions of God tend to be easier to grasp, and confidence in them seems easier to maintain when intermediate ingredients in them become habitual appearances tending to function as immediate (naively realistic) inferences.

Turning from mental contributions to uncertainty or certainty in imagining to contributions by our bodies and the existing real world, we observe both the stabilities, regularities, and unities, and the changes, varieties, and novelties existing and occurring which make contributions. The regularities of day and night, sunrise and sunset, with mensual and annual regularities and variations, the remaining contours of the earth's surface, the variations of wind, and rain, and clouds, the endurance of trees and perennial vegetation and the recurrence of annuals, the endurance of human and animal life, with evidences of birth and death, sickness and disease, variations in energy, ambition, achievements and frustrations, all have contributions to make to feelings of confidence and doubt in persons. Although each of these may make its own effects more directly on a person's attitude, some make their effects primarily through ways of conceiving and imagining based in both personal and group experiences, and increasingly in cultural conditioning as both kinds of knowledge and methods of education become more abundant and utilized in making human adaptations.

The more we explore the world (discovering new kinds of fishes, plants, insects, birds, chemicals, stars, etc.), the more we are impressed by the multiplicity of kinds, the complexities of beings and processes, and the endurances of what is unchanging and the surprising novelties emerging from changes. Expanding acquaintance with the real world has begotten the folk-saying: "Truth is stranger than fiction." Initial ventures into what was previously unknown tend to be fraught with feelings of uncertainty. Persons experiencing more frequent success in novel adventures often develop attitudes providing considerable confidence motivating additional ventures.

Our bodies continuingly condition our experiences and contribute to the kinds of knowledge possible and to the certainties and uncertainties in such knowing. We become conscious of such conditions when blindness, deafness, and other sensory deficiencies limit our knowledge. We become conscious of such conditions when we cannot see or hear clearly, for distances, in darkness, or with competing lights and noises. We become conscious of such conditions when our memories fail us, and when our energies to move ourselves or to move other things to help us see better, for example, diminish. Knowledge of an object just beyond our reach is limited by the length of our arms. Knowledge of an animal we cannot catch is limited by our abilities to run. The whole body of knowledge gathered by physiologists provides data regarding the kinds of abilities and limitations which our bodies provide as contributions to our ways of knowing, and to the confidence and doubt resulting from their contributions.

In addition to our minds, the real world, and our bodies, each of which has its own contributions to make to certainty and uncertainty, we need to recognize the roles of our efforts to adapt to the apparently real world, both in appropriating its apparent benefits and avoiding its apparent evils and in attempting to control it, exploit it, to produce more benefits from it, and to be more successful in avoiding its apparent evils. When we try to control something that is apparently real (whether to change it or to keep it from changing), if we succeed, then we tend to develop confidence in our ability. If we succeed again and again, then our confidence tends to increase. If we fail, we tend to lose confidence. If we succeed some times and fail some times, then we experience a mixture of confidence and lack of confidence. The abilities of problem solvers in bringing adequate imaginative proposals for solutions is itself a factor in the nature of knowledge, as well as of certainty and uncertainty. John Dewey has emphasized the role of imagination in dealing with problems: well begun is half done.[12] But normally, remaining uncertainties relative to future encounters with problems generate an attitude of tentativity, commonly regarded as essential to an adequate scientific attitude.

To what extent is organic unity inherent in imagination experienced with confidence? Each of the factors considered above (mind, the real world, our bodies, and our abilities) is involved in its own organic unity or rather its own multiplicity (or organic unity) of organic unities. A mind is an organic unity, and it has its own organic unities, which we expect to examine later. Each image is a whole of parts. It may retain its unity of structure for example, or fade into something appearing to have an opposing nature. Movie and television advertisers have become experts in reversing perceived images and revising them in fantastic ways for the purpose of attracting and keeping attention. Although viewers may be bombarded by explosive and contradictory scenes, the continuity provided by viewers being "glued to" their television screens seems to serve as a unifying force conducive to dream-like confidence. Evidence: the annoyance of children called away from viewing. However, a mind concerned with its own integrity regarding beliefs seems to demand a principle of consistency when seeking to rely on imaginative conclusions regarding permanent practices.

The real world often appears to us as "a universe," some kind of whole inclusive of all things, which holds them together, even if only in "mere space." Concepts of the unity of such a universe vary, but people (and cultures) do tend to achieve them. Each apparently real thing embodies whatever organic unity its image provides. Each investigator will be satisfied with his image of an apparently real thing only when he has some grasp on its organic unity, although failures of many to achieve a satisfactory unitary grasp have led to willingness to regard more analytic, and pluralistic, images to serve their purposes.

Human bodies are organic unities. Each body is one body, and exists by retaining its basic unity. Each of its organs and cells has its own organic unity. Some people think that organic unity is better exemplified in biological species than in physical or social organisms. Vision as a bodily function involves a multiplicity of organic unities, and provides visual images that have their own organic unities. Gestalt psychology became famous because of its emphasis upon the unity, that is, the organic unity, inherent in apparent objects in human perception. The confidence that we have in the knowledge obtainable through visual perception is thus a function of, or is mutually immanent with, a multiplicity of bodily organic unities.

Our abilities to solve problems involving interdependent dialectical interactions between mind, body, and the real world function successfully to the extent that some new organic unity is achieved thereby. The problem tends to be conceived as some kind of whole with parts needing adjustment to remove the inconsistencies or conflicts and some reorganizing synthesis to enable the process under way to function more smoothly. The organic unity involved in solving problems, where satisfactory solution brings a kind and degree of unity of pluralities inherent in its solution, is a fundamental character of such solutions, and serves as a basis for confidence in our images involved in it.

    **d. Language.** Although language involves much more than printed words existing as apparently real objects, restricted reference to it here is intended to exemplify presence-transcending inferences involving intuitions serving as bases for certainty (absence of uncertainty) upon which we tend to rely with confidence. Although the processes for learning a language may be slow and difficult, language learning is a normal part of growing up, and educated people spend most of their waking (perhaps also sleeping) time having their awareness occupied with appearances of linguistic significance which mold and direct their understandings and purposes.

    Development of language presupposes the existence of other minds and of successes in communication of some common meanings, and usually a whole cultural history providing a stock of words, printed materials, literature, etc., facilitating increasing communication. Attention to language here is limited to its role as a common means of transcending presence and especially as appearing to have a reality independent of the reader (knower) which is observable, communicable, preservable, recallable, and also controllable, useable, and changeable at times. To the extent that we naturally function as naive realists regarding words, their meanings, sentences, paragraphs, chapters, books, libraries, etc., we seem to intuit them uncritically. Errors, not only misprints, but also ambiguities, inconsistencies, and contradictions also appear, and give rise to doubts, some momentary and some more enduring.

    Although one may have pre-linguistic knowledge and even acquire nonlinguistic knowledge through new experiences later in life, most if not all of human knowledge, in educated adults, exists in linguistic form, and is accepted, appreciated, and used in terms of language. Language structures thinking, and in some respects educated minds become primarily linguistic structures. Whenever a new experience occurs, minds tend to interpret what appears in terms of previous experiences and these interpretations tend to be linguistic. Thus, the role of language in constituting knowledge, and serving as a means for inferring, for most intermediate inferences and surely for all mediate inferences, is not only foundational but permeates it thoroughly and is a primary means for seeking and achieving still more knowledge.

Problems of truth and validity of inferences tend to be stated in terms of language; and logic, as a science of valid inference, had some beginnings in Greek theories about logical implications of the grammatical structure of language. Logicians have developed more abstract concepts and have not only (for example, in "material implication") sterilized abstractions completely from their empirical and linguistic sources but have done this so completely that they no longer properly apply to language intended to interpret the real world. Yet even understanding such sterilized inferences itself requires language only incompletely sterilized. Different kinds of abstract logic depend on intuiting differing restrictions upon symbol usage. But any validity postulated to exist in inferences of each restricted type depends upon ability to intuit such restrictions in such inferences. Postulated certainties remain relative to postulated restrictions.

Language involves organic unities of many kinds at many levels. Each occasion for thinking about any appearances involves its own organic unity. Each word having some unitary significance has its own organic unity. If one becomes concerned with spelling, then each letter is observed as a unit of some kind that somehow incorporates all of its functions, either on a particular occasion or in its multiple uses in language. A sentence, expressing a complete thought, has a unity incorporating all of the words as parts. A paragraph is usually designed to incorporate sentences all pertaining to the same subject.

The same is true of intentions regarding chapters, books, courses of studies, specialized libraries, etc. Although the kinds and degrees of unity inherent in different words, sentences, paragraphs, chapters, and books vary considerably, those theorists insisting that each of these exists as an independent unit quite unrelated to its companions fail to understand the nature of organic unity and its role in intuiting, inferring, and thinking linguistically. A study of language is a study of organic unities of many kinds. Failure to recognize this is a failure to understand language.

Logics abstracted from language and reconstructed with restrictions on unities (even intending to exclude unity entirely) may postulate intuitable principles of validity for their specialized purposes. But any restrictions on, especially any exclusion of, organic unity as inherent in apparently real objects, in presence-transcending inferences, and in meaningful language, impose restrictions on ability to understand them and tend to contribute to debilitating our ability to know. Studies in language and logic are inadequate until one has studied organic logic.

e. Other persons. In spite of the intimacy evident in infant-mother association, an infant does not acquire much "knowledge" of either itself, its mother, or the real world until it becomes aware of distinctions between itself and mother and, doubtless, others in its environment. Awareness of, and some knowledge of, other persons is inherent in becoming human, not merely as a member of a biological species, but as a being able to have some understanding of itself as both similar to and different from some other persons. Awareness of what appears to be another person already involves presence-transcending inferences. I cannot report on how and when infants become able to distinguish between appearances as merely apparent or as apparently real, but that they do become naive realists sooner or later seems natural and normal and, although they early express fears and anger, the question about when doubt or uncertainty first occurs deserves additional investigation. But presence-transcending inferences involving the appearance of other persons are among a person's earliest inferences.

Presence-transcending inference apprehending appearances of other persons is essential to being human and is a precondition of most human knowledge. Such apprehending involves some awareness of both samenesses and differences, both between the inferer and each other person and between other persons. Apprehending both samenesses and differences involves organic unity of such samenesses and differences. Thus organic unity is present in, inherent in, knowledge of other persons.

Although one person may "know" another person without the other "knowing" the one (as when a mother knows her newborn child, or as when one person is asleep or is a casual passerby), most human knowledge, involving communication, presupposes two or more minds participating in presence-transcending inferences relative to each other. When two people are communicating (whether in conversation, in cooperating in lifting a child, or dancing, wrestling, or in merely looking at each other), they normally infer that each has some belief (at least partially true) about the other regarding both samenesses and differences (even if not clearly conceived). To the extent that double inferring generates feelings of association, organic unity is generated in such apparent communication. Such organic unity may be temporary, tenuous, and evanescent; or it may become enduring and stable; or it may function variably with changing conditions. But organic unity seems inherent in the knowledge involved in communication between human minds.

Communication involves dialogue, or at least reciprocating dialectical processes. When one person's presence-transcending inference apprehends the appearance of another person as really existing and as acting as an agent in responding to being apparently apprehended, the other person normally also becomes involved in his own presence-transcending inference in apprehending the first person and his active agency in his apprehending. Dialectic exists when one person, who has influenced another person to respond to his action on that person, is in turn influenced by action of the other person responding reciprocally to influence by the first person. By being influenced reciprocally, a person has his own being changed (even if only minutely) as a result of action by another, caused by the being and nature of the other but also caused partly by his own action influencing the other. Such dialectical interaction involves at least some element of self-causation, that is, whatever influence upon one's self is contributed by one's influence upon the other which has returned to one's self through the reciprocating responses of the other.

During brief conversations persons sometimes produce enormous effects, both upon other persons and upon themselves. Scaring another person may cause that person to kill you. Prolonged and recurrent conversations, such as those between husband and wife, teacher and pupil, business, professional, recreational, religious, etc., colleagues, tend to result in increasing quantities of dialectical influences upon each of the participants. To the extent that ideas initiated by one person become embodied in another, something of the being of the first becomes embodied in the other. When both of two people have influenced each other in many ways, each has its own being thereby embodied somewhat within the being of the other. Not only does communication involve interaction and interdependence but also mutual interexistence of a partial kind. Knowledge taught by teachers may remain embodied in pupils for a lifetime, existing as potential and sometimes actual causes of the ways such pupils live their own lives.

Such dialectical interexistence involves its own organic unity, or series of organic unities, or organic unity of organic unities, when participating in dialectical discoursing continues to mold the minds and lives of different persons in complexly different ways.

Inferences about, and communications with (or merely from) other minds, may be indirect as well as direct: through writing, books, television, libraries, and influences upon the culture of a civilization. Organic unities relative to such inferences vary greatly in kind and reliability. But their omnipresence provides us with conditions for further perpetual inquiry, and continuing efforts to improve the quantity and quality of our feelings of certainty and reduce the dangers of uncertainty and false knowledge.[13]

**f. Knowledge.** Although this entire book is about knowledge, and the foregoing has been about knowledge, attention is called here only to how people come to regard knowledge as not merely something existing within human minds (which is actually the only place that it exists), but as if constituting a great body of objects that can become known to persons at particular times but which somehow has a being independent of them. This idea, even ideal, is encouraged by the seeming embodiment of language in printing, in books, and in libraries. It has generated ideals of omniscience attributed to some perfect deity, to Plato's Ideas, and to A.N. Whitehead's "eternal objects" constituting the "primordial nature of God." To the extent that knowledge is so regarded, it functions as an apparent object of presence-transcending inferences, and so is mentioned here.

## LARGER, MORE COMPREHENSIVE, KINDS OF INFERENCE

In addition to the four directions of presence-transcending inferences, sketched above, we must recognize many kinds of inferences that transcend even these four directions. Some may include only two directions (such as past and future, or self and objects), some may include an environment surrounding the self-as-inferer in many ways, and some may intend to be all-inclusive of the universe as a whole. Each of these kinds of more-comprehensive inferences involves a conception of participation, even when the participation is primarily negative (for example, when one fears or feels antagonistic to or isolated from other things, near or far, large or small). Participation (being part of a whole) involves some mutual immanence in its organic unity. So each of these more comprehensive presence-transcending inferences involves some mutual immanence in its organic unity. The range of variations in such organic unity is, of course, tremendous.

Such inferences mentioned here include: 1. Past-present-future. 2. Enduring self. 3. Environment, including a.) body, b.) real world, and c.) more comprehensive wholes.

**1. Past-present-future.** The distinctions between present and past and continuity of present and past, and between present and future and continuity of present and future, naturally beget inferences about continuity of past, present, and future. Although awareness of some continuity of inferred future, present and past appearances may be intuited within a single presence (including as many as seven temporally distinguishable units), intuitions involved in inferences of continuity of present and past experiences and inferences about continuity of present and future experiences tend to involve inferences of durational continuity extending beyond (transcending) presence. When one infers a time period (unity of temporal continuity) extending beyond presence, such inference involves a concept of the present participating in the longer continuity.

No feeling of uncertainty need occur when making such inference about participating. The presence within which the inference is being made is interpreted as part of a larger whole or longer period of time within which it participates. Awareness involving such organic unity provides intuited confidence in existing continuity. Abstracters and generalizers about such participation tend to objectify and reify time and its continuity as an essential characteristic of existence.

**2. Enduring self.** Inferences about self often include more than inferences about it as a direction within presence. Self too is inferred to have had a past and to have a future or to be about to exist in the future and is inferred as existing continuously during past, present and future experiences, awarenesses, and agencies. In these ways a self is inferred to exist more comprehensively than in any single presence and to exist in a way that includes all of its experiences. An enduring self is an organic unity that unites its past, present, and future parts as well as all other kinds of parts, of which there are many.

Enduring self includes enduring mind. One's mind exists as part of one's self in ways comprehending past, present, and future awareness either continuously or recurrently in ways involving its own continuity as a whole in which all such recurrent awarenesses participate as integral parts. Each mind is a whole of parts. It is a dynamic, complex, organic unity that exists as a continuing whole transcending each presence upon which it depends for its active functioning as a knower. Mind is an organic unity not merely of its own parts but also an organic unit incorporating all of its dialectical interdependencies with other minds and other things, large and small, with which it interacts. A mind's knowledge of the rest of the world both transcends particular presences and is incorporated as parts of its own nature and functioning. A mind's multicomplex mutual dependence upon its body constitutes some of its essential parts and contributes vitally to its organic unity and to its ability to endure and incorporate comprehensively.

**3. Environment.** All that surrounds an existing presence may be regarded as its environment and as opportunity for presence-transcending inference. Such regard includes inferences in the four directions (past, future, subject, objects), inferences regarding self (including mind) as enduring longer than such presence, inferences regarding body as an enduring organic unity upon which mind and presence depend, inferences regarding the apparently real world as a continuing organic complexity of complexities, and inferences regarding more comprehensive wholes including all of the foregoing. The present section entitled "Environment" is limited to considering a,) the body, b.) the real world (including other persons), and c.) more comprehensive wholes.

**a. Body.** Postponing detailed consideration of the mind-body problem until later (Chapter 5), we here examine presence-transcending inferences concerned with awareness that the "physical" body with which mind and presence seem to depend (and interdepend and are actually mutually immanent) endures beyond presence, having had a past (usually many years) and its biological, etc., antecedents and causal processes, and to have a future (unless terminated by sudden death, etc.), as well as enduring during each presence. Such intermediate inferences are normal parts of knowledge, except perhaps in infants, the senile aged, and persons suffering from some kinds of illness or other mentally debilitating abnormalities.

Persons normally believe (infer) that they have bodies that begin to exist before birth and continue to exist until death, as conditioning actualities within which mind and presence exist. Mind, which has its own continuity, depends for its continuing to exist within the body upon the body's continuing. Although some people adopt and maintain mistaken theories about the ability of minds to exist independently of their bodies, no genuinely reliable evidence is yet available to substantiate such beliefs.

The purpose of mentioning "body" here is not to provide opportunity for detailed discussion of physiology but to exemplify how inferences regarding body illustrate more comprehensive presence-transcending inferences. Problems regarding the variability of organic unity present in such inferences recur. Obvious complexities in the body invite tremendous varieties of such inferences, including many that are false. The seeming facts that mind and presence interdependingly participate in the bodily (including brain) processes call attention to the constant (or at least recurrent) role of participatory inferences (about the participation of presence and mind in the bodily activities) either as explicit or tacit features of many other kinds of presence-transcending inferences. Awareness involving spontaneous participatory inferences seems obvious in most activities where one's overt bodily action is involved in knowing how to manipulate a tool. Persons normally attain some knowledge of their own bodies and both extents and limitations of such abilities by acting experimentally in their adaptations to things and persons in their environments.

How comprehensive each person's understanding of his body becomes seems quite variable with different persons. The skills and prowess of workmen, whether farmers, laborers, or manufacturers, and of athletes exemplify such variations. Personal opportunities, social experiments, and cultural encouragements or discouragements all influence achievement of knowledge. The trustworthiness of each person's inferences about his body also varies with experience, acquired caution, and the reliability of advice from his teachers and colleagues, including levels of culture development involving scientific discoveries and tests available to him.

Each person's accumulation of knowledge exemplifying intermediate inferences about his body tends to become enormous. In educated adults, it intermingles with knowledge involving mediate inferences and this involves additional variations in truth and reliability. As we shall observe later, some naively realistic and some intermediate inferences seem more reliable than some mediate inferences, and some mediate inferences seem more reliable than some naive and intermediate inferences. Some inferences involving intermingling of mediate and intermediate inferences are more reliable and some less reliable than either alone. Seeking to understand the quest for certainty continues.

One feature of the Organicist theory is its calling attention again to the organic unity of the human body as a functioning whole, which somehow remains a whole of parts from the time it emerges as a fertilized ovum until degenerating when death destroys the functional unity constituting something essential to its living existence. The organic unity of the human body as a whole, mutually interdepending with its numerous environmental conditions, is itself a continuing condition of the existence of life, mind, presence, and inferences. The multiplicity of organic unities involved in its various atoms, cells, organs, and systems are all involved as parts of, as participants in, the organic unity of the body as a whole, which continues to be a whole of parts as long as it lives and throughout the numerous changes both within and without and in its inner-outer interdependencies.

Theory of knowledge needs to recognize the continuing dynamic existence of the body as an organic unity, and as an organic unity of continuing organic unities, as an essential condition of knowledge, both in its origin in each mind and in its accumulation, recollection, organization, and use in thinking and acting. Details of just how organic unity of the body as a whole itself participates in particular acts of knowing and particular processes of knowing that develop their own varieties of organic unities, including those involved in each particular inference, are something for further, future, exploration. The reliability of particular inferences seems variably interrelated with the organic unity of the body as a whole, as is evidenced by additional difficulties in knowing when persons are affected by illnesses and other physiological deficiencies.

**b.  Real world.**  Just as organic unity (including multi-leveled organic unity) characterizes the human body, so organic unity (including multiplicities of multi-leveled organic unities) characterizes the real world. Reliability of presence-transcending inferences about the apparently real world depends on both the sameness and differences (both unique, irreversible, and regularly recurrent) observable in it. The organic unity of samenesses and differences, and of wholes and parts, of things both stable and changing is essentially inherent in the dynamic structures of physical and other processes that constitute the real world.

The stability of the earth upon which we stand, the continuing influences of gravitation holding us to the earth, the relative stability of the air we breathe, the water we drink, and the foods we eat, the relatively stable atmospheric pressures, wind velocity, and the regularly recurring days and nights, seasons, years, and the behavior of plants and animals habitually adjusted to such orderly remaining and orderly changing, all function as conditions in terms of which we exist as knowers. The reliability of our knowing depends upon stabilities and regularities in our environment (and in numerous conditions upon which our more immediate environments depend) as well as the abilities (depending on organic unities) within the human body and mind. Understanding the nature (including organic unities) of each kind of thing is the aim of knowledge of the apparently real world. So constant attention to the role of such organic unities in the real world as conditions of reliable knowledge is needed by epistemologists as well as all other knowers.

Although the organic unity of particular real things, such as plants (such as trees) and animals (such as cows), seems obvious enough for intermediate inferencing, much of our knowledge these days is indebted to scientific investigations involving inferences that are clearly mediated. But before we plunge into discussion of mediate inferences, we should recognize that intermediated inferences have served mankind well for millennia and that, although mediate inferences do have some additional advantages, the reliability of intermediated inferences will continue to be a concern of epistemologists, and other knowers, and will continue to provide evidence of their reliability (and unreliability) in addition to whatever reliability (and unreliability) mediate inferences provide.

Other persons (to say nothing of animals and their knowledge and reliable or unreliable behavior) and their organic unities, and their organically unified mutually interdepending with their environments and each other are parts of the apparently real world influencing our knowledge of it. Culture constitutes an increasingly important part of our real world, increasing more as we reconstruct our world more often in terms of our mediated inferences, artificial designs, and novel structures and processes. The reliability, and unreliability, of ideas and practices embedded in cultures is a continuing condition of the reliability of knowledge.

We now rely on growing understanding of the history of civilizations, including the primitive origins of ideas and language, as exemplified in varying conceptions of *mana* (invisible power) and in varying ways of personifying such power as means of understanding and dealing with visible manifestations of obviously (i.e., inferred as obvious) invisible power (ability to cause effects).[14] Although culture enables children to benefit from the achievements of their parents and other ancestors in many ways, culture also has a way of retaining stability regarding conceptions and practices that outlast their original services, benefits, and usefulness.[15]

Consequently, both the staying power of custom and tradition and the gradual (sometimes drastic) decaying of institutional forms when newer problems develop (so that older concepts and practices no longer serve) are themselves factors in the nature of knowledge about the real world as conditioned by culture. Obsolete ideas often become so firmly embedded in a language that some minds become incompetent to apprehend new ideas needed for solving new problems. When people become unable to recognize that loyalty to obsolete traditions is counterproductive as far as the knowledge needed for adaption to new conditions is concerned, their abilities to know degenerate and now-false ideas are mistaken as true. The role of cultural obsolescence of knowledge will continue to be a problem for epistemologists, and knowers, for all time to come. I do not propose dreaming of some epistemological utopia where everyone knows everything, or at least no one has any false knowledge of the real world. Uncertainties inherent in cultural lag will continue.

c. **More comprehensive wholes.** Persons participate not merely in their minds and bodies, and in the real world including societies and culture, but also in larger wholes encompassing all of these in various ways. I do not here propose some hierarchy of levels of the organization of existence. I have elsewhere suggested some proposals for a metaphysical scheme.[16] Epistemologists should examine, and probably accept, the conclusions of competent scientists in all fields, including astronomy, physics, chemistry (more about this under "mediate inference"). But I have proposed that organic unity is an omnipresent constituent in existence, including any existence of the universe as a whole.

Questions about the nature of existence, levels of existence, increasingly larger and smaller units of existence, including the universe as a whole and any possible smallest kind of unit, will continue to plague scientists and metaphysicians. I expect to continue to support the proposal that existence, being dynamic, always both generates a larger universe as a whole (so that no whole of the universe is absolute in any but a momentary sense) and ceases in whatever respects its parts (and its interdependence with such parts) becomes past. In the same way I propose that no absolutely smallest particle can exist, or can exist more than temporarily, in any absolute sense.[17] Thus even at any supposed highest level (universe as a whole) and lowest level (smallest particle), the concept of organic unity provides a needed element in explanations.

Questions about the relative certainty (absence of uncertainty) regarding more comprehensive wholes will continue to plague, and challenge, us, and lead us on to further investigations. Participation of persons in these larger wholes will continue, even in the absence of understanding and true knowledge of them, just as they did in millennia past. I do not propose any factors or forces in the powerfully determining organic unities of these larger wholes in enabling the gradual emergence, growth, and development of the universe in ways that human beings have evolved within it. One can only marvel at what has occurred and is justified in regarding it as miraculous. But one contribution of Organicism to metaphysics and epistemology is its continuing emphasis upon the role of organic unity at all levels of existence and of the need or understanding the nature of organic unity both in the existing universe and in our ways of achieving knowledge of it through apprehending appearances and presence-transcending inferences.[18]

# D. MEDIATE INFERENCE

By "mediate inference" or "mediated inference" here is meant a presence-transcending inference that tends to regard explanations of the nature of supposedly real things as quite different from the way that apparently real things appear through immediate (naive realistic) inference and through intermediate inferences. Many, often most, inferences about apparently real things made by educated adults seem to be complex integrations of immediate, intermediate and mediate inferences or inference factors. Hence the following discussion, which aims to emphasize mediate inferences and the mediate ingredients in other inferences, will fall short of clear depiction of any idealized fully mediate inferences.

When error appears, that is, when intuition of what appears to be real also appears erroneous, then distrust of intuited appearances motivates seeking elsewhere for something to trust. But, in the absence of some self-evident assurance of certainty, possibilities regarding appearance of error seem to recur in mediate inferences as well as in intermediate and naive inferences. So caution about errors regarding mediate inferences is needed. In fact, judging by the history of discarded theories, even in theories that have been accepted as reliable for long periods of time, prospects for finding errors in mediate inferences may be as great as or greater than for immediate and intermediate inferences.

Although "mediate inferences" are described as "presence-transcending" for purposes of consistency in developing my theory of kinds of inference, some theories often ignore presence altogether, especially those holding that science is or ought to be "completely value-free" and "completely objective," meaning completely unrelated to anything subjective. My view is that, whenever a theorist (or inferer) forgets to recognize the continuing (even if only continuingly recurring) basis of inference (and theory) in presence (present awareness of appearance), that theorist abandons what is foundational to all knowledge, truth and certainty. Recognition of the ease with which speculative inferences about explanations of the real nature of real things are regarded naively, that is, as naively or uncritically as a naive realist regards color or beauty of a flower as real, should warn us that mediate inferences (and theories) continue to require caution and constant critical attention. The need for retaining an attitude of tentativity (not holding on too tightly) regarding all mediated inferences is itself a foundational principle in Organicism as a theory of knowledge. I stated this conclusion earlier: "Scientists, too, have no better tests than dreamers."[19] "The moment doubt disappears completely from any organistic thinking, dogma exists. . . .To neglect to regard Organicism as hypothetical is to misinterpret its intent."[20]

The history of philosophy and the sciences records a vast collection of theories, ancient, modern, and contemporary, Asian and Western, etc., about the nature of being, or existence, including the nature of the real and how appearances are related to it. Theories differ regarding how different ultimate reality is from awareness of appearance. They differ regarding the ways in which intuited appearances are close to or far from ultimate reality, and about causal relations between them.

For example, just as immediate inference is perhaps best exemplified by Naive Realism and intermediate inference is best exemplified by Representative or Critical Realism, so mediate inference may be best exemplified by what has been called "Scientific Realism." However, what is meant by "Scientific Realism" is itself subject to interpretation because what has been meant by "science" is itself interpreted differently by different theorists. Some limit the meaning of science to the physical sciences. But others add the psychological and social sciences, and psychiatry. My view is that the term "science" should be used in a sense that is broad enough to incorporate all of the sciences, all of the investigations of problems using the scientific attitude and methods. The philosophical sciences (epistemology, metaphysics, axiology, etc.) should be regarded as such.[21] We are warranted in using the term "Scientific Realism" to refer to mediate inferences only if we intend to refer to all of the sciences, including epistemology and its endeavor to understand the nature of knowledge, truth and certainty, founded in awareness of appearance in intuition and immediate inference.

When attempting to generalize about "mediate inference," I am confronted with the task of selecting representative examples rather than surveying encyclopedic extensions, not merely regarding all kinds of knowing but also regarding each kind. My selections here are guided partly by desiring to make comparisons with the kinds of knowing treated in the previous sections. Examples will be treated knowing treated in the previous sections. Examples will be treated under "the four directions of presence-transcending inferences" as 1. time (including past and future), 2. self, 3. the real world (including a. perception, b. conception, c. imagination, d. language, e. other persons, and f. knowledge).

## FOUR DIRECTIONS OF TRANSCENDENCE

**1. Time.** In Chapter 1, "Intuition," time was considered in terms of awareness of appearance of change, repetition, and duration being intuited directly. Although limits of duration (from beginning to end) of a presence seem not to appear, awareness that presence is not unlimited seems implicit and is exemplified by attempts to grasp together in a single intuition several apparent units (usually three, maximally seven).

In considering immediate inference, we observed examples of apparently real (naively realistic) change, repetition, and duration. For example, one may be aware of the rapid movement of one's fingers when playing a piano. Again, one may not be clearly aware of limits of awareness, that is, of beginnings and endings of apparent durations; nevertheless awareness that such apparent durations have limits seems implicit. Awareness of some limits may be explicit in changes in overt movements of hands, for example, or in the "keeping time" units metered by metronome or baton. When music involves a familiar melody, mental contributions to feelings of temporal extensiveness seem to permeate even each moment of awareness of change, repetition, duration.

In considering intermediate inference, we can observe awareness of change, repetition, and duration in many things: walking, eating, breathing, talking, feeling pulse, moving things about, driving an automobile, sunrise and sunset, day and night, months (moons), seasons, years (judged by seasons), stages in life (birth, infancy, youth, maturity, old age, death), and artificial time pieces, such as clocks and calendars, and consequently customary recurrences such as payments for rent, utilities, taxes, interest, and bus, train, plane, radio, and television schedules, etc. I judge that persons commonly feel no gap between their naively realistic inferences about momentary durations and inferences about longer periods appearing as days, months, years, when and because they feel themselves as participants in observable temporal processes of various kinds. Awareness of larger and more comprehensive periods of time, which seem normal as persons mature, may appear as natural extensions of more local time experiences. Intermediate inferences can include ideas of everlastingness, and of existence either without or with beginning and either without or with a final end.

When considering mediate inferences regarding time, we encounter multiplicities of theories of time that have developed historically.

Although experience commonly incudes awareness of distinctions between past, present and future and of participating in each, including some minimal actual (nonspecious) duration in presence, some theorists have claimed that "only the present exists." What is past no longer exists; what is future does not yet exist; so only what is present exists. Such theories are involved in the question: "How long is the present?"

If a person accepts the duration of one's own presence as "the present," one encounters evidences of variations in the durations of presences, within self and (by inference) others, and may encounter questions about whether other beings, insects for example, have units of awareness of much shorter durations. Theravada Buddhism and Zen Buddhism have theories of "momentariness." Some Existentialists, identifying *existenz* with each act of will, also advocate a doctrine of momentariness. A.N. Whitehead has a metaphysical theory of "actual occasions" which merely occur, that is, come into being and go out of being without any more duration than is needed for a moment of "concrescence" within which all existence somehow achieves organic unification before its momentary manifestation becomes permanently past.

Another well-known (if silly and self-contradictory) theory claims that the present is an infinitesimal instant in time (analogous to an infinitesimal point in a spatial line) between a nonexistent future and a nonexistent past. Reducing time to such an infinitesimal instant not only eliminates all possibility of duration, all existence which involves past, present and future as well as duration, and all intuition of duration in presence, but also implies that any statement of the theory itself, requiring more time to make it than an infinitesimal instant, does not exist, and is thus in effect implicitly self-contradictory.

Some theorists have claimed that time is an unbroken continuum without beginning or end and thus is continuingly present everlastingly. Hegel included all of history, past, present, and future, as somehow unified within his Absolute which involves an unbroken unity of all being, even though each period takes its own time to occur. Some theists, idolizing God as perfect in knowledge and awareness, describe temporal everlastingness as "God's now."

Some theorists deny existence to time, except as an illusion. Advaita Vedanta claims that ultimate reality, *Nirguna Brahman*, involves no time, neither duration nor events, no distinctions between moments, or between past, present, and future. *Maya* (illusory appearance of distinctions, including temporal distinctions) is an evil which yogic efforts aim to eliminate. Madhyamika or Sunyavada Buddhism also eliminates time from ultimate reality, *Sunya* ("Absolute Nothingness"), by saying that it neither exists, nor does not exist, nor both exists and does not exist, nor neither exists nor does not exist. Yet it also postulates a similar nondifference between *Sunya* and *Suchness*, time as ordinarily experienced.[22]

Some theorists distinguish between "time" and "eternity," where "eternity" is conceived as timeless or as timelessness. The difficulties of relating the two are encountered. For some, the two are different in kind, equally real, but essentially unrelated. For some, eternity is prior and more real: God, being eternal, had being both before and after created existence, which therefore had a beginning and end of time. Time is conceived not only as temporal but also as temporary;

whereas eternity is conceived as being whether or not time exists. Of course, what is timeless has being during all time, and thus it has become easy and common popularly to mistake, or identify, what is eternal with everlastingness, that is, something lasting throughout all time (in spite of the contradiction between concepts of timelessness and all time). Plato described time as a "moving image of eternity." Just how eternally static forms magically embody themselves in temporal processes remains unexplained even by postulating a creative principle.[23]

Some theorists reduce time to numbers, and adopt the symbol "t" to represent it. Time is reduced to a system of measurement or to what is measured by such a system. "If it can't be measured, it doesn't exist." Those who regard numbers as timeless again reduce time to something timeless. In spite of all of the successful uses of mathematics in engineering marvels, there is something silly, and false, in interpreting mathematical equations involving the symbol "t" as justifying the view that "time is reversible."

Some theorists are evolutionists, holding that processes of emergence and development of different kinds of things involve complicated kinds of changes, each of which "takes its own time" to develop or, rather, generates time as a temporal aspect of its processes. Time is thus an emergent characteristic of emerging existences. The character of time depends on the other characteristics of each emerging being and thus "behaves" differently in different parts of the universe and at different times "in history." This theory accounts for the occurrences of presences having different durations, and for temporal variations in fantastic speeds and galactic events. It may also be associated with theories of "space-time," where time is interpreted as a fourth dimension of space and participates in "curvatures" allegedly accounting for other difficulties encountered in physical and astronomical phenomena.

The foregoing theories of time exemplifying mediate inference may function as intermediate inferences to the extent that they have come into popular usage and have been accepted uncritically as true. The common confusion between timeless eternity and temporal everlastingness and the common use of "t" as a symbol in mathematical calculations of physical processes may be cited.

In proposing an Organicist theory of time as exemplifying mediate inference, I hope that it too may become more commonly accepted as a more adequate interpretation of the nature of time. The Organicist theory of time originated partly from immediate, partly from intermediate, and partly from mediate inference. Examination of immediate inferences about temporal experiences, prompted especially by a continuing quest for certainty became increasingly critical after my life-disturbing doubts (as a Christian fundamentalist college freshman), and pursued as a doctoral dissertation (1931-32) involved in examining other theories of time stated in contemporary philosophical literature, produced evidences both about the nature and limitations of presence and the variable temporal extents of presences, my own and others. This resulted in a tentative conclusion that, although the durations apprehended in presence were not "specious" (as William James stated, having been influenced by others) but actual, no theory of an absolute present or of absolute simultaneity could be accepted as true.

This conclusion generated for me the problem of how to formulate a theory of time accounting for multiple actual presents of variable lengths. Examination of commonly accepted intermediate inferences about time, including regarding days and nights, months (moons), and years as natural phenomena, for example, and the (nature-based) artificially measured periods of clock hours, minutes and seconds, and calendar weeks, months and years, and historical periods of centuries and millennia, and U.S. Bureau of Standards efforts to locate a most reliable unit of temporal measurement, yielded evidences about the existence of actual units of change and time that must be taken into account in formulating any adequate theory of the nature of time.

The Organicist theory of time involving mediate inference was, and is, interinvolved with its other metaphysical conclusions, especially those about change and permanence, wholes and parts, polarity, organic unity, dialectic, and eventually with its Diagram of Types and concept of "Organicity." It was first published in "A Multiple-Aspect Theory of Time," *Southwestern Journal of Philosophy*, 11:1-2, (Spring-Summer, 1971): 163-171, and republished as Chapter 11 in *Metaphysics: An Introduction*.[24] This theory incorporates its both-and logic and ideas of hierarchy, theories about there being no largest whole of the universe exempt from temporal passage and no smallest particle of existence exempt from some temporal duration, and postulates no completely absolute beginning or ending but accepts all of the recurring multiplicities of beginnings and endings (each absolute in its own way) as constituting all of the beginingness and endingness embodied in existence.

2. **Self.** In Chapter 1, "Intuition," self was considered as implicitly involved in any awareness of subjectivity inherent in subject-object conditions of the agency of an apprehender, or awarer, in the awareness-appearance polarity proposed in the definition of intuition constituting presence. Explicit awareness of self seems unnecessary in simple intuition.

Some theorists claim that a self cannot apprehend itself as subject, but only as an object, so self-as-subject is in effect unknowable. This view, premised on a logic of excluded middle and a theory of types (levels) excluding each other, deduces such impossibility. But this theory is false, or at least partly false. Granted that, to the extent that a self-as-subject is not self-as-object, it is not known as an object. But, to the extent that one apprehends self-as-subject as self-as-object, such self-as-subject is thereby apprehended, at least to that extent. But also self-as-object functions interactively in larger wholes, not merely implying, but actually apprehending, the functioning of self-as-subject as a part, participator, in such larger wholes explicitly. When we accept the theory that subject and object are organically related rather than divided by an excluded middle, the problem inherent in the claim that a self cannot apprehend self-as-subject becomes a pseudo-problem.

Awareness of a subject as a presence-transcending agency already involves inference, and persons normally do infer that a self-as-subject exists enduringly as an apprehending agent which is an essential condition of the existence of knowing. Even though a person may become unaware, in the sense of not being present as an object in the focus of attention, of self, much, even most, of the time, the continuing actuality of personal agency in all awareness causes frequent recurrence of awareness of such agency. How awareness of such agency appears in different presences varies considerably, depending upon multiplicities of factors in the ways such agency functions on particular occasions. Normally, sooner or later persons immediately infer that a continuing self exists, and naive realistically postulate its having a real existence ("real" here means existing even when the presence in which its appearance is apprehended has ceased). Belief in the existence of a real self is a normal consequence of continuing immediate inference. Each person acquires a stock of ideas about self from varieties of experiences, including its functioning as the agent of desiring, perceiving, bodily acting, feeling frustrated, fearing, feeling satisfied, etc. These normally intermingle with ideas accumulated through intermediate inferences.

Concepts of self are shaped gradually through dialectical interactions of subject-objects processes occurring in presence, including awareness of apparently real objects (functioning in their multiplicities of ways) and awareness of self as an apparently real agent interacting with these objects in various ways. I cannot survey all of such ways of interacting and resulting self-conceptions (many of which I can never know, at least in the experiences of other persons). But I do propose as a fundamental principle of the nature of self and of our knowledge of self that persons naturally and normally tend either (or, varyingly, both) to conceive themselves as different from and opposed to objects or to conceive themselves as the same as (in some sense the same as) such objects through conceptions of functioning as participants in larger wholes including them. Although such inferences may occur immediately, most of the vast array of kinds of identifications and oppositions embodied in a self's conceptions of itself involve intermediate inferences.

The more functions that a self finds itself performing, both as agent and patient, conceived as opposing other things, including persons, and processes real and imaginary, the more self-conceptions tend to become more numerous and more complicated as a person matures. Each person tends to identify self with body and all of its organs and functions. An infant tends to identify itself with its mother and often resists needs for separation and growing observations of opposition. A child may at first feel opposed to clothes which bind or inhibit action and prefer nudity as conducive to unrestricted activity. But becoming accustomed to clothing, not only for warmth but also when associated with pride, usually leads to identification of self with one's clothes; and cleanliness, primping, decoration, jewelry, cosmetics, and fine clothes often become important concerns with which a self is occupied. Principles regarding the ways in which a self employs different conceptions in shaping (and reshaping) self-concepts and feelings of identification and opposition are important epistemological principles. Not only do they provide clues to our knowledge of selves but also to the ways in which selves know, for self-conceptions tend to infect and to determine in part our concepts of, and ways of knowing, other things.

I have discussed the roles of identification and opposition in self-conceptions in more detail elsewhere.[25] Here I mention only some common problems inherent in self-conception as ingredients in the nature of knowing.

A chief problem with which Organicism is concerned is self as an organic unity, with self-conceptions, singly and somehow together, as organic unities and their adequacy in revealing and shaping a self's actual nature, and with the variable interactions of self as an organic unity with other persons and things as organic unities. Although there is more to a self than its self-conceptions (its nature as dependent upon the nature of body, mind, physiological health, environmental conditions influencing its nature and functionings, diseases, etc.), each self has a continuing problem of self-identity through time (that is, through its temporal experiences) and of feelings of personal integrity as it functions variably in differing situations and with variable success or failure in dealing with problems that confront it. When uncritical about such problems, a self seems not to have them in the sense of being unaware of them. But the very confidence with which persons proceed in knowing and acting depends on the confidence they have about their own capacities (as knowers and actors) which depend on their self-conceptions and the apparent reliability of such conceptions.

Some persons develop very rigid conceptions of themselves. Some develop more flexible conceptions and even enjoy new adventures in which new conceptions, or new aspects of conceptions, of self are required. Advantages and disadvantages of rigidity and of flexibility can be observed. The more rigid a conception, the more unified and integrated it appears to its conceiver, and, often, the more confidence with which such a conceiver normally thinks and acts. The more flexible a conception, the more it is able to integrate new features into its conception and to attain a more extensive and more complicated kind of organic unity of self. Also, people tend to vary regarding such rigidity and flexibility, in different social, etc., situations, in different stages in life, in different conditions of sickness and health, and with developed skills and habits of action in problem situations. The variations in such relative rigidity and flexibility are themselves factors in the organic unity of a self as a continuing kind of being and continuing kind of knower.

The importance of social roles and social, including cultural, environmental, and both the opportunities and necessities for dialectical interactions involving variable operations of the principle of reciprocity, needs to be stressed in developing and maintaining self-conceptions. The influences of the self-conceptions of others, and of theories about the nature of self retaining cultural credence, need to be recognized.

The Organicist theory of self as mediate involves multiple applications of its Diagram of Types to the various polarities observable in self-conceptions. These will not be developed here. But recognition of other theories of self, as eternal soul separable from the body, as an evanescent epiphenomenon completely reducible to brain functioning, as an *atman* actually identical with *Nirguna Brahman*, as an eternal form (Platonic Idea) manifest in a particular body, as a momentary self-deceptive apparition swarming with *chetasikas*, as a momentary act of existential will, as a soul predestined for heaven or hell completely determined by God, or as a momentary self-enjoying, self-suffering actual occasion concrescent in processes limited by eternal objects in the primordial nature of God, all are rejected as inadequate, each for its own reasons. The roles of subatomic particles and waves, DNA and other hereditary determining and determined functions, and of other factors in the nature of existence yet to be discovered, all may be expected to have bearings on additional mediate conceptions of self. Any adequate Organicist theory will have to consider them and take them into account. The quest for certainty will continue to be conditioned by problems confronting the epistemology resulting from additional evidence concerning the minimal and maximal limits of unity and plurality of the organic unity of a self, and of the roles of self-conceptions in the ways a self knows and feels certain or uncertain in differing circumstances.

3. **The real world.** Mediate theories about the nature of objects, whether perceived, conceived, or imagined, whether of other persons, language, or knowledge, and whether of particular things as objects of present observation of larger, more comprehensive wholes (including body, mind, environment, and the whole universe) within which persons participate, either as ingredients or as relatively isolated parts, tend to evolve into comprehensive philosophies about the nature of existence, knowledge, and values. Many of these arise from specialized problems and perspectives but some of them achieve greater comprehensiveness.[26] Even a brief survey of all of the

multiplicities of philosophies, and influential theories historically accepted in the major sciences, is not possible here. The following samples must suffice for present purposes.

a. **Perception.** Knowledge of the apparently real world through perception may involve inferences, immediate, intermediate, and mediate. The complicated conditions, including organisms, mechanisms, chemical, electrical and electronic processes, both within and outside of the body, involved in perception cannot be reviewed here. My introduction to the subject, 1925, through Woodworth's *Psychology*,[27] studying the views of Roy Wood Sellars and other epistemologists during 1929-32, reading H.H. Price's *Perception*,[28] and references to many psychology textbooks and articles since then, have kept me alert to technical problems involved in perceptual inference. I still regard psychology, which formerly was regarded as one of the philosophical sciences ("branches of philosophy"), as dealing with problems essential to understanding the nature of knowledge and, indeed, of philosophy generally. Reintroduction of concerns called "philosophy of mind" seems to be a rather thin and specialized attempt to recover concerns fundamental to the nature of philosophy. There is a fundamental sense in which philosophy is itself a psychological science. And investigation of the essential conditions of the nature of knowing, including sensation, perception, conception, imagination, memory, anticipation, reasoning, feelings and emotions, which have become the responsibility of psychologists as scientists, are all involved in understanding the nature of knowledge, and the possibilities, and truth and certainty, regarding inferences about the real world.

As an example of mediate inference by a psychologist, I select the following statement: "In vision, for example, one speaks of a target, which seems to be the stimulus but, since it is not the photic energy itself, it is not the stimulus. The target is what the experimenter . . . may see -- that is, it seems to be what is presented to the object or observer to report upon in an experiment. Actually, what stimulates the observer is the photic energy that no one sees. But what the observer describes may or may not tally with the standard description."[29]

What is apprehended as an apparent object now seems likely to have very little revelatory knowledge of the actual physical (chemical, electrical, electronic, etc.) processes functioning as stimuli. Psychological theory today interprets perceptual inference as revealing very little about what actually exists in the real world. Truth, as interpreted by the copy theory, escapes us almost entirely. The apparent regularities, both remainings and changings, that appear for apprehension and interpretation must serve, since they are all (together with inherited mechanism, organs, instincts, and habits of adapting) that is available to a person's organism (including brain and mind) for use in "knowing."

Although conception, induction, and communication with other minds provide additional data and means for interpreting appearances, any quest for certainty based on perception, and upon mediate inferences made by psychologists about perception, discovers little basis for assurance that such inferences are very reliable. Yet, even with such little assurance as we have, the successful ventures for living, for designing and guiding lifetimes, for building cities and empires, scientific laboratories and moon landings, do provide us with confidence that we do have some reliable knowledge. Extending knowledge of psychological and other processes and providing additional kinds of reliability, and of assurance in such reliability, in knowing is a continuing task of epistemologists.

**b. Conception.** Observation of similarities and differences apprehended in apparently real objects and processes results in conceptions which, when mediated by scientists, may become specialized technologies and philosophies of science. The organic unities involved in conceptions expanded into generalizations about an infinitely complicated real world have been stretched amazingly, and some have been stretched beyond retention of essential unity. Inconsistencies in theories about the real world have become obvious to anyone studying the history of science where theories accepted as true, often unquestioningly true, are later abandoned as false. The influence of university departmentalism in isolating scientific specialties from one another has resulted in interdisciplinary ignorance which aggravates humanity's problems of knowledge.[30]

Increased recognition of the interdependencies and mutual immanence inherent in the nature of things and of the need for attending to them in guiding research (in universities, think tanks, and private corporations) by adopting the Organicist philosophy of the essential omnipresence of organic unities could improve the quality and quantity of our understanding of the real world and, hopefully, our assurance that our understanding is more reliable.

c. **Imagination.** Although seemingly some imagination (some contributions of how the mind takes what is given) is a universal condition of perception and conception, and of knowledge generally, explicit and intentional stimulation and exploitation of imaginative abilities in art (fine and practical) and in the efforts of scientists to construct more adequate systems of interpretation, better exemplify the extensive uses of mediate inferences. The fantastic suggestions in science fiction are scarcely more fantastic than some of the proposals made seriously by scientists anxious to achieve an imaginative breakthrough to greater actual understanding. The fantastic speculations of mathematicians, theoretical physicists, astronomers, and computer wizards only occasionally result in fruitful, or useful, hypotheses. In the absence of available crucial experiments some of these fantastic hypotheses achieve widespread acceptance for years, even centuries, in ways inhibiting research in some areas.

Examples of mediate inference are plentiful for readers of contemporary physics. For example: (1) Most persons are able to interpret present apparently real space in terms of three dimensions. Such immediate inference is often extended intermediately to four dimensions of space-time. But a request to think of n-dimensional space, where n can mean six dimensions, or six hundred dimensions, or six million dimensions, involves mediate inference. (2)

Astronomical black holes are explained as invisible supermasses of energy ($10^{-8}$ times the mass of the Sun), "formed from the collapse of supermassive stars.... Most intriguing of all is the possibility that very small black holes -- as small as $10^{-8}$ kg -- may have formed black holes during the first fraction of a second after the universe began. ...There is no observational evidence that such primordial black holes actually exist, but they are of great interest to theoreticians because their properties are determined by quantum mechanics as well as relativity."[31]

Thomas S. Kuhn, in his *Structure of Scientific Revolutions*,[32] has dramatized the pervasive influences of speculative hypotheses in stabilizing and restricting commonly accepted conceptions of the nature of things for long periods. The influence of untestable, or inadequately tested, hypotheses resulting from imaginative attempts to understand has been tremendous. At the same time, we will, indeed we must, continue to employ imagination, not merely in each momentary perception, but also in constructing our scientific hypotheses and philosophical theories in our continuing quest for understanding truth and certainty. Cautious consideration inspired by increasingly adequate theories of the nature of imagination is desired.

d. **Language.** The existence of language, with its long history of development, is itself something miraculous. The invention (or discovery) of grammar, concern about phonetic uniformity and significance, the need for multiplicities of interlinguistic translations, the invention of artificial languages, the multiplicities of mechanisms for transmitting language (wireless, telephones, radios, movies, television, satellites, lasers, and networks), and the efforts to reproduce language mechanically all continue to be amazing.

Although doubtless language began with animal-like grunts, interpreted at first through immediate inference, the ingeniously complicated secret codes and code-breaking systems of military intelligence involve many varieties of mediate inference.[33]

Hubert G. Alexander, Chairman of the Department of Philosophy, University of New Mexico, for many years, authored *Time as*

*Dimension and History*,[34] presenting a double-aspect theory of time similar to my own "Multiple-Aspect Theory of Time" but based in his study of the grammars of several languages, a specialty in which he was genuinely competent. His major works, which I find highly agreeable, are *Language and Thinking*[35] and *Meaning and Language*[36].

Language, which normally becomes incorporated into the nature of selves and minds, is a common prerequisite ingredient in most mediate inference. The organic unities inherent in the nature of words, sentences, grammars, etc., as well as of minds and inferences, continue to function as essential ingredients in mediate inferences about the real world, with all of its complexities, speedy processes, initiations and terminations, existences and nonexistences, and our doubts and assurances about it.[37]

e. **Other persons.** Although infants acquire knowledge of other persons through immediate inference, mediate inference is replete with theories, often partly reliable and often wildly irrelevant, about the nature of persons, including their bodies and minds, which are employed variously in assuming knowledge of other persons. The nature of persons, both generally and in each person, is so complicated that varieties of conditions, habits, differential functionings, attitudes, and beliefs make assurance of understanding other persons very difficult. At times, persons develop feelings of sympathy and achieve habits of mutual cooperation which generate feelings of assurance of mutual understanding. Such persons may develop feelings of loyalty and convictions of certainty about these other persons. Oftentimes such convictions prove justified. But evidences of efforts of societies, for example, to achieve consensus regarding conceptions of common interests reveal that failure to agree seems more common than agreement, even though some basis for agreement is already a basis for the existence of the society.

How to obtain reliable knowledge of other persons will continue to be a major task of epistemologists, psychologists, sociologists, etc. Again, recognition of the roles of organic unities within each person, in human association, and in each of the kinds of communicating and participatory endeavors, should facilitate pursuit of such tasks.[38]

**f. Knowledge.** Knowledge itself, originating in immediate inference, has become an object of endlessly complicated mediate inferences. The investigation of and formulation of an Organicist theory of knowledge itself exemplifies mediate inference about knowledge. I tentatively accept the conclusions proposed by "objective relativists" claiming that commonly accepted knowledge by groups of people achieves a kind of realistic status (existing in other minds whether a particular mind knows it or not) which can achieve a sufficient stability to function reliably.[39] Culture does become institutionalized in the minds of all people and its unchanging features provide a basis for stability, and hence reliability, of many useful kinds. Although the "cycle of institutional development"[40] needs to be recognized as having its effects on culture also, the currently continuing stability of institutionalized knowledge is a significant factor in understanding the nature of knowledge and is something that epistemologists need to recognize as an essential condition of much mediate inference.

The organic unities involved in the nature of culture function here in ways that need to be understood as conditions of much knowledge, and of some kinds of assurance which cultural stability makes possible. Institutionalized fanaticisms will continue to prove provocative to both those interested in political harmony and to epistemologists who need to try to find ways to convince and assure persons with mistaken fanaticisms that they should abandon their false views and try to adopt true views. It now seems that even more reliable knowledge will be needed by epistemologists if they are to succeed in such attempts.

## LARGER, MORE COMPREHENSIVE, KINDS OF INFERENCE

Although larger, more comprehensive, kinds of inference have been implicit already, when not explicit, in the foregoing, we may note that, with some exceptions, larger and more comprehensive kinds of inference seem more likely to involve mediate inference. Although some speculative theories about the nature of the universe, or even of some large portions of it, may seem very disconnected from the apparent realities in immediate and intermediate inferences, a tendency remains quite constant for speculators, at least, to feel somehow as participants in the universe as they scheme it.

Some persons seem habituated to restricting inferences to local or nearby apparent realities. But others may become habituated to experiencing at-homeness in the cosmos and even spend much of their time, concern, and assumed knowing with more distant or more comprehensive objects. Believers in cosmic deities, one or many, and in the primacy of unity in constituting ultimate reality (as in the doctrines of *Nirguna Brahman* and *Sunya* or the Neo-Platonic One), often believe and act as if their views about the universe are true and good and certain. The extents to which such beliefs may be justified, for purposes of personal satisfaction as well as in terms of realistic evidences available, remain constant problems for epistemologists.[41]

Faith in some reliably enduring cosmic unity serves a need of those who lack awareness of the omnipresence of organic unities in less comprehensive inferred areas of existence. Familiarity with the nature and omnipresence of organic unity and mutual immanence should retard tendencies to go to unfeasible extremes in making mediate inferences about the structure of the universe and the place of persons in it.

The foregoing treatment of mediate inference is extremely inadequate, given the multifarious and multitudinous examples available in all of the general sciences, each of which has its own collection (not always consistent) of mediate inferences, especially in its more theoretical explanations.

Theoretical physics and mathematics tend to be extremely mediate in their theorizing whereas engineering involves a constant intermingling of mediate, intermediate and immediate inferences. Practicing engineers seem unlikely to keep in mind our distinction between immediate, intermediate, and mediate inferences. Engineers usually proceed with more confidence when, and because, they tend to have naively realistic attitudes toward all of their apparently real objects and, especially when enjoying experienced successes in applying their theories, tend to regard their understanding of theoretical objects with as much confidence (feeling of certainty) as when they proceed naively. That problems arise and consequently doubts (sometimes temporary and sometimes more enduring) occur and tend to involve all three kinds of inference (immediate, intermediate, mediate) seems likely. Problems that arise in engineering may be primarily of one of the three kinds of inference, and at times (especially in more complicated problems) may involve all three kinds, that is, doubts regarding each of the three.

The remainder of this work on theory of knowledge will involve inferences and, although my preference is for pursuing inquiries illustrating intermediate inferences more than mediated inferences, the numbers and kinds of information increasingly available through more and more specialized sciences tend to force consideration of more and more mediated kinds of concepts as relevant to understanding the nature of knowledge.

Another way of expressing the Organicist theory of inference is presented in Appendix I, "Subject-Object Theories," which includes an Organicist partial treatment of subject-object, apparent-real self, apparent-real object, and subject-penetrating-object and object-penetrating-subject polarities. Although the basis for each of these polarities originates in immediate inference, their exposition in terms to the Diagram of Types obviously involves intermediate inferences, and the technical extremes, named "extreme middlism and "extreme equalism," may be regarded as resulting from mediated inferences

seemingly required to complete a statement of implications inherent
in the nature of polarity.[42]

# Three
# GENERALIZATION

## A. WHAT IS GENERALIZATION?

Generalizing is a process occurring whenever a person becomes aware that two or more things are the same in some way. Each sameness of two or more things is named "a universal." It is named "a universal" because it is something that is common to all of the two or more things. Each of the two or more things that are the same in some way is named a "particular." It is named "a particular" because it participates in a universal as one part (or particle) of the universal as a whole.

Universals and particulars are conceived as existing interdependingly, or as being by nature mutually immanent. The nature of a universal is to have particulars as parts. The nature of a particular is to be a part of (as being one of the things in which the sameness constituting the universal exists) the universal.

Generalizing about merely apparent objects may not involve awareness of any distinction between, or interdependence of, universals and particulars in what appears. The same is true about what appears as apparently real objects. But when persons generalize intentionally, they naturally attend to both the particular objects being generalized about and the sameness (or samenesses) being observed. The universals are observed to be embodied in the particulars.

Because much thinking abstracts, it has become convenient to distinguish two kinds of universals: A universal considered together with all of its particulars is named a "concrete universal". A universal considered as abstracted from all of its particulars is named an "abstract universal."

The word "generalization" has two accepted meanings. First, it means a process of generalizing. Generalizing is a process of observing or creating an awareness of sameness in two or more things. Second, it means that which has resulted from a process of generalizing. A generalization is a statement of a universal. Both of these meanings are used in this chapter. Which meaning is intended should be evident from the context. Expected use of generaliz*ation* should not imply indifference to the importance of prior generaliz*ing* involved in the originating of most observed universals.

In popular usage, persons often generalize without intending to refer to exactly all of the things in a collection. They may be uncertain about whether all of the things embody the universal, and be willing to be indefinite about whether all or only some (many or most) are included. Although persons tend to find this way of generalizing very useful practically, I intend to use the term "generalization" as connoting inclusion of all of the particulars involved in a universal.

How to begin a chapter on generalizing in such a way as to provide a sound initial grounding of theory in some obviously foundational way escapes me. Although my aim is to treat the problem of knowledge by observing some essential ingredients in its nature, and to point out clearly some of the bases which seem obvious after surveying the field, in my attempt first to analyze basic parts and then to gradually synthesize all of the parts in some comprehensive whole, I am confronted with the fact that experience functions holistically and that the objects appearing in consciousness often are already dynamic complexly integrated interdependent wholes having multivariant significances implicit in their natures.

I choose not to repeat the criticisms rightly raised against traditional empiricist and rationalist theories of the origin of ideas. But I find that, by beginning in the middle, so to speak, I am challenged to explain complexities by a method that is analytic in ways that lose much of what is obviously involved. My experience is not a "blooming, buzzing confusion," as William James has said, but it is

a rich conglomeration of intermingling varieties of apparent objects appearing continually with varying attention to what appears. "The organized wholes in immediate experience are original data: the beginning, not the end-product, of mental activity."[1] "It takes a very recondite and special interest to limit ordinary direct observation to color, line or texture, an attitude of abstraction that is very remote from the usual way of observing things."[2]

I must begin in some way, and following the topics outlined in the articles, "Intuition" and "Inference," is adopted as a suitable expedient: Generalizing within presence. Generalizing immediate inference. Generalizing intermediate inference. Generalizing mediate inference.

# B. GENERALIZING WITHIN PRESENCE

All of the statements constituting the chapters, "Intuition" and "Inference," are already generalizations. Thus, in one way, treatment of generalization has already advanced to great lengths. But the topics examined can now be attended to for the specific purpose of trying to understand the nature of generalization. Intuiting, inferring, and generalizing have distinguishable natures. Even though we have already generalized about intuition and inference, additional generalizations about the nature and kinds of generalization seem needed for an adequate account of the nature of knowledge.

Is there a simplest example of generalization? Whenever two appearances appear to be the same in some way (they are already the same in appearing or in being appearances), that sameness is a universal. Such a universal is intuited. A person may intuit without generalizing, or without being aware of a universal, but a person cannot generalize, or be aware of a universal, without intuiting.

Is there any limit to the kinds or complexities of generalizations apprehendable within presence? Although limits do exist regarding what may appear in presence (and these limits vary in different

persons as well as in the same person at different times), any awareness of two or more appearances (no matter how complex the appearances) as the same in some way constitutes awareness of a universal. For example, if one is aware of a kaleidoscopic festival parade on a busy city street as continuing (and the apparent continuing is being grasped in two or more instants within one presence), awareness of such sameness, or of any sameness in the two or more instants, is awareness of something universal. That is, awareness of the appearance of two or more complex dynamic gestalts as being the same in some way constitutes a universal (also a generalization). The point being emphasized here is that any apparent samenesses of two or more organic unities function as samenesses that can be generalized about. Awareness that two apparent opposites are mutually immanent and are the same in sharing such mutuality, involves both some universality and some generalization. Awareness that an apparent whole and its parts are both alike and different, and are also at least partially mutually immanent, involves generalization and universality. Generalizations apprehendable in presence can range from the simplest to the most complex.

Since existing things that appear as apparently real objects usually are very complex in nature, the recurrence, or simultaneous appearance, of two or more complex objects also constitutes an apparent complex universal. The kinds of knowledge occurring even within one presence can be extremely complex, and variations in the kinds of combinations of characteristics existing in two or more apparently real objects complicate the kinds of knowledge experienced. Distinctions of kinds of combinations also occur in presence because they occur in the existing things causing awareness of apparently real objects. They also often occur in dreams and imagined objects. Knowledge of kinds is a kind of knowledge. Combinations of characteristics not only occur in particular objects as system gestalts, but recurrence of such objects involves a recurrence of systemicness, and thus, even within a presence,

universal systems and universal kinds of systems may be apprehended. Systems involve organic unity, and the sameness of the organic unities of two systems may be apprehended in a presence even when not present in the focus of attention.

Although each presence appears as continuous and thus as an undivided whole, it may also contain many apparent objects. When it does, it exists as a whole of parts embodying organic unity. But also when what is apprehended is apprehended as an organic unity, it also may be apprehended as a universal (that is, as an organic-unity universal). Such a way of apprehending seems to be involved in all observation of dynamic objects even when the organic unity is not attended to or apprehended as such. Every universal is already an organic unity, a whole (the sameness embodied in the particulars) and its parts (the particulars) existing interdependingly. Universals apprehended within a presence are organic unities, and the presence (as a whole and its parts, including any apprehended universals) is an organic unity, even when its organic unity is not attended to or apprehended as such.

Since Organicism presupposes that organic unity is omnipresent in existence, and thus in each existing presence, how does it explain the claims of yogins to achieve awareness in which objects and duration are completely absent? Each person can, I believe, experience moments of seemingly complete rest in which what appears appears as completely static and in which awareness remains unchanged. Does this mean that organic unity is missing? Is what is apprehended as a moment of complete rest a whole without parts? If, as a claimed (or hoped for) ultimate basis for reliable knowledge (seeming certainty) is to be located in intuition, in awareness of appearance without intermediation, then when awareness apprehends what appears as a completely static appearance, must we not accept as a fact that a whole without parts can exist in presence and that organic unity is absent? Although the answer must be yes so far as particular moments of consciousness are concerned, the Organicist theory contends that the multiplicities of conditions causing the existence of such moments are sufficiently suffused with multiplicities of organic unities that the production of some moments of organic unities in which the unity or wholeness predominates and of other organic unities in which the plurality of parts predominates makes possible the occasional appearances of complete rests. Yogins promote actualization of such occasions.

**1. Time.** I have generalized about two dimensions of presence, appearing as pairs of polar opposites, that is, past-future and subject-object, which not only recur constantly but seem to be present almost universally. Generalizations may occur not only about each of these four kinds of directions but also may occur within each of them.

A person may, when hearing a succession of sounds, such as those of an alarm clock, apprehend them as all alike as sounds and as embodying a universal of such sounds. One may observe each of the sounds as passing, so that a direction of such passings is also repeated with the occurrence of each successive sound. A sameness of such repeated direction may be observed as a universal. As each sound ceases and becomes past, any awareness of such repeated cessation can be generalized as a universal. And any awareness of repeated apparent becoming past can be apprehended as a universal of such becoming past. Intuiting a generalization about successive alarm-clock sounds normally includes awareness of regularity in the repeated successions. Intuitively apprehending a generalization about a person's conversation may include irregularities. Thus generalization may be about either or both regularities and irregularities. But any generalization about irregularities will involve observing processes having differences that are at least alike in being differences and often alike in being like kinds of differences. All genuine novelties are alike in being genuine novelties, and such likeness, when generalized about, functions as a universal.

A person may, in ascending a stairs, be aware of a succession of achievements in advancing into the future, and generalize about the sameness reembodied in each step. Thus one may apprehend generalizations both about passage into a past and advancement into a future, and both simultaneously (when hearing an alarm clock or climbing a stairs) all within a presence. When such successions are extended, generalizations may be extended through expanding presence and extending beyond presence. Repeated experiences of such extensions yield generalizations about an immediate past and an immediate future, and may serve as bases for inferring generalizations about an extended past and an extended future.

Surely nothing is more common in ordinary experience than an awareness that two or more objects appear to be alike in some one way or many ways. Awareness of an apparent sameness of two or more apparent objects constitutes an apparent universal. Some apparent objects appear as apparently real objects. Awareness of an apparent sameness between two apparently real objects constitutes an apparently real universal. All this can occur within presence, and also may occur through expanding presence and through expanding beyond presence.

**2. Self.** Although much awareness of objects neglects attention to awareness that a self or subject is involved in such awareness, a person may also be aware that the same subject recurs or continues the same during an awareness of two or more objects and that such sameness exists as a universal when attention is focused on it. Such awareness of a subject (that is, in any subject-object awareness) as a universal can occur entirely within presence, or through expanding presence, or extending beyond presence.

Also, since objects normally are objects for subjects and subjects normally are subjects for objects, a subject-object sameness normally exists in awareness as a condition whether or not present in the focus of attention. A person may generalize about such a subject-object universal within presence or through expanded presence or through transcending presence.

Although there need be less doubt about apparent universals apprehended within presence than about those involving presence-transcending inference, habits of doubt acquired from attending to presence-transcending generalizations may actually infect a person's way of "giving" to what is "taken" when the sameness of two objects appears as given when the objects are apprehended as presented within presence.

# C. GENERALIZING IMMEDIATE INFERENCE

**1. Time.** When presence-transcending immediate inferences continue to remain the same, or to recur as the same, universality exists in such sameness. When a person is observing for a first time an apparently real object (for example, a tree), the awareness of continuance or recurrence involves a generalization as the awareness continues or recurs. When the object is complex, its systemic complexity and organic unity are embodied in the generalization even if attention is not focused on such embodiment.

When a person is aware of a series of objects disappearing from sight, as when bubbles are observed disappearing down a drain or when portions of the pavement disappear under a moving automobile, any sameness observed in such repeated appearance of disappearances constitutes a generalization and embodies a universal. When a person recalls blowing out all of the lighted candles on cakes during three successive birthdays, the recollection of the samenesses (birthdays, cakes, candles, blowing out all) embodies a complex universal. When a person reads, with a naively realistic attitude, about the rise and fall of ancient dynasties, one's awareness that the dynasties were all alike in being dynasties, in rising and falling, etc., involves a complex of universals. All of these examples illustrate generalizations and universals pertaining to pastness, and are themselves all alike (and thus universals) in pertaining to pastness. But also, what is being emphasized here, when universals appear as embodied in continuing or recurring after-images, disappearances, memories, and accounts of past histories, the nature of generalization and universality is such that it can be so embodied.

When a person is anticipating continuing or recurring enjoyment of successive swallowings of a favorite beverage or succulent flavors while eating a meal, such anticipations of recurrence embody a generalization and a universal. When a person drives an automobile, and observes approached objects and approaching vehicles, one normally retains a persistingly alert attitude of anticipation. Generalization and universality exist in such continuing and recurrent alertness and anticipation. When a door-to-door salesman plans to call on several potential customers, the salesman often expects some common kinds of response. Any awareness of such expected commonness exists as a universal in the salesman's present awareness. (It may or may not be realized as anticipated.) When a person enrolls in a college, one becomes aware of several courses to be taken, and one's awareness that they will all be the same in some ways (for example, for three semester-hours credit) and that some kinds will be the same in some ways (all given in the history department) thereby embodies anticipated universals, as well as universals of anticipation. These examples illustrate generalizations pertaining to an apparent future. They illustrate how the nature of generalization and universality is such that it can be embedded in these ways.

When a person is looking out of the window of a speeding train, one's observation of seemingly passing objects normally involves not only both their sudden recurrent appearance and their rapid recurrent disappearance but also their almost simultaneous appearance and disappearance. Generalization and universality can thus be embodied not only in awareness of becoming past and of becoming future but also in awareness of both together simultaneously. The more complicated awareness of passage becomes, the more complicated is the universality embodied in such awareness.

Naively realistic immediate inferences of objects not only may infer the existence of apparently real universals in objects, for example, two or more chairs being alike in having four legs, but also involve the sameness in two or more acts of inferring the existence of such chairs and their sameness. Universality is present in all naively realistic inferences to the extent that they are the same in any way, including being naively realistic inferences.

**2. Self.** Immediate inference regarding the existence of a real self as subject in subject-object relations may infer not only that a self continues or recurs in functioning as aware but also that such continuing or recurring functioning embodies a sameness existing as a universal. When such inferences become involved in the awareness of new objects or new kinds of objects causing differing responses of a self as subject, any observable sameness in the new responses of a self as subject may be generalized about, not merely as a sameness of self but also as a sameness of a new kind of self-response. Generalizations about an immediately inferred real self may be both stable and enduring or variable and various.

Immediate inferences combining naive realistic appearances of both objects and subjects normally occur transparently but nevertheless embody universals constituted by any samenesses present in their recurrence. Recurrent variations in subject-object interactions may include awareness of feelings of satisfaction, confidence, conviction, uncertainty, confusion, or fear. Generalization is by nature such that it can function in relation to all other kinds of immediate inference previously outlined, including the larger, more comprehensive kinds, such as participation, mind, body, and environmental surroundings.

# D. GENERALIZING INTERMEDIATE INFERENCE

The importance of "intermediate inferences" in constituting "knowledge" should not be underestimated because they constitute most of our inferences in everyday living. Inferences are here named "intermediate" when and because they involve both some acceptance of objects as being real in the way they appear as real and retain some trace of uncertainty regarding whether and in what ways what is real about the objects is also different in nature from the way it appears. Thus intermediate inferences range from almost complete acceptance of what appears as real (as in immediate inference) to almost complete doubt about the revelatory capacity of such apparently real appearances (as in mediate inference). Thus the kinds of generalizations and resulting apparent universals vary enormously in nature and kinds.

**1. Time.** In each person, knowledge of the past is a product of both the uniformities in biological heredity, physiological functioning, environmental conditions, and the social and cultural traditions in which a person has developed and is living. Thus generalizations involving intermediate inferences about what appears as past (times, processes, places, people, objects, groups, culture, etc.) involve both relatively stable and continuing conditions of many kinds and also the peculiar conditions occurring often with novelty (at least for the individual living adaptively), both unique novelties and novel kinds of situations in which novelties occur.

Since biological development has provided tendencies to see (hear, smell, taste, touch, etc.) objects as real and as real in ways conducive to adaptation and survival, it has also provided tendencies to infer with confidence the ways in which objects appear as real. But uncertainties inherent in adaptive processes resulting from awareness to adapt as desired also conduce to caution and induce doubts about whether what appears really is as it appears. Hence generalizations about uncertainty regarding apparently real things is itself a product of the nature and conditions of biological adaptation. Thus generalization is such that much of it results from the need for and nature of intermediate inferencing in relation to apparently real objects, past, present and future.

Knowledge about what is future tends to be experienced as more uncertain than knowledge about what is past. That apparently real future experiences will occur seems normally assured except perhaps for those expecting death. But how they will be experienced is conditioned by past failures of generalizations about intermediate inferences so that present intermediate inferences about the future tend to be suffused with uncertainty and thus conducive to alertness, attention, and an attitude of inquiry. It is true that some persons anticipate with serene confidence most of the time and that others seem to be always tense with anxiety. Generalization is by nature such that it occurs in intermediate inferences about what is future, whether anticipated with serenity or anxiety.

Generalizing is processual and thus proceeds temporally in ways involving futurity. When each additional particular in which a universal is observed appears first as anticipated and thus as future, does any uncertainty inhering in intermediate inferences about what is future condition the generalizing process? Although persons may differ regarding such feelings of uncertainty, generalization is by nature such that uncertainties inherent in any intermediate inferences about presently apparent universals being also embodied in particulars expected to appear in the future also condition such generalizations. Acceptance of a doctrine of "working hypotheses" as essential to scientific method is normally accompanied by insisting on an attitude of "tentativity" regarding all hypotheses, thus integrating generalizations about uncertainty (and uncertainty about some generalizations) as inherent in the nature of the quest for reliable knowledge by such method.

**2. Self.** Knowledge of self involves generalizations, and generalization is by nature such that it can yield knowledge of self. All generalizations are acts of observation by a self. So all generalizations are self-dependent (dependent on a self). Each self is by nature a generalizing process, both in generalizing about other things, in generalizing about itself, and in generalizing about interrelations between itself and objects. A self is also in a sense a generalizing process, with or without awareness of existing as such a process, by generating or regenerating itself as the same self through continuing or recurring existing. That is, a self is a progressing concrete universal existence whether or not it becomes aware of itself as such in any distinctly conceptual way. So intermediate inferences about the nature of self, and of self as a generalizing process, seem warranted.[3]

Knowledge of apparently real objects occurs in most people mainly in the form of intermediately inferred universal generalizations. Generalization is by nature such that we can generalize about perceived objects of many kinds and about many different ways of perceiving. It is such that we can conceive objects of many kinds and complexities, as concrete or abstract, as instantaneous, varyingly enduring, or even timeless, and as obviously so or as extremely vague, unclear, chaotic, and self-contradictory, or as nonexistent. Generalizations occur regarding images, and ways and kinds of imaging, and feelings, and desirings, and how these are projected as apparently real objects of art and beauty and ugliness.

Most generalizations in adults appear in language, too often naively projected as having some kind of real existence, whether in sound waves, or on printed paper and in libraries, in some eternally real subsistence, or merely in other minds. Recurrent doubts about fully understanding, not only one's own language but especially foreign languages, tend to become more important as one learns more languages or more about languages, causing generalizations to appear more intermediate and less immediate. Generalizations about other persons begin in infancy and tend to mature along with generalizations about self. Although some persons gain seemingly complete confidence in their knowledge of, and trust in, other persons as understood, most knowledge of other persons includes generalizations involving uncertainty, even mystery, and sometimes fear. Learning to generalize about how other persons generalize, often quite differently, is one way of extending our understanding of the nature of generalization.

Knowledge of the real world, that is, the apparently real world, as known through intermediate inferences involving it both to appear as real in the way that it appears and to appear in some way or ways as more than it appears, involves generalizations normally infected with uncertainty. When a person is engaged in solving a problem, then at least two kinds of uncertainty may be involved. (a) When a person is confronted with a problem, one does not yet have a solution. Then one normally experiences uncertainties about whether one can attain a solution, about whether one's first (or second or third) hypothesis will work, and about how much testing or working with the hypothesis satisfactorily will be needed if a solution is to be found and accepted. (b) When a person has a proposed solution, uncertainty regarding whether there is more to what appears than is apparent and what its nature is often remains. Since two kinds of uncertainty occur in such situations, we may inquire about how they are related. Each of the two kinds may be complicated and variable. But can both be reduced or overcome? If a person believes that one has solved one's problem satisfactorily, then the uncertainties related to the problem may be eliminated, although the generalized solution to many kinds of problems retain sufficient uncertainty that tentativity is retained as an essential characteristic of the scientific attitude and method. But uncertainties about ways in which what appears real appears to be more than appears may be such that they can never be eliminated, even though, with continuing efforts to understand, uncertainties may be reduced somewhat although also uncertainties may increase as our efforts reveal that there appears to be even more of the more than what appears than appeared earlier.

Some persons may be quite unaware that these uncertainties are of two kinds and simply have vague feelings of uncertainty. But the more a person (or a task force, a society, or a civilization) is concerned about knowing more and more about what appears to be more than appears, then more inquiry into its nature is pursued deliberately. Although it seems impossible to reproduce all of, or all of any part of, existence in minds, that is, in awareness, and in generalizations, the fact that we have had some success in learning more about what appears to be more than appears encourages us to continue our inquiries and serves as a warrant that our ignorance and uncertainties may be reduced. Recognition that generalizations about the impossibility of complete knowledge of the real world (existence) are warranted itself involves a generalization about such generalizations. Agnosticism is a necessary ingredient in any adequate theory of knowledge to the extent that some kinds of knowledge are not possible. But the inevitability of some agnosticism need not inhibit efforts to act on the faith that some more of what appears is more than what appears may yet become apparent. More knowledge of the real world seems in prospect for humankind even if the process of attaining it also reveals still more about existence that we do not, perhaps cannot, know.

I now turn to generalizations about larger, more comprehensive wholes, that is, to generalizations inclusive of the generalizations about our four directions (past, future, self, and objects) and to ways that they describe massive and extensive integrated wholes, such as societies and civilizations, embodying organized complexities of many kinds. These range from smaller organisms, such as a swamp, a family, a circus, a festival, a village, a university, through metropolises, nations, federations of nations, to civilizations, to humankind, to the earth, to a galaxy, and to the universe. Inferences and generalizations about all of these conceptions of apparently real massive and extensive organized wholes have bases in personal experiences and tend to have their apparent reality accepted. When a person reads about a dynasty with unfamiliar cultural traditions, one already has some ideas about family and cultural systems at the same time one is aware that there is much more to such dynasties than appears in one's awareness.

Most inferences of civilized adults are intermediate inferences. Not only does the food that a farmer's wife prepares appear to be as real as it appears, but she also knows that the food is a product of many causes and conditions of the earth's agricultural system which she does not understand. Not only is a national dictator familiar with the personnel and fortifications that he depends upon, but he also knows that multiplicities of conditions, such as jealousy, willingness to endure submission, weather, enemies, competing loyalties, etc., are too many and too complex to rule with complete assurance. Although a chemist has much demonstrated reliable understanding of many chemicals, the complexities of combinations and the uncertainties about the nature of energy organized in subatomic particles keep him uncertain about their nature.

Most experienced adults apprehend the organic unities of the complex objects in their environment both somewhat as naively realistic and somewhat with uncertain wonder about the mysteries of their existence and nature. But the naive familiarity and critical uncertainty become organically unified, with amazing variations. The nature of time remains very much a mystery. And self-conceptions include familiarity with one's awareness, interests, attitudes, body, and ways of functioning. But also persons often wonder why they exist, of what they really consist, and what makes them function in the ways they do. Most self-conceptions involve intermediate inferences and generalizations. "What is knowledge?" Almost any answer will involve intermediate inference.

# E. GENERALIZING MEDIATE INFERENCE

"Mediate" or "mediated" inferences, as these terms are used here, refer to inferences that what appears as real also involves something both more than and different from what appears as real. Each kind of apparent more than and different from what appears as real involves an additional kind of mediate inference. Each kind of mediate inference may generate a generalization about such more than and different from what appears as real (and possibly about how that more than and different from what appears as real is related to what appears as real).

A fundamental difficulty in discussing mediate inference is that, no matter how much more than or different from the inferred being is from what appears in immediate inferences and intermediate inferences, it cannot be completely more or different, because it functions as a projection intended to apprehend a real object and thus is like all other projected intentions in being a projected intention. In every subject-object polarity something of the subject is immanent in the object. So even in mediate inferences to objects most unlike other objects, something of the nature and intention of the inferring subject remains implicit or immanent in the object as it appears.

But a mediately inferred object is significant because of its mysteriousness when compared with objects in ordinary experience. Although the uncertainty inherent in inferring the existence and nature of what appears as more than and different from, hence other than, what normally appears, tends to remain inherent in the inference, when people have repeated making the inference so that it becomes habitual, and a culturally established habit, its uncertainty tends to diminish and to become part of a creed of "believers."

Mediate inference may be exemplified in primitive thinking. Anthropologists report a plethora of generalizations about invisible powers. For their scientific purposes, anthropologists have generalized about many such primitive generalizations by adopting the Polynesian term *mana* to name a general invisible power common to all of them [4] Faith in the practical generalization, that a thing is what a thing does and that when something is done there is something that does it, is common to human nature and human (and other animal) ways of knowing. Generalizations about visible causation naturally lead to generalizations about causation by invisible causes when actual effects are observed and no evident cause is observed. When something appears to be caused but no cause appears, then a person naturally infers, and generalizes, that an invisible cause is present. Primitive and traditional cultures are replete with examples of accepted explanations of both unique and recurrent examples of causation by invisible powers. Analogics are called up to depict the invisible power as a deity of some kind, having form like some animal (as in totems) or giant or wizard. A history of developments in Hindu theology well exemplify this process. [5] They lead eventually to *Nirguna Brahman*, which is conceived as the being of blissful awareness purified of all else. It is mediately inferred to be completely freed from all distinctness, form, time, desire, life (and thus completely other than ordinary experience), and yet as a negation of all negations, it is a product of human interest in negation, and in perfection of purity. Why any being should be is a complete mystery. Why Brahman is also both completely powerless to cause and yet is the causal source of all else, emanated or incarnated as *maya*, remains an ultimate mystery.

Contemporary physics is replete with mysteries and physicists compete with each other for professional advancement and Nobel Prizes by mediately inferring, and supposedly demonstrating, the existence of some particular kind or form of physical structure or power. Energy is a central concept in physical science. Everything in the universe embodies energy. What is energy? On the one hand, nobody knows. It is a complete mystery. Why energy exists, and why all existents embody energy, continues to be a complete mystery. On the other hand, the nature of energy should be obvious to everyone, because, if energy is what energy does, and if energy does everything that is done, so to speak, then we cannot fail to observe its nature in the ways existing things function. Although energy is thus believed to be present through its effects in what appears in presence, and in immediately and intermediately inferred things and processes, there remains something about it that is inexplicable, and to this extent knowledge of it involves mediate inference.

In addition to the mysteries remaining after continuing the study of chemistry and astronomy, and now biotechnology, the mystery constituting the mind-body problem, for example, of how mental energy and brain energy can seem to be so different in nature and yet interact dialectically in multi-complicated ways, continues. In spite of all the published volumes of scientific findings, in libraries and data banks, and commonly accepted "scientific laws" revealing something about the nature of energy, the remaining ignorance, and uncertainties, about its nature requires retaining a large amount of inferential mediacy in our knowledge.

**1. Time.** Generalizing mediate inferences may extend in any of our four directions (past-future, self-objects) as well as including all of them and extending beyond them. Although existing as temporal beings and intuitively accepting their temporal nature, persons have little understanding of the nature of time. Although conceptually accommodating days and months and years, even centuries and millennia, and hours, minutes, seconds and even milliseconds, and times for eating and excreting, sleeping and waking, and rhythms of lungs and heart and sunrise and sunset, and energy from periods of rest and fatigue from periods of work, the nature of time as a universal characteristic and condition of existing remains unclear. So theories about the nature of time are invented, some simple and obvious, some having partial plausibility, and some deepening its mysteriousness.

Questions about the nature of time are so many and so complicated that it may seem that no theory of time can be adequate. Is time a container of all the events that occur within it and all of the things that come into it, remain in it, and go out of it? Or is time merely an aspect of, or an ingredient in, existing things and processes? Is it everlasting or did it have a beginning, and will it have an end? Is there such being as eternity (timelessness)? If so, how is it related to time? Some claim that God, who is eternal (timeless), created the world and thus created time as a period within which the world will exist. (How souls can remain eternally in Heaven after the end of the earth remains unclear. If God is eternal, God is both before and after the earth which God created. Thus God is everlasting in the sense of lasting as long as the earth and its time. But after the earth, and time, ceases, the being of God may be eternal, but how can souls be eternal and still be alive, i.e., temporal?)

Are there many times, and lapses of time, as with the Hindu "Days and Nights of Brahman"? Brahman manifests the world for an aeon (a "Day") and then does not manifest the world for an aeon. *Ananta*, unendingness, is an unendingness not of each aeon but of the series of "Days and Nights." But the view of Advaita Vedanta is that all time is illusory (*maya*) and hence unreal except as an illusory manifestation of an eternal being. This view, like the above, has both intermediate and mediate ingredients, but at first acquaintance, belief seems to call for stretching imagination into accepting an unbelievable mystery. Of course, when a person, or a society or civilization, accepts a belief in a mystery as true, and becomes accustomed to its belief, the mediate characteristic of the inference recedes from obviousness and it tends to be accepted as a familiar immediate inference.

Is time continuous or discontinuous? Some holding a mathematical view of time as consisting of instants just as a line consists of points externally related to each other, claim that, since what is past no longer exists and what is future does not yet exist, and what is present is a durationless instant, the apparent duration of any presence is a specious illusion. William James called it "the specious present." Bertrand Russell proposed that existence exists for an instant and then does not exist for an instant and that all being consists in instantaneous sections of a universe proceeding temporally instant by instant. "The whole process of nature may, so far as present evidence goes, be conceived as discontinuous."[6] Minds saturated with mathematical measurements may find Russell's proposal as immediate or intermediate inferences, but they remain mediate for me.

If existence is essentially temporal so that nothing can exist without time, is time essentially existential so that there can be no time apart from existence? Is there a single time, or are there many times, as many as there are existing processes? Does time flow smoothly, or does it sometimes flow faster and sometimes slower? Does it have different speeds in different kinds of existence, different areas of the universe, at different periods in history? Does time have "width" and "thickness," like space, not just a line (of instants) and a plane, but also a cube, and thus have "volume"? If so, does its volume vary? Regularly or in erratic waves? Does it sometimes stop and then start again? Is time dialectical? If existing proceeds dialectically, must not time proceed dialectically?

Turning to the past in our past-future polarity, does the past exist? After-images and memories presuppose a yes answer. But if what is past is not present, has it not ceased to exist? (After-images and memories are present in awareness, and have not yet passed from presence.) Can what becomes past remain past everlastingly? Or may what is past be "reborn" in another present?

My view is that existence occurs in organic unities, having hierarchical levels of unities, each of which has its own duration and present unit of time, so that we have present minutes, present hours, present days, present months, present years, present centuries, etc., or present heart-beats, present breaths, present waking, present menstrual period, etc., such that time is multi-leveled in its being ingredient in the multi-leveled processes of existence. No present is a mere instant, no matter how short comparatively, and no present is everlasting. The multi-variant lengths of times involve the multivariant pasts and futures of each present. Many pasts and futures are contemporaneous with each present. So what becomes past does not become so completely, but, just as "old soldiers never die, but just fade away," what becomes past becomes past gradually. Persons becoming acquainted with my theory regard it as requiring mediate inference. But, given my familiarity with it, my inferences seem primarily intermediate. But some mediacy remains in my inferences, because I continue to regard existence itself, and thus the existence of anything, as an ultimate mystery.[7]

Inferences and generalizations about the future are as various as those about the past. Immediacy is present when anticipating the taste of a spoonful of soup just entering your mouth. Intermediacy characterizes inferences about plans for marriage, political election, moving to a new location, and retirement. Mediacy is added when we generalize about an afterlife, the future evolution of galaxies, and potentialities for generating several species of super races.

**2. Self.** By "self" we here refer to the subject-object polarity present in awareness of appearances. Self is more than subject. Although its presence as subject in awareness, functioning as that which is aware, is intuited, and is conceived in terms of the ways it functions as subject, generalizations that each person makes about it normally involve also immediate, intermediate, and sometimes mediate inferences. A self as subject normally immediately infers that it continues within and controls its body. A self as subject normally intermediately infers generalizations about its interactions with its environment, its past experiences, its learning abilities, its intended actions. Although whenever a self may wonder about what it is, how it came to be, how its future may develop, mediate inferences speculating about its nature tend to develop.

Suggestions available in culturally inherited doctrines include inferring that a self is an eternal soul separable from its body, is an illusory and ignorant manifestation of *Nirguna Brahman*, is a temporary collection of atoms, is a mechanistic epiphenomenon, is destined to become a Mormon deity, is predestined for a future in Heaven or Hell, is all good because God (as conceived by Christian Scientists) is omnibenevolent and has the power to prevent any evil. When a person dreams or imagines self in any of a variety of fantastic ways, mediate inference may be involved. But most mediate inferences about self seem to retain more intermediate ingredients than do inferences about objects.

Objects, as our two-directional subject-object polarity implies, are objects for subjects. Some (perhaps most) objects appearing in awareness appear as if real. Immediate inference generalizes about each object and each kind of object as being as real in just the way that it appears. Intermediate inference generalizes about objects in many different ways, depending not only on the kind of object but also on the kinds of errors or inadequacies appearing as a result of immediate inferences. Culturally-inherited explanations about the nature of apparently real things as objects contribute to intermediate inferences, exemplified by learning from textbooks, reading directions from manufacturers, and listening to lectures in training sessions.

Dissatisfaction with intermediately inferred generalizations has produced enormous varieties of mediate inferences. The histories of the sciences, religions, and literature are replete with examples of fantastic ideas at first unbelievable because so different from ordinary and culturally-established beliefs. Persons seeking to induce others to accept the fantastic generalizations must be very persuasive, and must appeal to some consistency with accepted immediate and intermediate beliefs. Evidence of inadequacy of accepted beliefs is normally invoked. Current concepts about anti-matter and chaos and black holes tend to be resisted by those unfamiliar with the inadequacies in recent and contemporary physics calling for more mediate kinds of speculation.

The unenviable state of much thinking in contemporary physics can be illustrated by citing titles from current publications. "Millisecond Pulsars Deepen a Cosmic Mystery."[8] "Quantum Chaos: Enigma Wrapped in a Mystery."[9] "Space Inversion, Time Reversal and Particle-Anti-Particle Conjugation."[10] "Strange Matter." The author of this article quotes MIT physicist Robert Jaffe as saying, "a theoretical physicists does not sit back and make up his mind to think great thoughts. . . .What we do is . . . invent some crazy theory and then try to prove it wrong."[11] Isaac Asimov remarks that "the present frontier of physics . . . has become a jungle of strange and mystifying events." Each new proposed discovery seeming to solve some problem remaining in accepted theory typically generates a whole new set of unsolved problems, leaving the hope for "a new, subtle, and intensely bright illumination of the physical universe" suffused with mystery, if not more hopeless than before.[12]

Turning to generalizations about larger, more comprehensive wholes, that is, generalizations inclusive of our four directions (past, future, self and objects), do we observe any additional characteristics of the nature of generalization? The more complications, including multiplicities of remaining mysteries, in each of the various sciences and other speculative ventures in literature, etc., that call for synthesis, or organisis, into an adequate world view provide additional problems with inherent characteristics. Concern for assurance or certainty about our inferences becomes more complicated as we seek more comprehensive kinds of knowledge.

Each of the sciences involves pressing inquiries into uncertain frontiers, each tending to adopt its own acceptable conclusions as presuppositions for further investigation. When these involve mediate generalizations with continuing mysteries and uncertainties, the problems of interdisciplinary understanding become fraught with complicated uncertainties. Philosophy, as a comprehensive science, is continually confronted with problems of trying to achieve some acceptable integration of multidisciplinary and interdisciplinary conclusions reducing the uncertainties as much as possible. Metaphysicians have always sought some pervasive integrating principle that will seem to provide assurance that existence in intelligible. This problem becomes increasingly difficult as each discipline discovers or invents new mediate generalizations, especially when evident contradictions continue to remain unresolved. But human nature seems inherently curious and provides continuing quest for understanding no matter how much absurd mediate speculations are proposed for exploration. The human predicament will continue to be plagued with many more complicated mediate speculations.

My own suggestions regarding some generalization about intellectual integration center about whole-part dialectical interactions involving both mutual immanence of polar opposites, holons and hierarchy, caused novelty, and omnipresence of both sameness and difference, addition and negation, initiation and termination, of whatever exists. In spite of my familiarity with my "Organicism," which I regard as primarily intermediate generalizations, I must confess that ultimate mysteries remain and mediacy continues to infect my perspective. But others seem to find my Organicistic concepts quite mediate, partly, I suspect, because people in each of the world's three major civilizations have typical preconceptions preferring more pluralistic (Western) or more monistic (Indian) or more explicitly harmonistic (Chinese) assumptions to serve as foundations for assurance.

I believe that most people will continue to remain naive realists most of the time, trusting immediate inferences naturalistically. Increased acquaintance with the established doctrines in traditional cultures promotes acceptance of intermediate inferences. But persons having intellectual curiosity and committed to pursuing inquiry into the nature of existence will engage in inferring mediate generalizations more and more.[13]

# Four
# MIND

## A. WHAT IS MIND?

A thing is what a thing does.[1] A mind is what a mind does. Inquiry into the nature of mind is inquiry into how it exists, what it is, and what it does, and its normal characteristics and ways of functioning.

Mind[2] exists. Or minds exist. As existing, each mind embodies all of the characteristics common to all existing beings.[3]

Mind is omniscient. Mind is omniscient, not in the sense of knowing everything that exists, but in the sense that all knowledge is mental. All knowledge is known by and in minds. Without mind, no knowledge exists.

Although presupposing that mind is completely dependent on body because mind and body are completely dependent on each other and are by nature at least partly immanent in each other, the primary purpose of the present chapter is to focus attention upon the nature of mind as mind. The organicistic theory of mind-body interdependencies is stated in the next chapter.

Intuition, inference, and generalization as presented in Chapters 1, 2, and 3 are characteristics and functions of mind, and their discussion is presupposed in preparing the present chapter.

This chapter is organized, somewhat arbitrarily, in eight sections, each summarizing one function, or kind of function, contributing to the structure and functioning of minds. The eight: observes, inquires, believes, desires, intends, organizes, adapts, and enjoys.

# B. OBSERVES

Minds observe objects. In doing so, they must be conscious. Minds are conscious. Although a mind may not be conscious always, and further studies about the nature of "subconscious mind" and "unconscious mind" and various levels of "depth psychology" are needed, when a mind becomes and remains unconscious for some time, it usually ceases to exist. Consciousness is a characteristic or function of minds. No consciousness exists apart from minds.

Consciousness varies in ways described as being "more conscious" and "less conscious," or "more fully conscious" and "less fully conscious." Doubtless such variations can be explained in terms of attentiveness, alertness, interest, desireousness, anxiety, fear, etc., and durational extents of presence and attention-span. Since they interdepend with brain processes, the conditions of cortical and neural health, energy, chemical stimulation or depression, fatigue, circadian rhythms, etc., are also involved.

Consciousness involves awareness and appearance. No consciousness exists without awareness, although awareness may become dimmer and dimmer until it vanishes. Awareness involves something of which it is aware, called "appearance," although appearance may be vacuous or an appearance without content. The nature of awareness and appearance were discussed in Chapter 1 as essential constituents in intuition. Intuition is always present in consciousness.

A mind observes. A mind observes whatever appears. (Appearances are caused by complicated mind-body processes, to be discussed in the chapter on mind-body.) Observed appearances are called "objects."

Observations often, or normally, arouse interest in objects. Interest involves as least momentary attachment of attention to an object. Although awareness may occur without awareness of interest, and without attention, or at least without alert attention, attention seems to be a necessary condition of awareness of any particular interest. Although it seems that one may have a generalized awareness of interest to which one is largely inattentive at some times, awareness of any particular interest seems to involve attention as a necessary condition. The nature of attention can be explored at length, especially since it not only varies in intensity, focus, span, simplicity and complexity, but also in speed and agility in functional responses. The presence of attention seems to be a necessary ingredient in the nature of knowledge, both in its acquisition and in any current use. It is required for memory, anticipation, self-awareness, and most other functions of mind.

# C. INQUIRES

Attentive observations often arouse interests. Although all interests are alike in being interests, interest in objects is conditioned by the kind of object that appears. Objects vary in nature somewhat by how they appear, how they are perceived, conceived, remembered, anticipated, how simple or complex, how dynamic or static, variable or fixed, how they are related to antecedents, consequents, or how correlated or interrelated with other objects, how they proceed or develop, how they may be used, what, if any, are their value connotations, any special significance, and whether or not they are involved in linguistic expressions, either incidentally or as essential to their natures. Duration of an interest depends on its "interestingness." Presence and duration of an interest normally competes with other interests, at least when a person has many interests to occupy attention. Interests vary in significance in many ways. Some are related to and generated by bodily needs, some by environmental demands, some by social requirements, some by a person's fundamental purposes, self-conceptions, sense of responsibility, and feelings of freedom to act, and awareness of opportunities of action, etc.

Interest in an object tends to involve commitment, sometimes merely commitment to continue to attend to or to observe the object. But often interests involve complexities that entice continuing commitment to attention to them. The particular nature of the object of interest will determine the nature, intensity, duration, and developments of an interest in it. When an interest becomes more intense, or more committed to attending to an object, a value character tends to emerge.[4] How much commitment engenders, or perhaps is engendered by, awareness of any value aspect of an object may be investigated. Probably increase in feeling of commitment tends to involve increase in some value aspects attributable to the object. The nature of value remains to be discussed below. But some feeling of commitment, even if very minimal, seems essential to the nature of interest in objects.

Does commitment to an interest in an object tend to generate interest in inquiry into the nature of the object? Whether merely as a matter of curiosity or as a matter of urgency, even emergency, a mind tends to inquire into the nature of an object to which its attention is committed. Although the courses of such inquiries vary in many unpredictable ways, depending on the nature of the objects and their apparent nature and significance, such inquiries tend to include interest in knowing more about both an object's internal nature and its external nature or ways of relating to other objects, and how these are organized to cooperate with each other. Often inquiry is guided by an interest in how the object may serve the person or any of his interests in some beneficial way. The more a mind commits itself to an interest in any object, the more complicated its interest tends to become, that is, in ways of functioning, in ways of continuing, in ways of varying and developing, and even in ways of terminating.

What effect does a mind's commitment to interest in an object have on, or in, or to the mind? A mind is what a mind does, and when a mind takes an interest in an object, that interest and the way it is taken constitutes in part what that mind is and how it functions. Etymologically, the word "interest" involves "est" or isness, being, *esse,* or a being with a nature, and "inter," or entering into the object as a being with a nature. If so, then to what extent does a mind commit itself when "entering into" an object by developing an interest in it? Such commitments are various and variable, but a mind ventures as a mind through committing itself to continuing its interests in objects. Such ventures may be momentary and whimsical or of deep concern to one's future welfare. Some may be novel and momentary, and some are habitual, assured, and unquestioning.

An interest is a mind's interest. The object of interest is an apparent object and thus a participant in mind as an appearance of which the mind is aware. The appearance of an object is always something of which a self as subject is aware. (The nature of self has been discussed elsewhere, i.e., in Chapters 1, "Intuition," 2 , "Inference," and 3, "Generalization," and will be discussed again below.) Although how much awareness of self and of a self's interest in the object is involved when an object appears in awareness varies considerably with different interests, and although awareness of self is often transparent, or largely missing, something functioning as a self or subject is involved more or less in every interest in any object. Although when an interest is momentary, or instantaneous, little interaction occurs between subject and object, when interest is prolonged and commitment is intense and the object is interpreted as of importance to the person, then interaction between subject and object increases dialectically. That is, any apparent change in the object involves a change in the subject's awareness of the object. How significant this is varies considerably, but it may not only influence a self's conception of itself and of the person and its environment, but may set in motion a process of considerable dialectical interaction between subject and object, especially, for example, if the object is an apparently real person with whom the person and its mind are in engaged in continuing conversation, or other interactions such as occur in a marriage, which are crucial in directing intentions and actions influencing the welfare of the person and its mind.

Such dialectical interactions occur not only between subject and object but also between object (and subject and object) and the mind. For a mind is an organic unity uniting all of its parts or functions and is constituted in part by the ways in which dialectical interactions develop, not only between objects, and between subject and objects, but also within itself as that larger organic whole within which these interactions occur. A mind as a whole is a whole of its parts, and thus is a whole including not only both subject and objects and their dialectical interactions, but also any dialectical interactions between these as its parts and itself as a whole of its parts. Dialectical processes occur both only momentarily and continuingly. Normally, a person acquires some life-long habits of thinking and acting through persisting interests requiring recurrence of similar and/or different dialectical processes constituting a mind.[5]

Interests leading to inquiry naturally involve interest in understanding the nature of the objects of interest. When some understanding seems achieved, then, if understanding seems incomplete, interest in more understanding normally occurs. The method of inquiry tends to vary considerably with the object being investigated, some requiring consulting other persons, books, libraries, laboratories, etc., for historical, cultural, or specialized data. The processes of successful inquiry have been outlined by John Dewey in his famous *How We Think*.[6] He has provided the outlines for a common-sense method, and one that serves as the basis for a philosophy of scientific method. I adopted many of his ideas in preparing my own summary treatment of scientific method in "The Nature of Science," Chapter 2 in my *Axiology: The Science of Values*.[7]

# D. BELIEVES

Minds believe. When an object appears in awareness, normally its nature is accepted to be as it appears. The word "belief" is not normally used to name such acceptance. But if and when something in the awareness disturbs such acceptance or when there are tendencies to question the adequacy of what appears, then doubt occurs. Intention to accept what appears as adequate understanding after doubt is called "belief." That is, although we tend to speak of beliefs as accepted doctrines, without intending to connote doubts regarding them, we also tend to regard beliefs as resulting from settling doubts. Doubt does not occur originally until a person has a particular belief to be doubted. Although willing acceptance of what appears as it appears is normal in human nature, persons who have experienced much doubting, especially regarding objects appearing to be dangerous to one's welfare or desires, also tend to develop habits of doubting, or habits of being cautious about readiness to accept what appears as it appears. Although one may develop doubts about the nature of appearances that are merely appearances, habits of doubting are more common regarding apparently real objects.

Although persons developing habits of doubting are often called "skeptics," Organicistic epistemology adopts the term "tentativity" to name an attitude tending to be both tenacious enough to continue to "hold on" to an appearance as long as it seems acceptable (in more complicated situations, as "workable") and tentative in the sense of willingness to "let go" whenever it seems unacceptable. Although habits of doubting and having attitudes of tentativity tend to be beneficial to a person's welfare whenever uncertainties are warranted, these habits can also become excessive and even dangerous to a person's welfare when they cause doubts that are not warranted.

The endurance of a mind involves the endurance of its capacity to believe. Whether such capacity emerges fully at conception, or birth, and continues undiminished upon approaching death, or during illnesses of various kinds, needs consideration.

Although beliefs normally occur without questions about their truth or falsity occurring or appearing, after a person has experienced false beliefs and undesirable consequences of such falsity, then one tends to retain some doubt about whether or not one's beliefs are true. How much such retained, or retainable, doubt functions on particular believing occasions varies considerably. Minds tend to (perhaps tend to prefer to) accept their beliefs as they appear, and thus as either true, or such that questions about truth and falsity do not intrude.

Whatever exists is. "Is" includes existing in all of the differing ways of existing, and these ways of existing find expression in language, in different tenses, including is, was, will be, could be, could have been, can yet be, etc.

Truth and falsity, or trueness and falseness, characterize beliefs. The truth and falsity of a belief involve a relation between "what is believed to exist" and "what exists." Each, "what is believed to exist" and "what exists," may be taken as basic in stating the nature of truth and falsity.

"Truth is a characteristic of a belief when 'what is believed to exist' 'does exist.'" "Truth is a characteristic of a belief when 'what exists' is 'what is believed to exist.'"

Some beliefs are intended as expecting that "what exists" is "what is believed to exist." Some beliefs are intended as expecting that "what exists" is "what is believed to exist."

"Believers may vary their intentions from time to time, sometimes intending that 'what is believed to exist' depends more on 'what exists' and sometimes intending that the relevant 'what exists' depends more upon 'what is believed to exist.'"

Variations occur in how much more of either intention is intended by a belief. Each belief occurs "with such specifications as are required by its peculiar set of conditions and such specifications as are unintended are irrelevant."[8]

Minds trust beliefs, or at least most beliefs, as being true. But when some seemingly true appearance also involves some seemingly false appearance, doubt often occurs. Doubt involves distrust of belief.

Persons normally prefer to observe, attend to, examine, accept, and use beliefs about apparent objects undisturbed by doubts. So, normally, they are concerned about elimination of doubts, and replacing them with beliefs which they can trust. Feelings of assurance that one's beliefs are true is more comfortable. Desire to remove feelings of distrust motivates efforts to remove such distrust, and to achieve a feeling of assurance that one's commitments to a belief are dependable.

Although all trusted beliefs are somewhat alike in being undisturbed by doubts or in having doubts removed satisfactorily, and although all doubts are alike in contributing feelings of uneasiness, uncertainty, anxiety, and concern (even when such feelings of satisfaction or concern may vary in intensity and duration), each doubt tends to arise on a particular occasion and to be constituted in part by some particular kind of apparent "is" that also appears as "is not so." Thus what will be needed to remove dissatisfaction with an apparent inconsistency will depend upon what appears as inconsistent. So, when we consider the ways and means for testing the truth of our beliefs when doubts about their truth occur, we need to remember that factors in each particular belief giving rise to doubt will determine what is required to remove the doubt.

Although many "tests of truth" have been devised by thinkers historically, most of them have been designed in ways consistent with basic philosophical presuppositions accepted or favored by such thinkers. But particular persons also, even when unfamiliar with historical theories, tend to reuse methods they have used before in settling doubts, unless the new doubt defies this practice.

# E. DESIRES

Minds desire. Persons desire, and although many kinds of conditions contribute to the origin, existing, and nature of desires, including biological and physiological conditions and mind-body dialectical interactions, the presence in awareness of desire seems to be an essential characteristic of its nature and existence. Since mind is needed for the actualization of desire, we may say that "minds desire." Without minds, no desires exist actually.

Some desires arise from bodily needs: for food, drink, rest, sleep, exercise, association, and protection from cold, heat, sun, wind, and rain. Some desires arise from more understanding: of self, objects, other persons, animals, plants, and interactive processes. Some desires arise from interest in acting, influencing, causing, controlling. Some desires arise from interest in enjoyment (by eating, playing, associating, learning, achieving), and in avoiding suffering (from injury, hunger, isolation, ignorance, and deprivation). Some desires arise from interest in acquisition, honor, appreciation, reputation, and feelings of security.

Desires normally involve some feelings of satisfaction and frustration, and variations in further responses to them. Although at times desiring may subside, and awareness may be void of content and any motivating urge, and even enjoy undisturbed contentment, most awareness is occupied by desiring of one kind of another, mildly or intensely, and interest in satisfaction and avoidance of frustration. In this sense, each mind's chief activity is, or involves, desiring.


# F. INTENDS

Although a person may intend when observing, inquiring, believing, and desiring, a person may also observe, inquire, believe, and desire while feeling indifferent or even imposed upon when doing so. Intention involves volition or will. Volition ranges from minimal to maximal intensity, from willing acceptance of what appears to willful insistence on causal influence. Will may range from intense willfulness to approaching will-lessness, with some intermediate rangings of willingness.[9] Since intention involves volition, it too can range in variations in intensity.

Intention normally involves desire. Although one may entertain a desire without intending to satisfy it, most desires of which a person becomes aware seem to involve intention to achieve satisfaction. Some desires may pertain merely to ideas, imagination, and additional observations. But most desires of active persons seem to pertain to objects and activities that are apparently real. When persons believe that they live in a real environment, of buildings, machines, persons, culture, and problems, they normally seek to survive, act, influence, and control whatever appears related to their interests. Thus persons develop intentions regarding possible or needed actions. Such intentions are mental, and function as actions of minds as agents.

Although desires and intentions may be simple (a person may desire to drink some water and then do so), many desires and intentions are very complex. Since persons often desire to obtain more than is possible, they often confront problems of having to choose between two or more alternative courses of desired action when only one can result in satisfaction. When a person is confronted with choosing between the satisfaction of two desires, the person is caused to decide. Decisions may be reasonable or unreasonable. When a person is confronted with two alternatives, one of which appears better than the other, what is the reasonable thing to do? To choose the one that appears better. Why? Because it appears better. Apparent betterness is the ultimate basis for choosing.

Oughtness consists in the power that an apparently greater good has over an apparently lesser good in compelling our choices. Persons act as they ought when they choose the greater instead of the lesser apparent good. Persons ought to intend to choose what is better or best. Such oughtness is the foundation of ethics. Each mind is essentially ethical when and because it intends to choose the better or best when confronted with alternatives. Acts are right when one intends to produce the best results in the long run. Minds thus act rightly when they so intend. Of course, it is the person who acts rightly, but since that person's intention is mental, the rightness, that is, the rightness of the intention, is mental. Minds may also act wrongly, but the causes of wrong decision and action involve complications regarding understanding, or misunderstanding, including ignorance of what is actually good and bad and best and worst.[10]

Intentions may be momentary when the problems calling for choosing and acting are momentary. Intentions may also be intentions to continue, to persist, to commit one's future life, including some future decisions. Persons sign contracts for future actions, including work, payments, and companionship. Some marriage vows state "Until death do us part" or "Through time and eternity." Some intentions may remain ambiguous, as willingness to venture in ways calling for additional decisions, choices and intentions. Life is problematic. Intention to continue to live normally involves a willingness to continue to confront and try to solve life's problems as they come along. Thus normally minds intend to be venturesome, although experiences with success and failure in achieving satisfaction often condition some minds to seek adventure and others to avoid it.

# G. ORGANIZES

Mind organizes. Each mind is an organizing organism in a person who is an organizing organism. Minds organize by becoming conscious. Con-scious-ness is a condition and function of "knowing together." Minds organize by intuiting, that is, by being aware of appearances, in each presence. Minds organize when transcending each presence by ignoring gaps in appearance to produce seemingly continuous awareness from waking to sleep. Mind organizes by attending to apparent objects, and participates in constructing these objects from the somewhat organized impulses supplied by the brain. How it does this, we do not know; but that it does seems obvious.

Mind organizes by remembering and contributing remembered appearances to present objects, interests, and processes. Mind organizes by anticipating, predicting, and becoming aware of predicted objects. Mind organizes by generalizing, that is, by noticing samenesses among objects, and making assertions about such samenesses. Mind organizes by regarding objects appearing to be alike as a class, and also observing differences between objects appearing as classes. Minds construct classifications. Minds organize by inferring, deducing, imaging, speculating, and solving problems.

The organization of some apparent objects is simple, such as a triangle, apple, or pencil. Some are much more complex, such as a person, a family, a city, a country, a science, a library, a corporation, a civilization, an army, or a war. All knowledge involves organization, and organization as conceived by organicism always involves organic unity. Each object organized by a mind involves both some unity or wholeness and some (few or many) parts, which may be of many kinds. Although a whole is not its parts and its parts are not its whole, and hence involves a multiplicity of negative relations between a whole and its parts and between its parts, each organic whole is a whole of both the whole and its parts and their negative relations, and also any tensions between their different natures and energies and many dialectical interactions among them as experience proceeds. Organically unified objects do not exist in isolation, except perhaps in momentary flashes in an otherwise vacuous awareness. But, especially when a person is observing a panorama of moving objects, each organically unified object also has organically unified interrelations with many other objects whenever all appear in presence together.

Although a mind's organizings are its own, it often is assisted by the organized nature of apparently real objects which it apprehends. Each person lives in a world of multiplicities of apparently real objects each having its own organized nature and organized, and often organizing, interrelations with other such objects. The organized nature of each and any organization of their interrelations and interactions tend to contribute to the way minds organize when influenced by them through perceptive processes. To the extent that a mind can intend to influence, through influencing the behavior of its body, and succeed in moving, changing, stopping, or even destroying, such apparently real objects actually, it functions as an organizing agency, through its causal influences in the actual world. Thus, a mind may contribute to the ways things existing in the real world become organized or reorganized.[11]

The history of cultures provides plenty of evidence of the consequences of minds influencing human behavior and to modifications in the plant and animal world and the physical environment. The organizations of houses, families, cities, schools, nations, institutions, and civilizations all embody influences of the organizing activities of minds. Some minds are now trying to modify the nature and behavior of planets, solar systems and galaxies. The magnificence, complexity, and constructive and destructive influences of minds, causally contribute something to organizing the nature and future of the existing universe. Some are now seeking to modify the organization of cells, chromosomes, DNA, etc., in ways that may reorganize heredity and the ways that humans organize themselves and organize the world.

# H. ADAPTS

Minds adapt, both to limitations imposed upon them by the conditions of existence, including those in brain and body, in physical, biological, social and cultural environments, and to the opportunities apparently available for action, desire and satisfaction.

Persons experiencing desires and satisfactions normally desire more satisfactions and thus to have more desires. Life consists in continuing to face problems and trying to solve them. Some solutions seems to remain satisfactory for long periods of time. Habits, customs, institutions result. Some are momentary and may be forgotten. Some solutions satisfy partly, or for a short time, but also frustrate partly, or for a longer time. Some proposed solutions frustrate completely.

Minds are constantly confronted with problems, and the general problem of desiring to solve problems in satisfactory ways has been, and will continue to be, a primary concern of all human minds. Experience provides plenty of evidence that minds cannot obtain all that they want. Minds sometimes respond to frustration of desires with anger. Sometimes they respond by redirecting desires. Sometimes they accept frustration as part of the way the world works. Gradually persons learn which kinds of desires can be satisfied and which cannot, or which more easily and which only with difficulty.

Self-evident wisdom regarding how to deal with frustration of desires was expressed by Gotama, The Buddha, as his discovered enlightenment: Desire for what will not be attained ends in frustration. Therefore, to avoid frustration, avoid desiring what will not be attained. When a person inquired about not knowing which desires will be satisfied and which frustrated, Gotama asked, "Do you desire to have more knowledge about which will be satisfied and which frustrated than you will attain? If so, then you are desiring even more frustration. You can avoid frustration as much as possible by being willing to accept the consequences of your desiring, which ever way it comes." He illustrated his view by referring to desires for another life. "If you desire a next life and there is a next life, you are satisfied. If you desire no next life and there is no next life, your desire is satisfied. But if you desire a next life and there is no next life, you will be frustrated. If you desire no next life and there is a next life, you will be frustrated. If you desire no next life and there is a next life, you will be frustrated. To avoid frustration, what is important is not whether there is or is not a next life, but your willingness to accept whichever comes."[12]

# I. ENJOYS

Minds enjoy. Persons enjoy, but feelings of enjoyment occur in their minds. The kinds of enjoyment (and suffering) are so many, and some so complicated, that adequate treatment of them is not possible here. Also, feelings and emotions are difficult, for me at least, to explain and define. They are foundational to any account of the nature of values, that is, of intrinsic values as ends-in-themselves, which serve as the bases for explaining the existence and nature and kinds of instrumental values.

Intrinsic goodness consists in feelings of enjoyment, and intrinsic badness consists in feelings of suffering. Four main kinds of intrinsic good and bad can be distinguished: Feelings of pleasantness and unpleasantness (especially pain), of satisfaction and frustration of desire, of desirousness (that is, enthusiasm) and apathy, and of contentment and disturbance. Awareness may be occupied by each exclusively or by two or more together in various interminglings.

Although a presence may be occupied momentarily by a relatively pure feeling, most awareness involves appearances in which feelings are intimately associated with, or appear as ingredients in, objects, including apparently real objects. When minds perceive real things as objects, they tend to project the contents of objects as apparent as if present in the real world. Such projections are of many kinds.

For example, persons may locate their feelings of pleasantness in their mouths as a sweet flavor, in their noses as a fragrant odor, in their ears as harmonious sounds, in their erogenous zones as voluptuousness, etc. To the extent that persons identify themselves with their bodies, and with these feelings, they tend not only to experience these feelings as parts of themselves but also to experience themselves as good. Such awareness of a person's goodness (or badness if painful, for example) exists in mind. Thus, minds feel, and minds feel as participating in the goods and bads within their bodies, or as being that in which the goods and bads are present.

But feelings of participation extend beyond one's body. Lovers normally project their feelings of intrinsic goodness into each other. Each is experienced as "lovely," or beautiful. Courtship and marriage often induce feelings of communion such that both experience appearance of feelings of overwhelming spiritual identity. Such feelings actually exist separately in their individual minds. But when conceptions of identity suffuse perceptions of mutual participation in shared enjoyment, the goodness may appear as an environmental aura of sublimity. Mother-child intimacies constantly, but variably, involve projections of goodness in each. Again, these feelings are mental and in each mind, but the mutuality of some interdependencies tends to beget conceptions of, and feelings of, sharing in some common good.

Cultures promoting ideals of family participation tend to produce enjoyments of such participation, while cultures promoting individualistic ideals tend to encourage ideals of personal independence. These ideals contribute to the kinds of feelings of enjoyment and suffering that persons experience, and minds are aware of, in varying ways that persons associate with one another. Each group in which a person becomes a member (village, nation, school, club, factory, army unit, football team, or scientific society) tends to induce a feeling of participation, and how a person projects feelings of goodness into the group and its processes, location, and reputation may vary greatly.

Some enjoyments are momentary, some last for an evening, and some endure recurringly in an acceptable lifestyle. Some enjoyments may be identified with a sip of nectar, some with an enduring royal marriage, some with a professionalized society providing security and advancement, some with the kingdom of all living beings, some with Mother Earth, and some with a cosmic spirit.

Religion, conceived here as concern for the enjoyment of the ultimate intrinsic values of life as a whole (not as "belief in God," except as an included instrumental example),[13] is mental. Minds are not only ethical, because programmed to choose the better or best of two or more alternative apparent goods, but also religious, because programmed to occasionally become aware of the remarkable significance of personal existence in the cosmos and the fortunate opportunities for embodying enjoyments and in participating in communities of enjoying persons. How clearly or vaguely persons conceive their cosmic existence may vary greatly with differing personal, associational and cultural influences. A history of the world's religions reveals astoundingly different schemes of human ideals. The ethical monotheisms of Judaism, Christianity, and Islam, each also multivariously conceived, and the omni-indifference of *Nirguna Brahman* with combinations of vigorous polytheisms in India, the naturalistic and humanistic ideas of Taoism and Confucianism in China, the Shintoism in Japan, added to the multiplicities of local native traditional variations, all serve to provide a sense of personal security (with numerous variations accounting for the ways evils are included) and plan for some final self-realization. But each of these culturally induced, and indoctrinated, ideals can function effectively only if and when also embodied in the conceptual systems acceptably believed in human minds. Normally minds are not constantly fully conscious of these ultimate intrinsic values of life as whole. Times and places may be established to encourage awareness of such enjoyments. Some people may be induced to become more fully preoccupied with such values, and become celibate nuns or yogins trying to isolate themselves from all but the beatific vision of divine perfection or to remove the veils of ignorance preventing intuitive identity of *atman* with *Brahman*. Unfortunately some systems condemn some persons to suffer feelings of "original sin," "total depravity," or necessity for constant *tapas* to assure the surplus of good *karmas* needed to achieve *moksha*.

The existence of enjoyments and sufferings in minds is the basis for all of the values, intrinsic and instrumental, in the human world. They are based in the nature of minds functioning in observing (including intuiting, inferring, and generalizing), inquiring, believing, desiring, intending, organizing, and adjusting (and dialectically interacting with brain, body, and environment). When minds project their feelings of enjoyment into the apparently real objects as they conceive and perceive them, they thereby create, or participate in creating, a world that appears filled with various kinds of good and bad, which they then may continue to appreciate or depreciate, exploit or suffer, and embody as means for motivation or, unfortunately, for depression.

Mind is not only omniscient in the sense that all knowledge is mental, but also omnivalunt (all-good and all-bad),[14] a newly-coined term, in the sense that all intrinsic values exist in minds, and all instrumental values, as means to intrinsic values as ends-in-themselves, acquire such value in serving such ends. A mind is what a mind does, and being omnivalunt is one of its important functions.

# Five
# MIND-BODY

Persons know. Persons, and knowledge, involve both mind and body. Each person is one person, is a person as a whole. Each person is an organized dynamic whole of parts. Two of each person's parts are its mind and brain (or nervous system) which so interdepend with the remainder of its body that the problem of understanding the nature of knowledge as involving both mind and brain is usually referred to as "the mind-body problem"

## A. WHAT IS MIND-BODY?

As parts of a whole person, mind and brain have natures constituted by their being parts of such a whole. They depend for their being and nature upon the being and nature of the person as a whole and the person as a whole depends on them, on their existence and nature, in constituting it.

Mind and brain are not identical. Each is and has its own being and nature. Yet mind and brain are the same in being and functioning as parts of the same person. A person depends not only on both of them but upon their natural ways of interdepending, interacting, interinfluencing, and interexisting as mutually immanent.

A mind can function only in ways permitted by its dependence on a brain, and a brain, part of which has its nature and function to serve mind, can function in ways permitted by its dependence on mind. Biological evolution has produced a kind of natural mutual immanence of mind and brain such that the nature of each is structured in ways that its natural functioning, and survival, is interinvolved with that of the other.[1]

# B. ONTOGENY RECAPITULATES PHYLOGENY

The biological principle, "ontogeny recapitulates phylogeny," applies not only to body and brain but also to mind and mind-body interdependence. Although a much-neglected part of evolutionary theory, it will not be demonstrated here. Stephen Jay Gould has reviewed the extensive and complicated history of the developments of this principle in his work, *Ontogeny and Phylogeny*. "Over and over again, we find an explicit appeal to biological recapitulation; since the embryo repeats the physical stages of remote ancestors, the child must replay the mental history of more remote forebears." He cites Piaget's views: "There are inborn components of reason, but they are not static: they themselves evolve in a definite way during ontogeny as the child assimilates external reality to its changing internal structures. Reason itself evolves in response to increased experience with the external world."[2]

# C. ENERGY

What energy is continues to be a mystery. Yet we know very much about it, since everything in the universe consists in energy or involves energy in some way. On the one hand, energy is energy, all energy is alike in being energy. But energy seemingly exists only in some ways or forms or functions, and so we know about it as what it does in the various ways that it functions.

Persons are energetic only because they have, or are, or consist in, energy. The energy in a person is of many kinds because many forms and functions are required: each kind of cell and organ uses energy in ways consistent with its nature and functions. Mind and body both involve energy. On the one hand, the energy in mind and body are the same. Energy is energy. On the other hand, the energy in each is different to the extent that it performs different functions.

Since mind and brain not only interact, and do so dialectially, some of the energy in mind and some of the energy in brain is engaged in functioning in and through such dialectical interactions. Dialectical interaction involves some actual exchange of causal influences and of the energy involved in such causation. Thus, to some extent at least, some mental and some brain energy are the same since each becomes embodied in the other. Yet also, to the extent that mind and brain have natures and functions that are different, the energy involved in such differing functions is also different.

In addition to the energies that are primarily mental energies and primarily brain energies, these also interdepend hierarchically with the energies functioning in other organs, cells, molecules, atoms, etc., and in both the person as a whole and the many kinds of energies in the environment of the person with which mind and brain energies also interact, whether directly or indirectly.

I have no suggestions regarding how different kinds of mental actions, such as perceiving, attending, intending, wanting, fearing, reasoning, remembering, etc., involve particular ways of using energy in influencing the brain, or how different kinds of bodily and brain functioning, such as pain, fatigue, hunger, disease, or exhaustion, etc., involve particular ways of using energy influencing the mind. But that mind and brain do influence each other in many ways and involve the energy needed for and suited to such ways seems obvious.

Mind-brain interaction involves not only some exchange of energy during each particular interaction, but habits of interacting, and especially when interactions are both very rapid and continuing (as when persons are shaking their fists, waving their hands, or writing), patterns of interaction develop, become stabilized as processes, and involve energy not only in the interacting influences but also in maintaining the pattern of interactions, in which the energy is functioning as both mental and physical.

I do not suggest that such momentary, or even long-extended, stability of interactive pattern involves some third kind of entity (even though I must regard it as substantial while continuing), but that the person as a whole is already a third or more-inclusive kind of energetic functioning. Persisting mind-body interactions are the person acting and functioning internally. I do not expect to explain how a person, as an organic unity of mind and body as organic unities, each having its own hierarchy of organic unities, manages the allocation of energy for so many different kinds, ways, level, and substantial processes. Although a person's nature functions habitually in many ways, some established by heredity and some by learning, each involving energy in its own particular ways, a person as a whole is partly a product of each of the many and various particular ways, including their occasional variations.

Discussions of mind-body interactions remain inadequate until the energies introduced into the body by eating, drinking, being warmed by heater or sunlight, cooled by wind and rain, influenced by other electronic, magnetic, gravitational, etc., forces, and until the energies in the body that become expended in work or sweat, exhaling and excreting, etc., are appropriately considered.

# D. ORGANIC UNITY

According to Organicism, "organic unity," a term intentionally connoting unity of unity and plurality, and unity of whole and parts, and unity of all polar opposites, is a basic explanatory term.[3] Each existent is an organic unity. A person is an organic unity. A mind is an organic unity. A brain is an organic unity. Each of these involves its own hierarchy of organic unities.

Concern here focuses on mind-body, or, more specifically, on mind-brain organic unity. Neglecting consideration of the many problems regarding how multiplicities of brain and brain-body organisms function and cooperate, attention is directed to problems of how mind contributes some additional unifying services to the brain's unifying functions.

The problem seems most challenging when we confront data regarding examples of bisected brains. Each brain has two hemispheres. Each hemisphere is both separated from the other by a deep vertical fissure and joined with it by a pons, or bridge, including a complicated pedunculus. Bundles of neurones from eyes, ears, and other sensory organs divide and terminate in the separated lobes of the cortex. Mind is not consciously aware of such separate terminations, but apprehends each apparent sensory product as unitary. Single objects are products of bifocal vision, and of a divided brain. How a mind, participating in, and functioning as a product of, a mind-brain organic unity is able to achieve awareness of a single object involving bifocal and divided-brain processes remains a mystery. Yet it should be no greater mystery than how billions of neurones achieve unification in each hemisphere. That mind, consciousness, and awareness do apprehend appearances as unitary is obvious to all. Normally such unitary appearance is understood as involving an organic unity unifying impulses terminating in both hemispheres.

Special problems arise as a result of surgically separated hemispheres resulting in persons with "split brains." Studies by R.W. Sperry have shown that persons can "perceive, learn, and remember independently, each hemisphere evidently cut off from the conscious experience of the other," and "behave as if each of the separated hemispheres had a mind of its own." "The structure of the conscious cerebral process is inferred to be such that some aspects of conscious experience may be separated by commissurotomy, while others, united through bilateral representation and/or brain stem mechanisms, remain intact."[4]

I must leave to other, including future, experimenters to provide additional data about how surgically divided brain hemispheres behave relative to mind-brain ways of functioning. But each person is an organic unity involving not merely two hemispheres of the brain, but also some hereditarily unifying functions in the nervous system ranging at least from those present in "the brains of all vertebrates--from frog to man."[5] The medulla, cerebellum, and thalamus, though of ancient origin, retain a unifying function while participating in more advanced and complicated unifying processes in the limbic system and cerebrum.

Even Sperry, who does not recognize my distinguishing mind entitively from the brain, asserts that "A cerebral process acts as a conscious entity, not because it is spatially set apart from other cerebral activity, but because it functions organizationally as a unit. ...The criterion for unit is an operational one."[6] Interpret each cerebral process as an entity, some of which participate in a mind-brain organic unity, functioning organizationally as an "operational unit." Even Sperry, speculating on possibilities for descriptions of "subjective experience...in objective terms," predicts that "they will be found to be expressible in term of emergent properties of higher-order cerebral processes, and further that these emergent phenomena will be seen to play a potent causal role in brain function that cannot be accounted for in terms merely of the neurologic and neurochemical events as these are traditionally conceived."[7] By combining emergentistic and structuralistic principles in more holistic explanations, Organicism already provides "what cannot be accounted for." But even more is needed for adequacy.

How does Organicism explain organic unity? Organic unity, which is unity of unity and plurality, seems best exemplified in the whole-parts interdependencies in each existing being. Each existing thing is both a whole and its parts. To be a whole is to be a whole of parts. To be a part is to be a part of a whole. So each, whole and part, by nature involves the other. Yet also a whole is not its parts and its parts are not the whole. Since each is not the other, some negation is involved in their relations. Thus, for a more adequate conception of the nature of a thing, a concept is needed that includes both its whole and its parts, the mutual involvement of their natures, and any negations between them (a whole is one and unitary and thus opposed to its parts as many and pluralistic). This more inclusive concept, organic unity, is that whole of a thing that includes both its whole as opposed to its parts and its parts as opposed to its whole. So organic unity is a unity inclusive of both plurality and negation in a more complex organization.

However, the Organicistic concept of organic unity is still more complex because it conceives each existing thing as being also related to other things, each of which relations functions as a kind of part of it. Each thing exists not only as a kind of entity, or being, having its own organic unity, but also as related to other things, many other things in many ways. Its concept of relations is that, when two things are related, they are both different and not each other in being two and like each other in sharing the same relation that is relating them. Thus, each relation itself has an organic nature, rather than, as some claim, being merely an external relation or, as some claim, merely an internal relation. For Organicism, each existing relation between two or more existing things is both external and internal because it involves both their difference (and some separation) and sameness (and some identity).[8] So each person is conceived not only as an organic unity, but also as organically related to other (even all other) things.

Although each thing's relations to other things will vary depending on the nature of the things related and the particular ways in which they are related, including being parts of larger wholes, having parts of their own, and cooperating or competing with neighboring things consisting of their whole-part organizations. To the extent that each thing is part of a larger whole and has parts that are also wholes of parts, it functions as part of, and as contributing to, a hierarchy. The concept of organic unity is thus inherently involved in hierarchy.

# E. HIERARCHY

Although each existing thing has a tendency to remain the same, to continue to exist as what it is, to exist as an entity, and thus to be static in some way, each is also dynamic and moving, again either in stably recurring ways or in ways that change it, little or much. It tends both to remain the same and to change, in varying ways, in all of its relations. It has tendencies in its relations to any wholes of which it is a part, to the parts which are parts of it as a whole, and to other things cooperating or competing with it.

Consider first a thing's relations to the whole of which it is a part. To the extent that a thing's survival depends on stable relations with such whole, its stability, either as remaining the same or as recurring in the same way, is needed. But things existing as dynamic have tendencies to change. Emergentists emphasize the tendencies of things to causally influence larger wholes, either to influence the larger wholes within which they already exist or to produce new larger wholes not yet in existence. Not only is it part of the nature of the parts of a dynamic whole to promote the welfare of that whole, but that whole, or the organic unity of the thing as a whole, often has a tendency to participate in the emergence and welfare of still larger wholes through cooperation with other things as wholes to become active parts of such larger wholes.

Persons, for example, are both by nature participants in, and thus parts of, social groups. Each person is born from a mother, and so for a long period is an internal part of its mother, and is nurtured and protected in infancy only by associating with others. It grows socially by participating in additional groups, of neighbors, friends, play groups, communities, villages, cities, states, nations, etc. Each person is by nature essentially social and tends to become more and more social as growth continues. But also, sometimes both opportunities and needs for the emergence of new groups occur. Children desiring to imitate parents sometimes organize to play house. When there is interest and urge in children to play house, they must cooperate in some ways needed by the game. Here there is a tendency within each child to cooperate in the emergence of a new level of existence, the organic unity involved in conducting the game. Sometimes the primary motives for initiating a new group have sources in higher levels, as when a parent or educator proposes and organizes the play group. Sometimes the primary motives are in the interests, energies, and motives of the children. The concept of hierarchy involves the concept of holons.

"Holon" is the name given to a whole (organic unity) functioning as part of a larger (organically unified) whole.[9] The Organicist conception of the nature of each existing organic unity includes its normal functioning as a holon or holons, for each existent may, and normally does, participate in many larger wholes, some of which, at least, are also parts of larger wholes which are parts of still larger wholes, etc., in an upward hierarchy. So the concept of organic unity involves a thing being not only a whole of parts but also being a part of one or more larger wholes. In this way, each existent is a holon.

Each person is a holon. But also a person's mind is a holon. A person's body is a holon (or a whole hierarchy of holons). And a person's mind-body organic unity is a holon. Although this conception of mind-body as a holon does not solve the traditional problem of how a person, seeming to be fully awake and fully aware, still fails completely to have any awareness of his or her brain and neural processes. But it does involve the claim that part of the nature of each, mind and brain, can be understood as involving its continuing and recurring cooperative interaction with the other in ways constituting it as an organic whole. A mind is not only by nature an organic part of a mind-body organic unity, by nature a part of a person, but also by nature an organic part of the social groups in which it actually functions influentially, including normal functions that are economic and political and sexual. Biologically, persons are programmed to have sexual interests involving other persons. So minds and bodies and mind-brain organisms are by nature holonistic in many ways.

Structuralists emphasize the biologically inherent programs for many kinds of holonistic behavior. Organicism aims to give equal emphasis to both structuralist and emergentistic tendencies inherent in human nature. Both are involved in the many kinds of hierarchies in which persons exist. This elementary discussion needs supplementation to overcome traditional conceptions of hierarchy as monohierarchical, with a single cosmic base of some lowest particle without parts and some largest whole that is not a part of some larger whole. Existence is multihierarchical, and the additional complexities involved in seeking to understand multiple hierarchies leave minds too amazed and "boggled" to warrant further pursuit here.[10]

# F. CAUSATION

Mind and body interact causally in many different ways. Some mental processes involve causation that is primarily mental. Some brain processes involve causation occurring primarily in the brain. Some processes are primarily mind-brain interactive and intercausal. Some processes are essentially joint mind-brain causation. Some are more specifically causal through influencing events in a person's environment or through influencing processes in a person's digestive, bronchial, and excretory chemical functions.

Permit me to generalize about the nature of causation as conceived by Organicism. Many scientists, including many who are Behaviorists, presuppose a deterministic doctrine assuming that nothing happens unless caused to happen in the way that it does happen. Furthermore, "cause equals effect" in the sense that (since energy [or mattergy] can be neither created nor destroyed) an effect is, in principle, exactly the equal to the energy in the cause. Form involves energy (as integral to the nature of each thing, quantum, or quantity of energy). Hence, in a completely deterministic system, nothing new can emerge. No new wholes can come into existence, unless they are merely collections of preexisting parts. But since the history of evolutionary processes gives evidence of the emergence of new kinds of beings, new organizations, new organisms, new wholes, and new holons, such a theory of causation is inadequate to account for the nature of living beings and of persons and minds, bodies, and mind-body interactive causation.

The Organicist Theory of Causation holds that the "C = E" theory is inadequate. Each effect is a product of a multiplicity of causes. Each effect in turn participates in a multi-causal process. The Organicist Theory of Causation can best be explained by symbols with stipulated meanings. Let all of the causes of an effect be symbolized by five C's, where the five are intended to represent all of its causes (all kinds of its causes) both immediately present and past. The effect is an effect of all of its causes. But since some of it was caused by cause $C^1$, some by $C^2$, some by $C^3$, some by $C^4$, and some by $C^5$, it is completely caused by all of its causes. But since an effect has a kind of being, entity, and unity about it because it functions as *an* effect, there is something in it that was not in any of its causes considered individually, nor in all of them together considered pluralistically. Thus something new, that is, something that did not exist before in any one of its causes or in all of them together collectively, comes into being. The Organicist theory claims that every causal process involves the creation of some novelty, no matter how much or little.

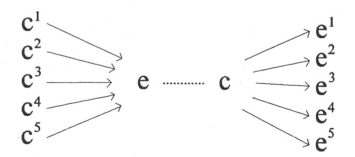

When anything which is an effect causes its effects, some of what existed in each of its causes is conveyed to these effects, and any all of what existed in all of its causes is conveyed to these effects. To this extent, C = E. But since some novelty is created in each act of causation, that which exists as new also enters into the continuing causal process. Of course, some of what existed as individual in each cause and some of what existed in all of the causes together also ceases to exist (novel non-existence?).

The Organicist view is completely deterministic in the sense that each effect is caused to happen in the way that it does happen. But it holds also that causal processes are such that some novelty is caused, or completely determined, by the uniting of many causal influences in the production of each unitary effect. This view claims to be both completely deterministic in the sense that whatever exists is caused to exist by all of its causes and to be what it is as a consequence of such causes and also emergentistic in regarding novelty (and new wholes and holons) when so caused.

Causation within mind-body organic unity may involve an effect having causes that are primarily mental, causes that are primarily physical, and causes that result primarily from the organically unified nature of mind-body as an organic unity. The nature of the organic unities that are effects of mind-body organically unified causes can be expected to be different from those that are effects of primarily mental causes or of primarily physical causes.

Abilities of persons to adapt to relatively new situations seem to be more adequate because mind-body organic unity causes may be more complex, more flexible, more ready to produce novelty in effected adaptation than causes that are merely mental or merely physical. Of course, survival requires both the ability to change (to survive through changing situations) and the ability to remain the same when remaining the same is needed for surviving through unchanging situations.

The functioning of a mind-body organic unity in managing the complex dynamic multiplicities of causal processes in each person is utterly amazing. Of course, the mind-body as causal manager is also an effect of many causal influences (managing influences) of the numerous centers of causal activity (including creative activity) elsewhere in the body, and of course, in the environment of each person.[11, 12]

# G. DIALECTIC

The nature of existing processes, including those constituting mind-body as a dynamic organic unity, involves functioning dialectically. Interactions between two things are dialectical when each causally influences the other in ways that introduce something (of the energy, existence, and nature) of one into the being, existence and nature of the other, so that after each such influence the other continues to be both what it was before being so influenced and what it is after being so influenced.

Dialectical language refers to such bothness as a "synthesis." As dialectical interactions of two things continue, each not only continues to add more syntheses to its being, but, since when it reacts reciprocally to the other, it does so as a being that includes in itself something of the other which thus involves the other in being partly self-caused to the extent that its causes of the other are participating in the other's causing it.

Thus mind-body processes involve multitudes of dialectical interactions in which each, mind and body, increasingly contributes more of its energy, existence, and nature to the other. Although a mind never ceases to be a brain's mind, so to speak, and a brain never ceases to be a mind's brain, their perpetually increasing dialectical interaction, involving increasing dialectical interexistence, causes them to function in ways in which each involves the other more fully.

Any persistently recurring dialectical interactions causing two beings to become more fully embodied in each other tends to produce a stable pattern of interactions causing such pattern itself to be regarded as a synthesis. Mind-body stable interactive patterns are not necessarily a "new synthesis" in each person because the very nature of their interactive patterns has been provided partly by the "ontogeny recapitulates phylogeny" biological heritage. Yet each new person must develop its own mind-body patterns of interaction in ways peculiar to the multiplicity of causal processes producing and maintaining it.

Since both mind and body interact dialectically in many different ways, that is, in ways relating to each of the kinds of interaction, mind-body processes must be regarded as multi-dialectical. Dialectical processes are involved both in changing and in remaining the same. When patterns of dialectical interaction become stable, as needed for some kinds of survival, then the causal processes involved tend to become regular, regular in ways needed for survival.

Persons interact dialectically, with other persons and with many other kinds of existences in their environment, and also establish habits of dialectical interactions conducive to their survival and happiness (and unhappiness and death) as well as depend on the needs and actualities of such interactions. To the extent that persons become aware of these additional dialectical interactions, they function in mind and mind-body in ways such that persons causally influence and are causally influenced by other things. Habits normally are habits of dialectical interactions. Thus, the kinds and quantities of ways that each person both embodies causal influences into its being and nature and embodies influences from itself into other things are amazing, and understanding them, or at least some of them, seems necessary for ordinary normal living.

That is, mind-body involves not only its own mutual immanence but also its own internal syntheses from dialectical processes involving influences from other beings, including persons, societies, cultures, as well as from temperature, pressure, agriculture, transportation, mining and war, etc. How thoroughly do these dialectical processes penetrate the nature of each participant? The Chinese concept of *Tao* (Nature) as consisting of *taos* (natures), each involving *yang* and *yin* as complementary opposites, implies that opposites are not merely interdependent but also mutually immanent. The existence and nature of each opposite embodies some of the existence and nature of its opposite. The way *tao* proceeds is by each of the opposites becoming the dominant nature of each *tao* in turn. "All that is springs from such alternation."[13]

How much of the complementarity of opposites as conceived by Taoists is involved in the dialectical processes just described through the increasing embodiment of each participant in the existence and nature of the other, as well as in the mind-body organic unity inherited from ancestors, remains uncertain to me. But I do find the concept of mutual immanence a useful way of conceiving mind-body as an organic unity.

The concept of mutual immanence may be extended to other, perhaps all, dialectical interactions (including social and other environmental interactions) and the influences resulting from them.[14] When we consider the levels of holons, higher and lower, and inquire into the influences that dialectical interactions between an organic unity at any one level and an organic unity several levels higher, for example, then the intricacies of the complexities involving partial embodiment, or reembodiment, of dialectical influences tend to become beyond normal comprehension. How much mutual immanence extends to more distant hierarchical levels remains a question for further investigation. The problem is further complicated when we recognize many interdependent hierarchies and how dialectic and mutual immanence function in relating to them.

Knowledge, which is located in minds, and mind-brains, is involved in such dialectical and hierarchical and mutual immanent conditions. Understanding its nature remains inadequate as long as these conditions are ignored. Simple reductions of knowledge to language and language to words and sentences grammatically analyzable on blackboards may result in diminished understanding when presented as a complete account. Each of the most general sciences has a contribution to make to a full account of its nature. Metaphysical, physical, and biological conditions of knowing too often are neglected by those rightly seeking some understanding by studying the nature of culture and the historical, social, and psychological conditions of knowing.

One purpose of Organicism as a theory of knowledge is to emphasize the importance of recognizing, and seeking to understand, more and more (ideally all) conditions of the nature of knowledge revealed by general and specialized investigations in the various sciences, and, of course to emphasize their cooperative interaction in the synthetic (or rather organic, as both synthetic and analytic) organic unities in moments of awareness and lifetimes of memory and habits of adaptation.

# H. CONCLUSION

Knowledge has its nature and location inherent in mind-body and all of the essential conditions of mind-body existence. The nature of knowledge is limited by such conditions and thus knowledge comes into existence having its nature both enabled and limited by such conditions. Any theory that fails to recognize the mind-body location and nature of knowledge remains inadequate.

# Six
# REASONING

## Part 1
## ANALOGY

All reasoning is by analogy. "Analogy is not a relatively poor use of logic; rather logic is a relatively good use of analogy."[1]

What is analogy? Analogy pertains to sameness and difference, to the way or ways in which some things that are the same are also different and to the ways in which some things that are different are also the same.

All existing things are alike in existing. Each existing thing is different from every other existing thing in being a thing. Therefore all existing things embody both some sameness and some difference in their relations with each other.

Thinking about existing is analogical because existing is analogical. When two or more things (apparent objects) are observed, they are observed to be both the same (in existing as appearances) and different (in being different appearances).

Inferring is analogical. Inferring is an act of intuition in which the intuiter is aware of an appearance that first appears both to be what it is as it appears and to involve something more than what it is as it first appears. Inferences are of many kinds. They vary both regarding the kinds of "more than" and regarding "how much more" of each kind. Variations range from complete absence of attention to any "more" as more to clear attention to any "more" and concern about its nature.

Three examples of kinds of inferring are examined: perceptual inference, linguistic inference, and implicative inference.

# A. PERCEPTUAL INFERENCE

For example, "I see a pen" states an inference regarding an apparently real writing instrument. The pen appears as an object in awareness. This awareness is intuited. It appears also as an apparently real pen. Its being apparently real is also intuited. If no doubts accompany this inference, the apparent pen and the apparently real pen are regarded as the same. When no difference is observed, the inference is accepted as certain, and no analogy is observed. Since psychologists and epistemologists do claim that there is some difference, questions about analogy remain theoretical for this inference.

When I ask, "What is that?" (referring to a new and peculiarly shaped pen), I am aware of an apparent object resembling a pen in some ways but also having unfamiliar characteristics (something "more"). Examining the pen and discovering that it is a writing instrument (having the essential nature of a pen), and that its unfamiliar characteristics do not inhibit its use as such and may improve its usability in some ways, I conclude that "It is a pen." It is both like a pen, as I previously conceived it, and unlike it as I previously conceived it. Being both the same and different, analogy is observed.

I have referred, in Chapter 2, to immediate, intermediate, and mediated inferences, all of which involve analogy, even though some thinkers accept most of their inferences as certain and neglect to observe analogy.

# B. LINGUISTIC INFERENCE

European languages involve grammatical structures, including sentences. Each sentence has a subject and a predicate. A subject is by nature a subject for a predicate. A predicate is by nature a predicate for a subject. The natures of subjects and predicates are conceived and defined in such a way that each involves the nature of the other in its definition. Because the subject and predicate of a sentence are both different in nature and the same in constituting the same sentence, analogy is present.

To say that the natures of subjects and predicates involve each other is to say that the nature of each is in some way present in the nature of the other and thus is immanent in the other. Subjects and predicates are by nature mutually immanent.

Each language has a structure consisting of several parts of speech, each of which is defined to perform one or more functions within the system. Each language is a system as a whole that has all of its parts as parts of its nature and has a nature that is immanent in each of its parts (because they are parts of it and being parts of it is what they are). Each part has something of the nature of every other part in it because it participates in the system, inclusive of all of its parts, which is immanent in it. All parts are the same in being parts of the language, and each part is a different part, so analogy is present in the parts. Mutual immanence involves analogy. Analogy involves mutual immanence.

# C. IMPLICATIVE INFERENCE

Implication presupposes definition. Abstracting concepts from perceptual inferences and linguistic practices normally involves concern for clarity of definition and assurance of precision in thinking.

What is definition? Definition of a concept involves assertion of its characteristics. For example, a square is something "having four equal sides and four right angles."

Concepts are also defined by relating them to other concepts. For example, a cube is "a solid with six equal square sides." Given this definition, a person can infer that "if something is a cube, it has at least one square side."

Concepts are universals. When two or more objects appear to be the same in some way, abstracting that sameness as a concept creates in the abstracting mind a universal. That sameness is named "a universal" because it characterizes *all* of the two or more objects.

After abstraction, many concepts are regarded as conceptual entities having their own definite nature without concern for the original objects. Many concepts are defined in relation to other such concepts in ways creating imaginative implicative systems. Logics are born.

Logicians, persons who have given much attention to the nature of reasoning, tend to deal exclusively with conceptions, with abstracted universals, and with relations between abstract universals as such. Although, when the interest of the logician is to use logic for understanding the nature of existence, interest in universals that also exist in real things is primary. Then, facility in relating universals, and symbols representing them, has naturally produced interest in generating new universals, universals that appear as inherent either in the nature of the abstracted universals or in relations emerging in ways of thinking with them.

When one universal concept is related to another, such as "persons" and "animals" when "all persons are animals" is already accepted as true, then this relation of inclusion is regarded as "implication." That is, because all existing persons are regarded as the same in being persons and all animals are regarded as being the same in being animals, and all persons are the same in being animals, the observation of inclusion is accepted as actual, and the generalization that all similar samenesses may result in abstracting "inclusion" as a concept, as a universal, and as something useful in relating concepts regarded as the same.

When abstracted, and regarded as a formal concept having its own nature, "implication" becomes a major intellectual instrument in reasoning and in explaining the nature of reasoning.

Is "implication" analogical? On the one hand, strict logicians intend that implication as a formal concept (universal) is by nature independent and self-standing in the sense that what is implied is the same as what implies, and that sameness is exact (exactly the same) to the extent that the relation of inclusion holds. Of course, there is more to what is meant by "animal" than by "person." But, although this difference is important regarding existing persons and animals, this difference is ignored as insignificant as far as the abstract concepts, "persons" and "animals," are concerned. The concept of "inclusion" is normally intended to be systematically ambiguous regarding how much inclusion is intended. So, on the one hand, implication is intended by many logicians to be concerned with strict sameness, and this is not analogical as intending to involve both difference and sameness in its meaning.

On the other hand, "implication" involves both sameness and difference, in many ways.

First, not only are what implies and what is implied two and thus different in being two, but also whenever there is more of something in the implied than in the implier or more of something in the implier than in the implied (e.g., as more in "animal" than in "person"), this more is a difference involved in the nature of such implication. Only when "A implies A" (the "law of identity") is the sameness complete in this way. [It is still incomplete in the sense that each of the two A's is a different A. The Platonic, and Logical Realist, assumption that A (or any abstract form) is timeless or eternal, seems to warrant the idea that no difference is involved when two A's are asserted as involving identity.]

Secondly, inferences occur in minds, and, even if the logician intends that abstract concepts, and symbols, have being independently of their being considered, they still exist in mind and exist as two and thus as different. Each inference that occurs in a mind involves that both what implies and what is implied are the same (in being involved in the same inference, and in the same mind) and different (in being what implies and what is implied).

Third, although some logicians try to retain the assumption that each concept is by (eternal) nature completely independent of all others, other logicians recognize that implications attributed to even completely independent concepts normally come to be involved in relations with others. Although not all logicians seem forced to go to the extreme of regarding all concepts as true because being consistent with the whole universe of concepts in some coherent system (as in the Coherence Theory of Truth), most logicians who become teachers submit examples of reasoning in which implicative relations involve concepts in concept systems that have additional implications for the concepts. For, even all supposedly completely independent concepts are alike in being completely independent and each one is different from every other one in being a different concept. There is no escaping sameness-difference relations no matter how abstract (or eternalistic) a logician tries to become. Implication involves analogy in some ways, even when logicians intend that it does not.

Fourth, I regard attempts to hold that exact implication involves sameness completely without difference as a natural tendency to go to, and to prefer, the extreme end of the sameness-difference range when interpreting apparent, including apparently real, objects.

How is implicative inference analogical? Implication involves both an implier and an implied. The implier implies the implied because it is the nature of an implier to imply. The implied is implied because it is the nature of an implied to be implied by an implier. Implication is analogical because implier and implied are the same in being part of the same implication and are different in being implier and implied. The nature of each involves the nature of the other. Implicative inference is analogical and involves mutual immanence.

The significance of regarding complete sameness and complete difference as ends of a sameness-difference continuum can be made clear by citing other views.

Those who state "A is A" (as a "Law of Identity")[2] require two A's, each of which, as items in the statement, is different from the other, and thus involve both sameness and difference in making the statement. Since the statement involves both two A's which are different and an assertion of identity, or non-sameness, it is self-contradictory.

Those who state "Nothing is both A and not-A"[3] are making a statement including both A and not-A. Since the statement is itself something including both A and not-A, its assertion that nothing is both A and not-A is self-contradictory.

Distinguishing between observing that implicative inference is analogical in involving implier and implied in being both the same and different, and asserting that implied and implier ("A is like B") are analogical, brings us to implication and inference as such.

"Implication," etymologically meaning "to enfold" ("en," or "in" plus "pliant" or "flexible"), has been appropriated by Western logicians to indicate the formal nature of concepts and how their definition can be (even must be) interpreted. Clear and precise definition of concepts is often understood to involve the concept of necessity, meaning that no alternatives are permitted. Complex concepts may be analyzed and abstracted parts may then be asserted to be parts internal to, or inherent in, them.

When implication is interpreted as logical necessity, inference is regarded as reliable. When the concept "animal" is defined to include "man," then the deduction, "If A is a man, then A is an animal," is regarded as necessary and "valid" (the accepted terminology). When implication is interpreted as mutual immanence of implier and implied, the inference is interpreted as reliable because the concepts "animal" and "man" do involve each other by nature (and when inferences are intended to be about apparently real things, as reliable, because real animals and real men are by nature involved mutually).

Questions naturally occur regarding how much implier and implied are the same and different. Sameness and difference may range from complete sameness ("If x is a square, then it is a rectangular four-sided figure."), when implier and implied are identical, to complete difference ("If x dies, then it will live forever."), when implier and implied are contradictory. When an inference asserts complete sameness, is it analogical? Analogy involves both sameness and difference. Complete sameness involving elimination of all difference remains by nature analogical because part of its nature is such elimination of negation. Complete sameness is thus both analogical in involving the whole range of sameness-difference in its nature and not analogical in eliminating all difference. Complete difference involving elimination of all sameness remains by nature analogical because part of its nature is such elimination of sameness. Complete difference is thus both analogical in involving the whole range of sameness-difference in its nature and not analogical in eliminating all sameness. All reasoning is analogical because it involves the conception that the ends of the range in two directions, toward complete sameness and complete difference, are by nature parts of the range.

Implication interpreted as logical necessity exemplifies reasoning by analogy presupposing as true the extreme sameness end of the sameness-difference range. Implication interpreted as mutual immanence accepts the whole range of sameness-difference (and all other such ranges as recognized by Organicism).

Problems of how much sameness and how much difference are involved in particular implicative inferences also range from one end of the range to the other. Each how-much involves its own kinds of concepts and their numerous kind of characteristics, and its own numbers of concepts and numbers of kinds of characteristics.

A Western logician, L. S. Stebbing, has claimed that "We can now make precise the characteristics upon which the strength of an analogical argument depends. Its strength depends upon the character of the initial resemblance and upon the relative comprehensiveness of the properties which are asserted to be connected. ...The more we can increase the total known analogy the more likelihood there is that we shall increase the number of important properties it contains; hence, the less likelihood of our overlooking an important difference or resemblance."[4]

# Part 2
# ORGANICITY

Reasoning is organicistic because existence is organicistic. (Any adequate theory of reasoning will base its nature upon or within a theory of the nature of existence. Major differences in theories of reasoning are due mainly to differences in their metaphysical foundations, or lack of them). An explanation of the nature of existence requires a language in which to express its nature. I adopt the common term "thing" to name anything that exists. Each thing is an entity, has being or is being, exists, and involves energy.

The central concept in organicistic metaphysics is organicity, which will be explained primarily in terms of organic unity. The problems of "the one and the many," which have plagued humankind from its beginning, are exemplified most significantly in problems of wholes and parts.

Each thing is a whole of parts. A whole is not its parts. The parts of a whole are not the whole. Yet every whole is a whole of parts. And every part is a part of a whole. Each, whole and parts, involves the other within its own nature. A whole cannot be what it is as a whole of parts without the parts. A part cannot be what it is as part of a whole without the whole. Hence, whole and parts are united by nature in a unity inclusive of the whole and its unity and the parts and their plurality. This inclusive unity I call "organic unity."

Reliable reasoning about organic unity is facilitated by understanding characteristics constituting its nature.

# A. INTERDEPENDENCE

A whole and its parts interdepend. Interdependence involves both some independence and some dependence. Each part, in being different from every other part and from the whole, has its own being and nature that cannot be reduced to its being dependent on them. To this extent it can be thought of as independent. The whole, in being different from each and all of the parts, has its own being and nature that cannot be reduced to its being dependent on them. To this extent it can be thought of as independent. (When each part functions also as a whole of its own parts, it has its own organic unity that is not reducible to the organic unity of the whole-parts organic unity. When the whole functions as part of a larger whole, its functioning partially in this way differs from its functioning as a whole of parts.)

Wholes and parts can differ in their ways of interdepending. Some parts depend more on their whole than other parts do. Some wholes depend more on some parts than on other parts. Some parts depend on other parts, and do more so on some parts than on others.

Organicity involves variations in such ways of interdepending, both in any stable condition and in all kinds of changes. When a part changes in any way, the whole which depends on it becomes changed also to the extent that the whole becomes a whole with a part that is changed in that way. When a whole changes in any way (e.g., as result of its role as a part in a larger whole), each of its parts becomes changed to the extent that it becomes a part of a whole that has changed in that way.

Interdepending involves causing. Changes are caused. When a whole changes by embodying a change in a part, it has been caused to become changed by the change in that part. When a whole is changed by a change in a part, it becomes a changed whole causing all other parts to be parts of it as a changed whole. Caused changes are variable, wholes being more influential at some times than others, and each part varyingly influencing the whole and each and all of the other parts.

Existence is dynamic, and organicity is present in such dynamism. In an organic whole, whole and parts influence each other continuingly. Such influences are reciprocal and dialectical. That is, when a part causes a whole to become different in any way, the whole, having become different in that way, responds with its changed nature to cause the part to become different (at least different in being a part of a somewhat different whole). Then, the part, being influenced by the whole in this way, responds by influencing the whole in a way caused by the way its nature is changed by being influenced by the whole.

Each dynamic organic whole embodies multiplicities of such dialectical processes, some of which become regularly recurring and thus causing new kinds of stability within it. Interdepending is dialectical. Reasoning about interdepending, to be adequate, needs to be dialectical.

Organicism is the philosophy of interdependence.[5]

# B. MUTUAL IMMANENCE

A whole and its parts are mutually immanent. A whole is a whole of parts which are inherent in its nature as a whole. Each part is a part of the whole and has its participation in the whole as inherent in its nature as a part of the whole. The nature of each, whole and part, has the being and nature of the other inherent in, or immanent in, its own nature.

Organicity involves the mutual immanence of whole and parts in constituting organic unity. Reasoning about organic unity involves organic unity in reasoning.

For example, "Mary is my sister," presupposes biological relationships between Mary and me involving the beings and natures of Mary and of me as implicit, if not consciously intended. Thus the mutual immanence of these natures in each other, biologically and conceptually, are present in such reasoning.

For example, "If Mary is my sister, then I am Mary's brother," is an inference stating an implication involving the mutual immanence of the natures of Mary and me, biologically and conceptually.

For example, "If Mary has three apples and I have two apples, together we have five apples," assumes that three actual apples and two actual apples are five actual apples. The being and natures of these apples constitutes them to be five in ways having the mutual immanences of their actual natures evident in the inferred addition. When numbers are abstracted from existences and achieve apparently independent being of their own, the mutual immanence of biological actuality is omitted, and the numbers acquire conceptual mutual immanence of their own such that three and two involve each other naturally.

That is, a number as a concept, even when the sources from which it has been abstracted have disappeared from awareness, has its own organic unity as a concept. Each number is a whole of parts, a whole integrating all of its ways of functioning as parts.

The number one, for example, functions as the parts of all other numbers, such as two, three, etc., in addition, subtraction, multiplication, and division, and in technical calculations. Yet it remains the number one. It is both complex in its varieties of functions and simple in its retaining its unity as a concept integrating all of its functions. Its simplicity as a unit and its complexity as multifunctional are mutually immanent. Such mutual immanence is inherent in its ability to exist as a concept that continues to function in the ways that it does. Without organic unity, the unity of its wholeness and parts, the unity of its simplicity and complexity, and some other unities, the number one would not be what it is.[6]

Organicism is the philosophy of mutual immanence.


# C. POLARITY

A whole and its parts are poles of a polarity. "Polarity involves at least three general categories -- oppositeness, complementarity, and tension." And these categories, "being essential to the nature of polarity, mutually involve each other."

"Oppositeness involves two posits, or positives, each of which is opposed to the other. Each is something negative relative to the other as positive. Thus each posit is both positive in itself and negative with respect to its opposite."

Complementarity involves "supplementarity, interdependence, and reciprocity." "Supplementarity pertains to supplying something lacking. The term 'supplement' (supply-ment) connotes better than the more commonly used term 'complement' (complete-ment), an incompleteness that needs and receives something that is lacking. Each of two opposites is incomplete in several senses. ...If 'complementarity' is interpreted as involving a double mutual supplementation of each of a pair of opposites by the other, then two supplementarities are required to constitute complete complementarity."[7]

Dimension (for "interdependence," see above) involves appositeness and poles. "Appositeness pertains to a closeness of relationship between two opposites which, in spite of their negation of each other, share something in common which is essential to the nature of each as a posit. To illustrate: 'good' and 'bad' are opposites and 'cause' and 'effect' are opposites, but 'good' and 'bad' together constitute value as a dimension (both are values) and 'cause' and 'effect' constitute causality as a dimension, whereas what dimension, if any, 'bad' and "cause" constitute is not immediately clear. Although any pair of opposites embodies a dimension, apposite opposites, such as 'good' and 'bad' and as 'cause' and 'effect,' constitute a dimension more obviously than inapposite opposites, such as 'bad' and 'cause.' ...The nature of two apposite opposites is such that each can be inferred from its opposite to the extent that it and its opposite share what is common to both."[8]

"Reciprocity involves at least two subcategories: symmetry and asymmetry. Oppositeness involves two posits each of which is, in a sense, equally (symmetrically) positive. Also, since each is not the other, and equally not the other, each is, in a sense, equally (symmetrically) negative. Oppositeness thus involves both positiveness and negativity equally (symmetrically). ...Symmetry presupposes asymmetry; for each of two opposites"[9] is not the other and has a nature that is different from the other and this difference constitutes a symmetry.

"Tension is a stretching of anything due to two or more divergent tendencies."[10] The whole and parts of an organic unity tend to vary in ways in which the whole constitutes more of it at some times and the parts constitute more of it at other times. Some of these ways occur in dialectic.

Organicism is a philosophy of polarity.

# D. DIALECTIC

A whole and its parts interact dialectically. Dialectic is a process of interacting between two or more things each of which is causally influencing the other in such a way that each develops through such interaction. That is, each, while retaining its own integrity, changes not only as a consequence of being influenced by the other but also as a consequence of its own influences on the other that in turn influence it. When a whole or its parts change in any way, each influences the other to be changed in some way, and each is in turn influenced by the other in ways involving any changes in its nature as a result of being influenced by the other.

Thus dialectic is inherent in organic unity, and the natures of both, whole and parts, embody dialectical processes inherent in their developing natures. Reasoning about organic unity, generally and with particular things, involves dialectical processes as implicit in their natures.

Dialectical processes in organic unities may vary somewhat by either whole or parts becoming more influential or may become stabilized as natural structural features of things. Awareness of dialectical features of things can influence ways of thinking and reasoning about them. How dialectic functions in higher-level organisms, physical, psychological, and social, needs recognition in scientific studies.

# E. HIERARCHY

A whole and its parts embody hierarchy. A whole is larger, and in this way higher, than any of its parts. Each part, which is also a whole of its own parts, is smaller, and in this way lower, than the whole of which it is a part. Since the whole-parts interdependence embodies hierarchy, hierarchy is inherent in the nature of organic unity.

Each thing, each organic whole, is part of larger wholes. Each part of an organic whole is itself a thing as a whole with parts of its own. For example, an atom is part of a molecule, a molecule is part of a cell, a cell is part of an organ, an organ is part of a person, a person is part of a family, a family is part of a community, etc., and earth is part of solar system, which is part of a galaxy. Hierarchy is important in the nature of organic unity because wholes of higher and lower levels influence each organic unity indirectly. Hierarchy involves each organic unity in being an organic unity of organic unities.

Each thing, each organic whole, participates in more than one hierarchy, for each of its parts is a whole with its own many parts hierarchically integrated, which many parts are also hierarchically integrated, etc., in ways descending in this way in many directions, and it participates in larger wholes which, as complexes of their own parts, tend to influence it indirectly in many ways. Existence is multihierarchical, and such multihierachicalness is inherent in, or immanent in, the nature of organic unity, and of each organic whole.

Reasoning about organic unity involves hierarchy implicitly even when hierarchy is unrecognized.

Concepts involve hierarchy, for some concepts, at least, are wholes with parts, and because expressing what can be expressed in language involves the concepts in the linguistic system and the way concepts occur as a result. Efforts to simplify and clarify concepts tend to abstract them from a rich multihierarchy of cultural accumulations.[11]

# F. CAUSATION

A whole and its parts are caused. Each causes the other when influencing it, both to remain the same and to change. But the organic unity of whole and parts also functions causally, for it is things that are causal relative to each other and not merely their wholes and parts separately. Awareness of the entitiveness and nature of the organic unity of things should provide some understanding of their causal power. For example, persons interact with each other causally as persons, not merely as parts of persons nor as wholes (souls?) abstracted from their parts. Organicity functions causally because things exist and function as organic wholes.

Organicity involves hierarchy. "My own hypothesis is that multileveled causation is a universal condition of existence and of each cause-effect situation."[12] Multihierarchical causation is also involved. What, then, is causation?

My analysis of causation differs from the common view that "C $\rightarrow$ E" or "C = E," that the amount of energy in cause and effect are equal. How energy empowers causation is unclear, but causation involves energetic influences. Causation does involve causes and effects, but in extremely complicated ways. Consider my analysis. "It claims that there is some novelty and thus some creation in every cause-effect situation." There is also some cessation or destruction.

How this appears to be so may be seen by considering what may be regarded as a minimum symbolism for causation. Every cause-effect situation involves a multiplicity of causes for each effect and a multiplicity of effects of each cause. All of the causes, simultaneous and successive, which participate in causing a particular effect, are symbolized by $c^1$, $c^2$, $c^3$, $c^4$, and $c^5$. If one thinks of an additional cause which he believes we have not considered, then he may add another $c^6$ or as many as will satisfy him that the symbols are sufficient to signify all the causes. Now the effect, $e$, which is caused by all of these causes, is caused by no other causes and is, in this sense, completely caused. There is nothing in the effect that was not caused to be there by the causes, singly and collectively. But notice that, nevertheless, there is something in the effect that did not exist in any of its causes. Insofar as it is an entity of an eventity, it has a unity about it, a unity of its own, that did not exist anywhere previously. This difference is not only a difference of the effect from each one of its causes taken singly, but also a consequence of the fact that it is one although they are many. That is, $c^1$ cannot be the sole cause of $e$, for $c^2$, $c^3$, $c^4$, and $c^5$ also are its causes. Likewise $c^2$ cannot be the sole cause of $e$ since it must share such causation with the other causes. Likewise $c^3$, $c^4$, and $c^5$. If $e$ is the joint effect of the five $c$'s there must be something about it which is contained neither in any one of its causes taken singly nor in all of them collectively, because their collectivity involves a manyness, and an external relatedness of each from the others, which does not exist in the effect.

The effect, as an existing entity, in turn functions as a cause of other effects. To the extent that it is caused by its causes, that is, continues in itself what existed in its causes, when it causes effects, it passes on to its effects what it received from its causes. But to the extent that it has a wholeness, unity, or entitiveness of its own, which did not exist in its causes, and which enters into its causal efficacy when it causes effects, it originates new causal efficacy that is different from that of its causes. To the extent that this is so, creation, both of what is novel in the effect and of what is new in the new causal efficacy which originates in it, is involved. According to this hypothesis, then every causation involves creation, both some new effect and some new cause. Such creation is partial, is aspectival, and is in some cases extremely minute. But in other cases novelty is great, and new kinds of causes are created. All causation involves creation.

"Such causation involves destruction also, for in whatever sense each of the causes of an effect had a unity about it which did not continue or recur in that effect, such unity ceased. Whether in the total causal processes in the universe there is exactly as much cessation as creation, I choose not to speculate.

"My hypothesis further accounts for apparent variations in the loss of and gain in energy apparently present in some kinds of beings by recognizing that causation is also multileveled. That is, for example, when atoms become organized into molecules, the molecular structure and substantial behavior involves energy over and above that constituting the atoms but also conditions, modifies, and incorporates some of their energy into itself as a molecule. A cell is caused to be by other cells in accordance with the causal laws of cell behavior and reproduction. But causal laws, behavior, and creativity involved in molecular causation influence cellular causation and are in turn influenced by cellular causation. A cell in a human body may be caused to come into being to serve the needs of that body, needs caused by a mind's desire to serve a social need such as for blood donation that is caused by a national group's decision to fight a war. That is, a cell may be both an effect of causal processes at molecular, atomic, and subatomic levels and at the same time an effect of causal processes at physiological, psychological, social, and political levels. It may also function causally at all such levels.

"Such multileveled causation provides opportunity for greater varieties of novelty and of new creations. It also reveals causality to be much more intricately complex than is usually supposed. It should discourage efforts to believe that causation can be understood reductionistically by the simple symbolism, $C = E$." [13]

Organicity involves multileveled causation as inherent in the nature of things. Reasoning remains inadequate in understanding the nature of things when its concepts fail to connote multileveled causation implicitly.

# G. PROCESS

A whole and its parts proceed. That is, they continue to exist through dialectical interactions in accordance with their mutual immanence, and both to remain the same in some ways and to change and become different in other ways. Each change is an event. An event is a unit of change. It has its own beginning, occurring, and ending, and continues from beginning to end. Such continuing is enduring, and each event involves the duration of its continuity.

Time consists in events and durations. Each continuous duration is an event. Events and durations vary, from that of a galaxy to a picosecond.

Consider "all of the heartbeats as events within a lifetime, which may also be regarded as an event, the latter is a higher, or more inclusive level, of time. Each complex organic unity that depends for its existence on all of several constituent organic unities is a temporally higher-level organic unity. The life of a person's cells depends on the occurrence of the events within each of its cells, which in turn depend on the occurrence of events within each of the molecules constituting the cells. ...Likewise our galaxy, presumably, is an organic unity constituted by sun and planets including our earth, which is constituted by molecules, atoms, particles, and so on. As persons, we exist...within...hierarchical systems of time...while our lives are events occurring within geological, solar, and galactic events."[14]

The commonly recognized mathematical conception of time as an infinitesimal present with no duration and no existing past or present is false. Representing time by a set of linear numbers does not reveal the actual nature of existing time. Use of the symbol "t" in physical equations is a fiction. These may have uses limited to the extent that actual units of time and temporal processes have linear features abstractable from them. Although measurements may use actual organic unities (how many heartbeats during one inhalation), common practice has adopted artificially rigid units interpretable mathematically. When a physicist interprets the equals symbol (=) in an equation to imply that time is reversible, the viciousness of this mathematical interpretation of time becomes obvious.

Organicism is a process philosophy. Reasoning about organic unities involves the nature of organic unities, including their processual nature.

# H. ENERGY

A whole and its parts are energies. An organic whole is an energy of energies. Energy exists as quanta. A quantum is an undivided whole. Each undivided whole exists as a quantum of energy. Each organic whole is a whole of parts, and the undividedness of its whole is a quantum. Each of its parts, being also a whole of parts, is a quantum while its whole is undivided. An organic whole is the whole of a whole and parts, and it too is a quantum to the extent that it continues to be undivided.

Existence is processual. To proceed is to both change and become different and to remain the same through change. Each organic whole proceeds through interaction of its whole and parts. Each change through interaction is an event. Each event involves the duration of its occurrence. The continuum of the duration of an event is an undivided whole, and thus functions as a quantum. Process is a procession of quanta.

How does a quantum of energy as an undivided whole change in any way? It is a whole of parts, and its parts may change (do change at least temporally in order to continue to exist). When a part of a whole changes, the whole changes by becoming a whole with a changed part. This change in the whole is gradual. The rates of change are variable. But each change of any part involves a continuation of the whole and thus the part participates in a continuum of being (energy) while the change occurs.

Energy changes are not abrupt (divided by an excluded middle) but are continuous. Energy changes take wave forms. Each wave is a continuum from its beginning to its end. Yet it involves variations in its nature as a quantum. The wave-particle theory of light exemplifies how energy proceeds. Light proceeds as both particle (quantum) and wave (continuum of change). I speculate that each ray of light involves a helix (or double helix?) containing the quantum as a continuum of being functioning as a particle with momentum. The rapidity with which the vibrations of the wavicle occur is amazing. But the process remains continuous and embodies a continuum within which the changes have the gradualness of the wave form.

Organicism is a philosophy of energy. Organicism is energicism. The Aristotelian distinction between matter and form has its counterpart in organicism as energy and organicity, except that, whereas form and matter are different in kind (divided by an excluded middle), the *erg* in en*erg*y and the *org* in *org*anicism are such that *org* is the form of *erg*, and *erg* is never without form or *org*. Not only are *erg* and *org* mutually immanent; *org* is the nature of *erg*. [No pure being exists. No pure energy exists. No pure *org* (nature) exists. Only organizing energy exists.]

# Part 3
# PRACTICALITY

Life survives through solving problems. Biological evolution has provided human beings with natural capacities for surviving in suitable environments. But eating, drinking, breathing, excreting, sleeping, associating, reproducing, etc., all require adaptive activities also. When problems occur, solutions are attempted. Some problems are solved without much effort. But some require reasoning.

Although each particular problem occurs with its own kinds of features, generalizing about problem solving has received excellent explanation in the pragmatic philosophy of John Dewey. His book, *How We Think*,[15] is classic. I adopt his views in stating my own pragmatic method of solving problems. It has been stated in my treatment of "What is Science?" It can be summarized in five stages.

# A. AWARENESS OF A PROBLEM

No problem, no science. Awareness of a difficulty in understanding provokes doubt about one's beliefs. The difficulty may be long standing or newly discovered. If one feels helpless, hopeless, or incompetent to deal with the difficulty, it does not become a scientific problem. One can, and relative to some kinds of problems must, accept one's incompetence. One must have a desire to deal with the problem and achieve a willingness to try to solve it before it can qualify as scientific.

# B. EXAMINING THE PROBLEM

Examination of a problem begins by observing it. This is initiated by an interest in the problem and by an effort to understand it. Although interest in understanding the problem tends to be continuous with interest in understanding its solution, initial efforts tend to be focused on understanding the problem. These are efforts to clarify the problem, i.e., both to mark out its boundaries and to analyze its ingredients. Such clarification aims to distinguish relevant from irrelevant aspects of the problem. It aims to provide bases for distinguishing relevant from irrelevant data (and consequently relevant and irrelevant hypotheses).

Initial examination of the problem is likely to include an effort to evaluate the importance of the problem, i.e., whether or not, and how much, effort should be exerted to solve the problem. This evaluation will involve others: Is the problem solvable? Is it solvable within the limits of time, money, effort and cooperation required? What are the probabilities that it can and will be solved? What values can be expected from achieving a solution?

Examining the problem is likely to generate questions about causes of the problem, how is it related to, or interrelated with, other factors in experience, and whether and how is it like or different from similar problems dealt with previously. These questions involve inferences about such causes, other factors and other problems. Problem solvers often remark that "Well begun is half done." The more fully one understands one's problem the more likely one is to achieve a workable solution. Thus thoroughness and carefulness in examining a problem are prescribed as beneficial in scientific method. The more highly socialized a particular scientific inquiry, the more attention needs to be paid to expressing clarifications in language easily and clearly communicable to other scientists. Accuracy as well as adequacy in observing, analyzing and communicating a problem are excellent ideals for a good beginning.

# C. PROPOSING SOLUTIONS

Solutions, to be adequate, must be clearly relevant to the problem. Initial suggestions often spring spontaneously from initial observations of the problem. But progressive clarification of the problem usually both refutes initial suggestions and leads to others seemingly more adequate. Trial and error thinking is to be expected. Some problems, when clearly understood, seem to generate solutions almost immediately. Other problems resist both clarification and obvious solution. When an important problem defies efforts to propose relevant solutions, scientists often try out "working hypotheses," hypotheses relevant to only some of the essential features of the problem. Then by exploring implications of such hypotheses, they may discover additional data relevant to further clarification of the problem or refutation of the working hypothesis.

## D. TESTING PROPOSALS

Two kinds of testing ("verification of hypotheses") can be distinguished: mental and operational.

(1) Any hypothesis suggested, early or late in an investigation, should be examined mentally before other efforts are expended on it. Criteria for a good hypothesis have been suggested: (a) Consistency, both within itself, with known facts, and with the prevailing body of scientific theory. (b) Relevancy of the hypothesis to the problem and evidence available. (c) Adequacy in comprehending all relevant factors, in revealing theoretical understanding, and in providing for testability and final solution. (d) Clarity and simplicity are desirable, but we should remember that clarity should include what is clearly unclear and that simplicity that reduces adequacy falsifies. (e) Communicability, especially easy communicability, when possible.

Although reasoning occurs at every step in the scientific process, it receives special emphasis during mental testing because mental tests are primarily rational in nature. Consulting with colleagues during mental testing tends to be especially beneficial, because deficiencies in the hypothesis, including any failure to embody the criteria of a good hypothesis, can be detected and corrected more easily before efforts are invested in costly operations. As science becomes more complicated, criteria for numbers and kinds of colleagues to be consulted tends to become established; at the same time, the more highly specialized a scientific investigation becomes, the fewer colleagues that are available for consultation. Growing awareness of the increasing importance of interdisciplinology should have the effect of encouraging, if not requiring, inquiry into and evaluation of implications of the hypothesis for other fields.

(2) Operational testing, often involving designing one or more experiments, aims to demonstrate the workability of the hypothesis. It involves observation of new evidence tending to verify or refute the hypothesis. Each science, often each problem, will require its own kind of experiments and its own kinds of instruments for measuring. Each kind of experiment will have its own kinds of criteria for excellence. In addition, operational testing is better (other things being equal) when it is more efficient (yields more evidence, verifying or refuting the hypothesis for less costs in time, money, equipment and effort), when it provides more conclusive evidence, and when it is more easily repeatable, as well as when it better continues to embody the criteria cited for mental testing.

The ideal experiment is called "crucial" because it is designed to determine definitely and finally whether an hypothesis is true or false. Crucial experiments seem very difficult to design, especially as problems become more complex and include greater quantities of factors. Increasingly, evidence is stated in terms of probabilities, including, where possible, estimations of probable error. So hypotheses tend to be "verified" only approximately, or in some degree, and, in many cases, only under specified limiting conditions.

# E. SOLVING THE PROBLEM

Problems may remain scientific even when they are not solved. Problems may remain scientific even when they appear to be unsolvable by presently known methods. But the aim and purpose of scientific method is to solve problems. Problems originating in doubt are not fully solved until that doubt has subsided and investigators feel satisfied that understanding has been achieved. The initial problem, plus additional problems arising during the investigation, determine the criteria for satisfactory solution.

If a doubt arises in a single mind, that mind will have its own criteria for settling its doubts. If problems do not become scientific until they become social, i.e., have been communicated to at least one other scientist, then solutions to problems do not become scientific until they become social, i.e., have been communicated to at least one other scientist. Problems of publication, distribution, reading and understanding solutions are involved in the way that scientific problems are finally solved. Does full solution require translation into all languages? As scientific periodicals proliferate with increasing numbers of specialties and as specialists complain that they cannot keep up with even specialized publications, do solved problems, i.e., those accepted by some as fully demonstrated, suffer from deficient solution in the sense of reduced attention by other scientists?

# Seven
# CONCLUSION

This book was originally intended as a companion to my *Metaphysics: An Introduction*. But it developed in a different way. Work began in 1975. Work was completed on Chapter 1, "Intuition," before 1968, on Chapter 2, "Inference," in 1985, on Chapter 3, "Generalization," in 1987, Chapters 4, "Mind," and 5, "Mind-Body," in 1990, and on Chapter 6, "Reasoning," in 1994. Since 1975 my views about organic unity shifted from emphasizing wholes and parts as interdependent to wholes and parts as more intimately unified as mutually immanent, a result of influences from Chinese philosophy.

## A. DEFICIENCIES

This book was originally designed to include several more chapters, on perception, knowledge of other minds, knowledge, and experience. But aging processes (I am 86 years old as I write) have diminished my abilities, so that omission seems better than deficient thinking or failure to publish the book.

No theory of knowledge is fully adequate until the mind-body problem (how does brain energy function also as mental energy when direct awareness of brain activity is impossible?) is solved. But this problem seems to have a nature that makes it unsolvable. This was obvious before beginning the book.

**1. Perception.** Another essential is a chapter on perception. I have accumulated piles of books, articles, notes, and references on perception in preparation for such a chapter. But confronting the problem today of preparing an even summary account of the complexities involved in perception is appalling. And current research by brain physiologists demonstrating correlations between brain activity and conscious experience is proceeding so rapidly that any comments of mine in this area would soon become obsolete. I have omitted the chapter completely.

2. **Mind.** The chapters on mind and mind-body challenge the prevailing psychologies, behaviorism and cognitive psychology (as well as all others), for failing to recognize both that mind has a natural substantiality, is presupposed in any attempt to deny or diminish its nature, and has developed biologically (ontology recapitulates phylogeny) in ways that make it mutually immanent with brain functions.

I had hoped to discover an organizing structure in mind. My first paper described fifty functions. Eight have been presented as examples. These are understood as functions of mind as mind. Even though never free from the immanence of brain functions in their nature, they are not brain functions as such. Mind has a substantial nature of its own. Its importance has been neglected by philosophers and psychologists alike. Mind is omniscient, not in the sense that it knows everything that exists, but in the sense that all knowledge is mental. Theory of knowledge depends on theory of mind.

3. **Mind-Body.** Mind-body mutual immanence involves energy functioning both as mental and physical. How it does this remains unclear. Instantaneous dialectical intercausations of amazingly complex functions require a continuum of unitary organization. The union exists as an hereditary intimacy caused by designs in the natures of both mind and brain functioning to serve the needs of each other in constituting the organic nature of the person seeking its own survival and welfare. How hierarchical structures and functions in the brain and in the mind support each other remains unclear. But that they do seems necessary. The sciences of physics and astronomy, music, and medicine all exist in minds and their instantaneous interactions with brains, to say nothing of productions of great beauty and wars of magnitudenous destructiveness. The mind-body problem

may remain unsolvable. But the concept of mutual immanence can contribute to understanding it.[1]

**4. Other Minds.** Theory of knowledge of other minds is complicated by problems in genetic psychology, sociology of knowledge, systems of communication, and varieties of individual differences. The chapter is simply omitted.

**5. Reasoning.** I have struggled for a year to produce a chapter on reasoning processes. The result is a patchwork of suggestions. But I have proposed that traditional logical implication and deductive reasoning can best be understood as the extreme sameness end of a range of analogies, involving both sameness and difference, as universal conditions of existence. The extremity of such way of reasoning limits its capacity to understand most of existence which embodies other varieties of analogy. Implication is not only analogical in nature, but involves mutual immanence, for what is implied depends for its implicated nature upon what implies it, and what implies cannot imply unless what is implied embodies its nature.

Reasoning is organicistic because existence is organicistic. The central concept in Organicistic metaphysics is organic unity, its solution to the perpetual problem of the one and the many. The section on Organicity explains how organic unity embodies interdependence, mutual immanence, polarity, dialectic, hierarchy, causation, process, and energy as contributing to its nature. It proposes that the *org* in *org*anic unity is the nature of the *erg* in en*erg*y.

Practically, reason solves problems. I have accepted John Dewey's proposal that much thinking, including scientific thinking, is best understood as involving five stages: awareness of the problem, examining the problem, proposing solutions, testing proposals, and solving the problem. Solutions successful in solving problems are used again for the same problems, survive as useful ideas, and are regarded as true as long as they are useful.

**6. Knowledge.** Knowledge, in addition to being mental, involved in mind-body problems, and perception and reasoning, includes all of

the ways, kinds, processes, and quantities of knowing that seem
printed in books and periodicals, stock our libraries and data banks,
and occupy our lives with learning, business, research, and
entertainment.

Epistemology as a science now needs to become concerned with the
epistemic influences of instruments used in knowledge industries.
These include rock carvings, slate pencils, crayons, pens, typewriters,
printing presses, copying machines, word processors, computers,
disks, tapes, audio-cassettes, video-cassettes, telephones, radio,
television, postal services, Fax, E-mail, picture telephones, electronic
directories, and communication networks. Each has become a means
for both aiding and limiting ways of knowing, for producing new
kinds of knowing and new kinds of ignorance. We are now flirting
passionately with artificial intelligence, virtual reality, and chaos as
more promising venues of investigation than the continuing quest for
understanding actuality.

Knowledge has been accumulating through customs, traditions, and
histories, by families, tribes, nations, religious sects, universities,
sciences or fields of inquiry, libraries, and now data banks. The role
of languages, and translation problems, in promoting knowledge and
limiting understandings, requires philosophy of language as well as
linguistic sciences to assist epistemologists. The tendencies toward
specialization, with emphases leading to "tunnel vision," causes what
is taught in university departments to be partly false. Responsibility
for assuring that what is taught in universities is true seems missing.
American Constitutional guarantees of free speech and press have led
to mistaking the right to speak as implying that all that is spoken is
equally true.

Ignorance and how to avoid it or diminish it is also a problem for
epistemologists. The limited capacities of minds, varying with ages
and personal peculiarities, are conditions of knowing. The limited
resources for learning in communities are conditions of knowing. The
production of specialized knowledge that ignores the knowledge of
other specialists about it conditions knowing. The inabilities for

exact translation among languages involves some ignorance. Now, with proliferating kinds of instruments useful in knowing, lack of availability generates new kinds of ignorance. Finally, thousands of articles and books published each day produce so much information that only a small percentage of it can be used. Knowledge accumulated in data banks has become so quantitative that searching for any limited quantity can be frustrating. We now suffer from publication pollution. Kinds and quantities of ignorance will increase.

Ignorance of a more pervasive kind should be obvious. There is more to existence than can be reproduced in any one mind or in all minds together. Recognition of this fact requires epistemologists to recognize the necessity for some agnosticism in any adequate theory of knowledge. A study of specialized kinds of needed agnosticism should be interesting. But overzealous agnostics, such as those phenomenologists who reject possibilities of knowing anything other than phenomenal appearances, should be discouraged. People do know, and know much, about existence. Tentative and pragmatic realisms need encouragement.

7. **Experience.** Experience is awareness of participating in existing beings (organisms) larger than one's self. It involves a feeling of belonging, even when what one belongs to includes harmful tendencies. It is exemplified in enjoying a healthy body, skillful habits, a respected family, a prosperous community, a strong nation, a peaceful world, and cosmic stability.

Different persons, in different cultures, experience themselves somewhat differently. Some Jews experience living as one of "the chosen people." Calvinists experience living with confidence in predestined eternal life. Christians experience being "saved" and secure in God's world and assured by Biblical and Church teachings. A Sufi experiences his own will as God's will (or God's will as his will). People of color often experience themselves as racial beings. Brotherhoods (tongs, gangs, secret societies) often generate feelings of belonging in bloody ceremonies. Chinese experience selves as family members, and personal integrity as involving feelings of family loyalty. Japanese Shintoists experience awareness of divinity as descendants from the Sun Goddess. Vedantists experience "atman is Brahman." "I am the embodiment of being."

Whereas knowledge, above, is devoted to sentences, perceptual objects, deductive arguments, and scientific conclusions, experience, examined here, involves feelings of awareness, vague or clear, of continuing as an embodiment of beings larger than one's self and of enjoying participation (or suffering fears, uncertainties, and anxieties if one has been so conditioned).

Wisdom, a subject neglected by epistemologists, must be experienced. Wisdom is not knowledge. Wisdom is not smartness. Wisdom is not intelligence. Wisdom is the willingness to accept things as they are. No one is wise until one is happy. Happiness consists in feeling that one has what one wants, but only because one willingly wants what one has. A person may be a lover of wisdom without ever becoming wise. But experiencing some love of wisdom is essential to being a philosopher. Epistemology is incomplete until it accounts for experience and wisdom.

I trust that the foregoing remarks about omitted chapters will serve as minor achievements, if the reader is in a forgiving mood.

# B. ACHIEVEMENTS

Some virtues of this book, as I see them:

**1. Intuition.** The treatment of intuition as an omnipresent condition of knowing and the precise definition of its nature as awareness of appearance are original (as far as I know) and are important as basic universal presuppositions of knowing. My systematic summary of essential functions of knowing, aiming to ground the quest for certainty in the absence of uncertainty in pure intuition, failed to give needed assurance because indirect evidence from eye-jerks implied illusory continuity of awareness. Nevertheless, intuition, as I have discovered-invented an account of its nature, is the ultimate locus of such certainty as is possible.

**2. Inference and Generalization.** These two chapters continue to develop the functions of knowing in Chapter 1, with continuing attention to their dependence on intuition, in ways that no one, to my knowledge, has done before. This is original. I hope that it will prove fruitful.

**3. Mind.** Mind has been neglected, mistreated, and, by Behaviorists, denied, for so long that negligence has become traditional. Here mind is claimed to be a substantial entity, existing in its own way as substantially as the brain exists in its way, and having a nature that is intuitable and understandable in terms of the ways that it functions. Mind is omniscient, not in the sense of knowing everything that exists, but in the sense that all knowledge is mental. Minds function in ways that are not reducible to brain activities. These ways should be recognized by epistemologists.

**4. Mind-Body.** Mind-body interdependence is so intimate and essential to the existence and natures of both mind and body that they should be understood as having mutually immanent natures, not only now but throughout biological evolution. Continuing dialectical interactions between mind and brain involve transmissions of energy which remains both the same as energy and different because functioning in structurally different ways. The nature of each is inherently structured to serve and be served by the nature and needs of the other. Although knowing always involves both mind and brain, some knowledge is primarily mental (e.g., mathematical) and some knowledge is primary physical (e.g., perception of sexual urge). Recognition of both the intuitive natures and mutual immanence of mind and brain in persons is essential to an adequate theory of knowledge.

**5. Reasoning.** Reasoning, which has been emphasized in Western philosophies, has been pursued to such extremes that abstractions, such as numbers, have been claimed to be not only real (have being whether known or not) and timeless (eternal) in nature but also as metaphysically foundational to all existence. Some physicists assert

that "If it can't be measured, it doesn't exist." My awareness that
reasoning, especially in its extreme forms, is not only discouraged but
also has been denied being in some Asian philosophies, has made me
recognize that some Western extremes are not only mistaken but also
false.

My response as an Organicist is to propose considering all
reasoning as devoted to relating samenesses and differences, or to
analogies. Analogies vary and range from more samenesses than
differences through more differences than samenesses. Deductive
reasoning exemplifies the extreme of requiring implication of extreme
(compete) sameness. But since I understand numbers, for example,
as mental, they remain inherently involved in the nature of reasoning
generally, and should be seen as exemplifying analogy in its extreme
form. Uses of analogy for predicting existings involve considerable
uncertainty, although principles for assuring greater likelihood have
been proposed.

Reasoning is Organicistic because existence is Organicistic. So
understanding organicity, the idea that all things exist as both one and
many, both whole and parts, involves recognizing that whole and
parts not only interdepend and are mutually immanent because neither
can exist without the other, but also involve the concept of organic
unity, a more intimate and inclusive union of whole and parts.
Understanding organicity fully involves understanding all other
universal characteristics of existence, including polarity, dialectic,
hierarchy, causation, process, and energy.[2] Intellectual inferences
usually involve abstractions ignoring all of what a person is not
aware.

Practical reasoning is involved in problem solving, the most
important function of living organisms. Survival, health, and welfare
require confronting problems of both changing situations and
remaining unchanged through them. The nature of practical reasoning
as employed in science, technology, and engineering, and in family,
community, and political living, has been explained by John Dewey
as needing five stages, often used unawares in common sense

solutions. Practical reasoning is situational. But it may involve quantities of principles, only some of which enter awareness. Theory of knowledge is theory of practical reasoning. All else in epistemology may contribute to understanding its practice.

# APPENDIX I
## Appendix to Chapter 2

## SUBJECT-OBJECT THEORIES[1]

Inquiries into the nature of knowledge immediately encounter a distinction between knower and known, often interpreted in terms of subject and object or of the subjective and objective ingredients in experience. Exploration of the nature of subjects and objects led to the formation of many theories, some of which involve further distinctions between an apparent (or phenomenal) self and a real (or noumenal) self as subject and between apparent (or phenomenal) things and real (or noumenal) things as objects.

The first purpose of this Appendix is to provide a comprehensive survey of the kinds of theories which such inquiry generates as possibilities. A new inquirer may then examine the possibilities and test each in terms of its characteristics to determine which seem needed for a most adequate theory of knowledge.

For this purpose two diagrams have been constructed intended to depict the possibilities: Diagram I, first, Part A, regarding theories distinguishing subjective from nonsubjective aspects, and second, Part B, regarding theories distinguishing objective from nonobjective aspects, and Diagram II, regarding theories involving relations between subjective and objective aspects.

Both diagrams are designed to depict distinctions between what is apparent, or what is present in awareness intuiting appearance, and what is not apparent, or what is inferred as being involved in knowing even though it is not in awareness intuiting appearance, here stipulatively named as "real." (The terms "apparent" and "real" may be interpreted as having meanings similar to Immanuel Kant's terms "phenomenal" and "noumenal," without necessarily involving all of his views with which they are interrelated and which thus may have additional implications essential to interpreting his meanings. I choose the terms "apparent" and "real" as having meanings more familiar to beginning readers and thus available to those who have not become acquainted with the technical language of Immanuel Kant.) The dotted line in the center of the diagrams is intended to depict distinctions between subjective and objective aspects present within awareness of appearance, and these are named "apparent self" and "apparent object(s)." The unbroken lines between "real self" and "apparent self" and between "apparent object" and "real object" are intended to depict distinctions between them without implying that the distinctions involve separations, unless separations are explicitly indicated, as in the second diagram. The two outside lines are intended merely to depict the limits of the aspects involved.

The first diagram is divided into two parts, the first, Part A, is limited to theories claiming to locate and to indicate the location of the subjective aspect of supposed subject-object constituents of knowing, and the second, Part B, is limited to theories claiming to locate the objective aspect of supposed subject-object constituents of knowing. Each part lists seven possible theories.

When a term is depicted as standing by itself, the depiction is intended to be interpreted as a theory claiming that the aspect depicted is all that is involved in constituting the subjective (in Part A) or objective (in Part B) ingredients in knowing. When a term is depicted as a theory claiming that one aspect involves one or more other aspects in constituting the subjective (in Part A) or objective (in Part B) ingredients in knowing, the terms are joined by a continuous underlining.

## DIAGRAM I

|  |  | Real Self | Apparent Self | Apparent Object | Real Object |
|---|---|---|---|---|---|
| A. Theories distin- | 1. |  | subjective |  |  |
| guishing subjective | 2. | subjective |  |  |  |
| from non-subjective | 3. | subjective | subjective |  |  |
| aspects. | 4. | subjective | subjective | subjective |  |
|  | 5. |  | subjective | subjective |  |
|  | 6. |  |  | subjective |  |
|  | 7. | subjective | subjective | subjective | subjective |
| B. Theories distin- | 1. |  |  | objective |  |
| guishing objective from | 2. |  |  |  | objective |
| non-objective aspects | 3. |  |  | objective | objective |
|  | 4. |  | objective | objective | objective |
|  | 5. |  | objective | objective |  |
|  | 6. |  | objective |  |  |
|  | 7. | objective | objective | objective | objective |

## Part A

1. The first theory, in Part A, claims that an apparent self, or what appears as that which is aware of appearances, is all that is needed, or is all that exists, as the subjective aspect of knowing. [E.g., Theravada.]

2. The second theory claims that a real self, or that which functions as the agent in knowing is all that is needed, or that exists, as the subjective aspect of knowing. According to this theory, the real self is the knower in which the knowledge is embodied. Whether or not the real self becomes in any way apparent to itself is irrelevant to the

actual existence   and embodiment of knowledge   in it as a foundational agent.

3. The third theory claims that an apparent self involves a real self, or something that is needed, or exists, as an agent of the act of awareness. This theory may be interpreted as a general theory divisible into subtheories differing, for example, regarding whether the two aspects are to be regarded (a) as identical, or as at times divisible (partly or completely), or (b) as having differing priorities such as being or enduring or acting.

4. The fourth theory claims that an apparent object is also subjective in the sense that all appearance, or all that is present in awareness of appearance, is also subjective.

5. The fifth theory claims that the only knowing of which we are aware is that which is present when awareness apprehends appearance, so both the subjective and objective aspects of knowledge must both be present in such appearance. Although apparent self and apparent object are not identical, in the sense that no difference exists between them, this theory claims that each involves the other as a condition of its own existence, since whenever awareness apprehends appearance, awareness involves both an awarer (self as subject) and what appears (as object); for without awareness there can be no appearance and without appearance awareness is aware of nothing. The only knowledge of which we are aware is that which appears, or that which occurs within appearance. Further claims about the need for, or existence of, a real self or real objects are regarded as superfluous and, indeed, as needlessly complicating.

6. The sixth theory claims that knowledge is of objects and that, although all knowledge is subjective in the sense that all objects known are apparent objects, nothing more is needed to account for them. Whether or not there are real (noumenal, hence unknowable) things is regarded as irrelevant to understanding the nature of knowledge. Whether or not there is a real self or even an apparent self functioning as an agent of awareness, or as an awarer, is regarded as irrelevant to the nature of knowledge because knowledge is

regarded as consisting entirely in objects known, i.e., objects presently appearing.

7. The seventh theory claims that an adequate understanding of the subjective aspects of the nature of knowledge involves including both real and apparent self and apparent and real objects. It claims that real objects must be included because a real thing can be an object of knowledge only by becoming an object for a subject, and it is this becoming an object for a subject that constitutes it as an object, and such becoming involves the agency and activity of a subject in endowing it with the objectivity involved in being an object for a subject. Although we can distinguish both the real and apparent aspects of self and the apparent and real aspects of objects, and although these may be regarded as having differential roles to play in constituting knowledge, all four are regarded as mutually dependent, and in some sense continuously integrated, ingredients in the subjective aspect of the subject-object nature of knowledge.

## Part B

1. The first theory, in Part B, claims that knowledge is of objects and that what appears in awareness as objects is all that is needed, or all that exists, as the objective aspect of knowing objects.

2. The second theory claims that the real things which become objects of knowledge are the real objects of knowledge and that, unless real things are known as objects, knowledge does not exist. Genuine knowledge is knowledge of real things which become known when they are known as real objects. [E.g., Logical Realism.]

3. The third theory claims that real things, which become objects of knowledge, must also appear as objects in order to be known. No knowledge exists without awareness of objects and when real things become objects of knowledge they appear as objects and appear as real. This theory may be interpreted as a general theory divisible into subtheories differing, for example, regarding whether the two aspects ("apparent object" and "real object") are regarded as identical, as at

times divisible (partly or completely), or as having differing priorities in importance as constituting knowledge.

4. The fourth theory claims that when real objects are known they not only must appear (i.e., become apparently real objects) but also must involve something to which they appear. Knowledge of apparently real objects occurs only when they appear in the awareness of that which is aware of them. Hence an apparent self is involved in the existence of subjective knowledge and is to be regarded as inherent in the unitary apprehension of real objects in such a way that without it, the apparent self functions as an ingredient in the knowledge of objects regarded as primarily objective, such knowledge could not exist. Inherence of an apparent self in the apprehension of objects warrants interpreting it as inherently objective.

5. The fifth theory claims that knowledge involves an apparent subject-object interdependent unity and that nothing more is needed. The unitary nature of such subject-object relationship involves the subjective aspect in the objective aspect of objects whenever knowledge occurs. Again, inherence of an apparent self in the apprehension of objects warrants interpreting it as inherently objective.

6. The sixth theory claims that an apparent self is all that is needed to account for knowledge since all objects must appear in a self in order to exist at all as objects. Thus any objectivity of objects depends for its existence upon it being an object for, and thus an object in, a self. To the extent that an apparent self is constituted by the objects inherent in it, it functions objectively or as embodying the objective aspects of knowledge.

7. The seventh theory claims that knowledge involves a real self aware of apparent objects, an apparent self, apparent objects, and real objects, in genuine knowledge. The act of knowing real things is a unitary action involving all four aspects. The four aspects may be distinguished but not separated or isolated from each other. Each may at times seem to function as the dominant ingredient in an act of knowing, but all are essential to its existence as knowledge.

# DIAGRAM II

|  | Real Self | Apparent Self | Apparent Object | Real Object |
|---|---|---|---|---|
| 1. | *subject* | *subject* <---> *object* | | *object* |
| 2. | *subject* | *subject* <---> *object* | | ? |
| 3. | ? | *subject* <---> *object* | | *object* |
| 4. | ? | *subject* <---> *object* | | ? |
| 5. | *subject* <--------------> | | *object* | ? |
| 6. | *subject* <--------------> | | *object* | *object* |
| 7. | *subject* <---> *object* | | *object* | *object* |
| 8. | *subject* <---> *object* | | *object* | ? |
| 9. | *subject* <---> *object* | | ? | ? |
| 10. | ? | *subject* <--------------> | | *object* |
| 11. | *subject* | *subject* | | *object* |
| 12. | *subject* | *subject* | *subject* <---> *object* | |
| 13. | ? | *subject* | *subject* <---> *object* | |
| 14. | ? | ? | *subject* <---> *object* | |
| 15. | *subject* <--------------> | | | *object* |
| 16. | *subject* | *subject* | *subject* | *subject* |
| 17. | *object* | *object* | *object* | *object* |
| 19. | *subject* | ? | ? | ? |
| 20. | ? | *subject* | ? | ? |
| 21. | ? | ? | *object* | ? |
| 22. | ? | ? | ? | *object* |
| 23. | ? | ? | ? | ? |

18. { (bracket joining rows 16 and 17)

The second diagram lists twenty-three possible kinds of theories intending to interpret the relations between subject and objects in knowing. Unbroken lines indicate that the two or more aspects underlined are to be regarded as involving continuity, interpretable either as identity or as intimate interdependence. The two-headed arrows indicate opposition, often understood as involving polar opposites. Terms standing by themselves are intended to be interpreted either as alone necessary for the existence of knowledge or all that is certain as necessary for knowledge. Question marks indicate that the theory claims uncertainty regarding the existence of the aspects or of their possible contributions to the nature of knowledge.

\* \* \*

The first four theories postulate subject-object interrelatedness interpreted as involving both opposition between apparent self as subject and apparent object as object and their interdependent functioning in constituting knowledge.

The first theory also recognizes both a real self and an apparent self, distinguishable but existentially identical, and apparent objects and real objects, also distinguishable but existentially identical in some fundamental ways. [It combines Theory 3 in Part A and Theory 3 in Part B of Diagram I.] [E.g., Representative Realism, Critical Realism, Pragmatism, Vaibasikas.]

The second theory postulates both a real and apparent self without requiring the existence of a real object in order to account for knowledge. [It combines Theory 3 in Part A and Theory 1 in Part B of Diagram I.] [E.g., Berkeley, Subjective Idealism, Yogacara.]

The third theory postulates both an apparent and real object and an apparent self without requiring the existence of a real self in order to account for knowledge. [It combines Theory 1 in Part A and Theory 3 in Part B of Diagram I.]

The fourth theory postulates both apparent subject and apparent object without requiring the existence of a real self or real object in accounting for the nature of knowledge. [It combines Theory 1 in Part A and Theory 1 in Part B of Diagram I.]  [E.g., Hume, Phenomenonalism.]

*  *  *

The second group of five theories (5-9) all postulate a real self as subject as essential to the nature of knowledge, but differ regarding the nature of and need for objective aspects.

The fifth theory postulates that a real subject apprehends an apparent object but remains uncertain about whether a real object is needed. [It combines Theory 2 in Part A and Theory 1 in Part B in Diagram I.] [E.g., Kant.]

The sixth theory postulates that a real subject apprehends an apparent object which involves at least some identity with a real object. [It combines Theory 2 in Part A and Theory 3 in Part B of Diagram I.] [E.g., Peirce.]

The seventh theory postulates that a real subject apprehends an object integratively involving not only an apparent object and a real object but also the contribution of an apparent subject in endowing the object with its objectivity (as object-for-a-subject). [It combines Theory 2 in Part A of and Theory 4 in Part B of Diagram I.] [E.g., Husserl, Vatsiputriyas, Samhkya.]

The eighth theory postulates that a real subject apprehends an object as an object-for-a-subject, thus involving the subject in the objectivity of the object, without being certain about whether or not knowledge requires the existence of a real object. [It combines Theory 2 in Part A with Theory 5 in Part B of Diagram I.]

The ninth theory postulates that the existence of knowledge requires the existence of a real self which functions or manifests itself as an apparent self within which all appearance exists. The appearing of appearances within a self is all that is required for the existence of knowledge (e.g., as in a dream. "Life is but a dream."). Any supposed need for recognizing or distinguishing apparent and real objects is regarded as uncertain. [It combines Theory 2 in Part A with Theory 6 in Part B of Diagram I.] [E.g., Sankara.]

* * *

The third group of five theories (10-14) all postulate a real object as essential to the nature of knowledge, but differ regarding the nature and need for the subjective aspects.

The tenth theory postulates that a real object can be known by an apparent subject without requiring that the real object be mediated by a distinguishable apparent object, and without presupposing as necessary a real self. [It combines Theory 1 in Part A with Theory 2 in Part B of Diagram I.] [E.g., Vaibhasikas, Sautrantikas.]

The eleventh theory postulates that a real object can be known by a subject without requiring that the real object be mediated by a distinguishable apparent object, but that a subject involves both real as well as apparent subjectivity whenever knowledge actually exists. [It combines Theory 3 in Part A with Theory 2 in Part B of Diagram I.] [E.g., Naive Realism.]

The twelfth theory postulates that a real object can be known by a subject but also that a real subject appearing as an apparent subject apprehends the object as apparent by endowing it with objectivity through the subject-object relationship. The postulated relationship between the subjectivity of the apparent object and the reality of the real object may involve questions and varying answers regarding any preciseness of this relationship. [It combines Theory 4 in Part A with Theory 2 in Part B of Diagram I.] [E.g., Sellars' Critical Realism, Whitehead.]

The thirteenth theory's postulates are the same as those of the twelfth except that it is uncertain whether an apparent subject requires a real subject for its existence and functioning. [It combines Theory 5 in Part A with Theory 2 in Part B of Diagram I.] [E.g., Sartre.]

The fourteenth theory postulates the subjectivity of a apparent object as needed for endowing a real thing with objectivity, but remains uncertain regarding whether either a real self or an apparent self or both are needed for the existence of knowledge. It presupposes that the existence of knowledge is already actually implicit when a real object manifests itself as appearance. [It combines Theory 6 in Part A with Theory 3 in Part B of Diagram I.] [E.g., Tendai.]

The fifteenth theory is like all theories in the second group in postulating a real self as subject and like all theories in the third group in postulating real things as objects, but it simply omits all appearances (apparent self and apparent objects) as contributing to the nature of knowledge (of real things by a real self; how such relationship can be considered knowledge remains to be explained). [It combines Theory 2 in Part A with Theory 2 in Part B of Diagram I.] [E.g., Jainism, Aristotle.]

\* \* \*

The fourth group of theories (16-18) all postulate continuity of the four aspects that have been distinguished in studying the nature of knowledge, but do so in fundamentally different ways.

The sixteenth theory postulates that all that exists is subjective and thus that any distinctions between apparent and real self and apparent and real objects must occur within such subjectivity. [It exemplifies Theory 7 in Part A of Diagram I.] [E.g., Spiritualism, Idealism, Yogacara.]

The seventeenth theory postulates that all that exists is objective in the sense that whatever exists is there to be observed and that any observing that is done is also done by the things that exist there. Any distinctions that one may desire to make between apparent and real self and apparent and real things must occur within such an objectively real world. [It exemplifies Theory 7 in Part B of Diagram I.] [E.g., Materialism.]

The eighteenth theory postulates not only the continuity or identity of the four aspects as subjective but also as objective and, further, of their subjective continuities as polarly (i.e., partially identically) related to each other. [It combines Theory 7 in Part A with Theory 7 in Part B of Diagram I and Theories 16 and 17 in Diagram II.] [E.g., Hegel, Organicism.]

\* \* \*

A fifth group of theories (19-23) is cited here to suggest unlikely possibilities regarding extremely limited postulates. Each of four theories selects one of the aspects (19. real self; 20. apparent self; 21. apparent objects; 22. real objects) and postulates uncertainty regarding the other factors. [They exemplify Theories 2 and 1 in Part A and Theories 1 and 2 in Part B of Diagram I.] [E.g., 19. Samhkya soul in *kaivalya* (omitting the uncertainties). 22. Materialism without knowers. Nihilism.]

The last theory (23) exemplifies complete skepticism, or agnosticism, postulating uncertainty regarding any necessity for any and all of the distinguishable aspects. [If the uncertainties are removed, this type is exemplified by *chit* in the *satchitananda* of *Nirguna Brahman*.]

\* \* \*

The foregoing survey of twenty-three possible kinds of theories pertaining to relations between subjective and objective aspects distinguishable in examining the nature of knowledge is oversimple and extremely stylized. The theories mentioned are suggested without assurance that they fit the types exactly. The views of other theorists may be cited that fit the types more adequately. The survey is intended to assist in a systematic study of types of epistemologies that may serve as a foundation for a more comprehensive, perhaps more widely acceptable, theory of knowledge. I propose some additional systematic suggestions in my effort to achieve a more adequate theory in the following section.

## THE ORGANICIST SUBJECT-OBJECT THEORY

A second purpose of this Appendix is to propose a theory intended to be more adequate than other theories (at least those considered in the foregoing) because it is based on the comprehensive survey of distinguishable subjective and objective aspects or ingredients. The theory proposes that all of the aspects distinguished be included in some way. The theory proposes further that all of the aspects be regarded not only as interrelated with but also as interdependent with, even if variably, each and all of the other aspects. Each particular aspect has its own contribution to make to the total complex whole of an act of knowing.

That different aspects are to be regarded as having different importance in constituting the whole is to be expected. Although attending to each of the aspects singled out for exclusive attention in Theories 19-23 aims to call attention to them as such, it both provides opportunity for explicitly rejecting each such theory as in any way adequate and opportunity for explicitly including the aspects within itself as comprehensive. Although Theory 18 is explicitly the most comprehensive in its inclusiveness, all of the other theories are also needed to the extent that each may depict a variation in the variable roles of aspects in particular acts of knowing. Theory 23 calls attention to the fact that, even after our proposed theory has been demonstrated to be the most adequate, some kinds and degrees of uncertainty plague our whole investigative enterprise, which requires a principle of tentativity as essential to the scientific attitude and method, including its use in stating a most adequate theory of the subject-object nature of knowledge.

A simple formulation of the proposed theory of the subject-object nature of knowledge, here called "the Organicist theory," may be stated as follows: The existence and nature of knowing involves subject-object relatedness including all of the foregoing distinguishable ingredients: real self, apparent self, apparent objects, real objects, and the unitary and interdependent functioning of each with the others in varying ways. These are in some sense subjective and in some sense objective, and are present implicitly or tacitly when not functioning as obviously important constituents in any particular act of knowing.

The first four theories may be regarded as the most useful in considering most common kinds of knowing, including knowledge of appearances as such and absence of awareness of a real self in much knowing. But the ways in which the other possible theories historically have been belabored by different theorists seem to warrant recognizing their claims as often partially justified when conceiving and proposing a theory incorporating all of the distinguishable aspects in some way.

A more complex formulation of the Organicist theory involves repeated use of its Diagram of Types to state more fully its way of treating issues distinguishing ingredient aspects as different, as opposites, and as polar opposites. The following three summary treatments of subject-object, real-apparent self and apparent-real object polarities exemplifying this more complex formulation (except that the contradictory statements for each positive assertion and the negative summaries) and joint assertion of the positive and negative summaries, considered essential for a complete statement of the theories have been omitted. (See *Polarity, Dialectic, and Organicity*, Chapter 2, especially pp. 47-59, for an example of such summaries and joint assertion.)

## Subject-Object Polarity

Twelve different theories about the subject-object polarity are stated. Each theory asserts something about knowledge that is included as an aspect (or "sense") in the Organicist's theory of knowledge.

1. Extreme subjectivism: All knowledge is subjective.
2. Extreme objectivism: All knowledge is objective.
3. Modified subjectivism: Knowledge is both subjective and objective but more subjective than objective.
4. Modified objectivism: Knowledge is both subjective and objective but more objective than subjective.
5. Extreme dualism: Knowledge involves both subjective and objective ingredients which are entirely unlike each other.
6. Extreme aspectism: Knowledge involves both subjective and objective aspects which are identical with each other (i.e., the aspects function together in constituting one act of knowing).
7. Modified dualism: Knowledge involves both subjective and objective ingredients which are more unlike than like each other.
8. Modified aspectism: Knowledge involves both subjective and objective aspects which are more like than unlike each other.
9. Extreme middlism: Knowledge involves both subjective and objective ingredients which are exactly equally alike and unlike each other.
10. Modified middlism: Knowledge involves both subjective and objective ingredients which are not exactly equally alike and unlike each other.
11. Extreme equalism: Knowledge involves both subjective and objective ingredients and involves their likeness (identity) and unlikeness (difference) exactly equally.
12. Modified equalism: Knowledge involves both subjective and objective ingredients and involves their likeness (identity) and unlikeness (difference) unequally.

The Organicist theory of the subject-object nature of knowledge partakes of all of the above theories by asserting that there is (1) a sense in which all knowledge is subjective, (2) a sense in which all knowledge is objective, (3) a sense in which knowledge is more subjective than objective, (4) a sense in which knowledge is more objective than subjective, (5) a sense in which the subjective and objective ingredients are entirely unlike each other, (6) a sense in which they are identical with each other (function together in constituting one act of knowing), (7) a sense in which they are more unlike than like each other, (8) a sense in which they are more like than unlike each other, (9) a sense in which they are equally alike and unlike each other, (10) a sense in which they are unequally like and unlike each other, (11) a sense in which their likeness and unlikeness is involved equally, and (12) a sense in which their likeness and unlikeness is involved unequally.

The subjective and objective poles of the subject-object polarity are mutually immanent. Such immanence is present in the subject-object polarity in such a way that all of the twelve senses distinguished in the foregoing paragraph can be understood to be present as implicit in it.

## Real Self--Apparent Self Polarity

Twelve theories about the real self--apparent self polarity are stated. Each theory asserts something about the nature of the subjective aspect of knowing that is included as an aspect (or "sense") in the Organicist's theory of knowledge.

1. Extreme realism: The subjective aspect of knowledge consists entirely of the real self as subjective.

2. Extreme apparentism: The subjective aspect of knowledge consists entirely of the apparent self as subjective.

3. Modified realism: The subjective aspect of knowledge involves both a real self and an apparent self but consists more of the real than of the apparent self.

4. Modified apparentism: The subjective aspect of knowledge involves both a real self and an apparent self but consists more of the apparent than of the real self.

5. Extreme dualism: The subjective aspect of knowledge consists of both a real and an apparent self which are entirely unlike each other.

6. Extreme aspectism: The subjective aspect of knowledge involves both a real and an apparent self which are entirely the same

or identical (functioning together as a single unity in constituting the subject).

7. Modified dualism: The subjective aspect of knowledge consists of both a real and an apparent self which are more different than alike.

8. Modified aspectism: The subjective aspect of knowledge involves both a real and an apparent self which are more alike than different.

9. Extreme middlism: The subjective aspect of knowledge involves both a real and an apparent self equally, i.e., consists of both exactly equally.

10. Modified equalism: The subjective aspect of knowledge consists in both a real and an apparent self unequally.

11. Extreme equalism: The subjective aspect of knowledge involves both a real and an apparent self and consists of both their identity and difference exactly equally.

12. Modified equalism: The subjective aspect of knowledge involves both an apparent and a real self and consists of their identity and differences unequally.

The Organicist theory of the nature of the subjective aspect of knowing partakes of all of the above theories by asserting that there is (1) a sense in which the subjective aspect of knowledge consists entirely in a real self, (2) a sense in which it consists entirely in an apparent self, (3) a sense in which it consists more of the real than of the apparent self, (4) a sense in which it consists more of the apparent than of the real self, (5) a sense in which the real self and the apparent self are entirely unlike each other, (6) a sense in which the real and the apparent self are identical, (7) a sense in which they are more different than alike, (8) a sense in which they are more alike than different, (9) a sense in which they are involved in it exactly equally, (10) a sense in which they constitute it unequally, (11) a sense in which their identity and difference constitute it equally, and (12) a sense in which their identity and difference constitute it unequally.

## Apparent Object--Real Object Polarity

Twelve theories about the apparent object--real object polarity are stated. Each theory asserts something about the objective nature of knowledge that is included as an aspect (or "sense") in the Organicist's theory of knowledge.

1. Extreme apparentism: The objective aspect of knowledge consists entirely of apparent objects.

2. Extreme realism: The objective aspect of knowledge consists entirely of real objects.

3. Modified apparentism: The objective aspect of knowledge involves both apparent and real objects but consists in apparent objects more than in real objects.

4. Modified realism: The objective aspect of knowledge involves both apparent and real objects but consists in real objects more than in apparent objects.

5. Extreme dualism: The objective aspect of knowledge consists of both apparent and real objects which are entirely unlike each other.

6. Extreme aspectism: The objective aspect of knowledge involves both apparent and real objectivity as aspects which are entirely the same (i.e., function together as a single unity as objective).

7. Modified dualism: The objective aspect of knowledge involves both apparent and real objects which are more unlike than like each other.

8. Modified aspectism: The objective aspect of knowledge involves both apparent and real objects which are more alike than unlike each other.

9. Extreme middlism: The objective aspect of knowledge involves both apparent and real objects exactly equally.

10. Modified middlism: The objective aspect of knowledge involves both apparent and real objects unequally.

11. Extreme equalism: The objective aspect of knowledge involves both apparent and real objects and consists of their likeness and unlikeness exactly equally.

12.  Modified equalism: The objective aspect of knowledge involves both apparent and real objects and consists of their likeness and unlikeness unequally.

The Organicist theory of the nature of the objective aspect of knowing partakes of all of the above theories by asserting that there is (1) a sense in which the objective aspect of knowledge consists entirely in apparent objects, (2) a sense in which it consists entirely of real objects, (3) a sense in which it consists more in apparent than in real objects, (4) a sense in which it consists more in real than in apparent objects, (5) a sense in which apparent and real objects are entirely unlike each other, (6) a sense in which they are identical (function together as a single unity objective), (7) a sense in which they are more unlike than like each other, (8) a sense in which they are more like than unlike each other, (9) a sense in which knowledge involves both equally, (10) a sense in which knowledge involves both unequally, (11) a sense in which knowledge consists of their likeness and unlikeness exactly equally, and (12) a sense in which knowledge consists in their likeness and unlikeness unequally.

The foregoing account of a proposed Organicist theory of knowledge is limited to its treatment of the subject-object aspects of knowing. A fuller account will include proposals about the nature and roles of intuition and inference, of organic logic, of polarity, dialectic, and organicity in problem-solving processes, mind-brain interdependence, and hereditary, learning, communicative, social, cultural, and linguistic as well as physiological, physical and environmental conditions of knowing.

Because the Organicist theory aims to be antireductionistic, it seeks to be as inclusive as possible regarding recognizing the multiplicities of factors involved in knowing. Its both-and emphases generate the kind of theory depicted in its Diagram of Types, including the negation of negations which have been omitted here.

For fuller exposition, see the original Diagram of Types in *Polarity, Dialectic and Organicity*, Chapter 3. It exemplifies Organicism's primary example of generalization.

# APPENDIX II
## Appendix to Chapter 6

## THE NUMBER ONE[1]

In a day when the supposed mathematical axiom, "A whole is equal to the sum of its parts," is challenged increasingly by those calling for "more holistic" explanations of the nature of things, a reexamination of the nature of numbers may help to clarify our problems. Abandoning the notion that numbers are eternal forms somehow subsisting independently of minds and adopting the view that "a thing is what a thing does," we can observe that numbers behave in many different ways.

The number one is selected here for examination. Thirteen questions about its nature are asked and answered to illustrate ways in which its nature as a number is inadequately described as "a sum."

### Simple or Complex?

Is the number one simple or complex? On the one hand, the number one seems not only simple, but the simplest element in number theory. All else depends on it, whether for addition, multiplication, division, or subtraction. On the other hand, when we consider all of the uses to which the number one is put, all of the ways in which it functions, and all of the services it performs for other numbers and other parts of number theory, we must recognize that it is complex in nature, perhaps even the most complex number in the sense that all other number complexities involve it, implicitly if not explicitly, at every step. My study, then, reveals that the number one is simple, even completely simple, on the one hand, and also complex, even infinitely complex, on the other. Being both simple in one sense or way and complex in another sense or in other ways involves it in being both simple and complex, in these different ways or senses, without contradiction.

The number one is simple. How simple? Is it not the simplest number possible? Not even zero which, as a number, was not discovered, or invented, until late in number history, is simpler. Zero is essentially both negative and universal in nature. It depends for its basic meaning both on being the absence of other numbers and on being the absence of all of them, e.g., one, fifty, one-tenth, and negative numbers.

Some impatient theorists seem to say: "One is one, and that is all you can say about it." Yet more can be said, even about its simplicity. As a unit, it is not two units, or three or four; it is only one. As a unit, it is undivided; it involves unity but not plurality. As a unit, it is a whole without parts.

Merely as a unit, it has no external relations. External relations, whether many or even only one, would involve the number one in being more than one, i.e., one plus its relations. Merely as a unit, it has no internal relations. Internal relations, likewise, would involve it in being more than one, i.e., one plus its relations. Merely as a unit, the number one is the simplest possible number.

The number one is complex. How complex? It is related to all other numbers and to all functions of all other numbers. Each of these ways of being related involves a relation which is its relation. At stake here is a theory of relations to the effect that a thing and its relations interdepend, in contrast to those theories that hold that a thing and its relations are completely independent of each other and that a thing is nothing but a product of its relations and hence is completely dependent upon them. As we demonstrate in the following, a thing's relations are parts of it, and the number one is complex in as many ways as it is related to other things. If it can or does enter into an infinite number and variety of relations, then it is, thereby, infinitely complex.

There is more to the number one than its unity, because it functions in many ways. Each of the uses to which it is put (including those which are labeled "erroneous") constitutes one of its functions. Each of the ways it "behaves" in the sense that it has a role to play in thought processes and in practical endeavors is one of its functions. In what follows, we explore some of the seemingly endless functions of the number one.

## Substance or Function?

If a substance is that which "stands under" or remains through change, then if the number one remains the same in any way through all of the functions (additions, subtractions, multiplications, divisions, etc.), then it is substantial and is a substance. According to the view presented here, the number one is a substance in this sense. Doubtless it is the most substantial number in the sense that, because it is used more than any other number, it is involved in more functions and more changes, and thus it remains the same through more such changes. I am not suggesting that the number one is a physical substance, but only that it is experienced as substantial as any other thing to the extent that it is experienced as remaining the same through as many changes.

On the other hand, the number one functions, as already stated. According to a functional theory (or pragmatic behavioral theory), a thing is what a thing does or how it behaves or functions. To understand the nature of a thing, discover all of the ways in which it behaves or functions, and these together constitute its nature. It is then inferred to be that which does all these things and that its being and nature are constituted, for the most part, by its doing them.

The theory presented here holds that the number one consists in both its substantial and functional aspects, and that these complement each other in constituting it. That is, the number one is not merely a behavioral or functional process (as John Dewey seems to claim, i.e., a functioning without a substance), but it combines both its functioning, behaving, acting, serving, and consequently participating in many changing situations, with its being substantial in whatever way it remains the same throughout all such functioning, behaving acting, serving, and changing. It could not continue to function unless it remains in some sense the same through changes. Substance and function are thus seen to be complementary aspects of each thing, including the number one.

In what follows, we shall be concerned primarily with the ways in which the number one functions. But in doing so, we presuppose that there is some fundamental sense in which it remains the same throughout such functioning, and, to the extent that it does, is substantial and thus a substance.

## Subjective or Real?

Is the number one subjective and mind-dependent only or does it have an existence independent of minds also? Nominalists say that numbers are names which exist only in minds. Platonists and Logical Realists hold that numbers, even if they do not "exist," i.e., have temporal being, nevertheless "subsist," i.e., have non-temporal, or eternal, being. Such real numbers may be known whenever the real numbers enter the mind as "in-form-ation."

The view presented here: (1) Numbers are mind-dependent. No numbers either exist or subsist outside of minds. (2) Yet there are three senses in which numbers may be regarded as real. (a) Relative to each mind, numbers may exist in other minds whether it knows them, or knows about them, or not. (b) Some real things exist in such a way that they are numerable, not merely arbitrarily, but naturally or by their very nature. Consider, for example, a woman who gives birth to a child, and then to another child. The one came first and the other second. They did not come with numbers attached; but they came in such a way that one who thinks in terms of numbers and thinks truly will regard them as numberable one and two. The attachment of such numbers is not arbitrary but natural, i.e., in accordance with the nature of the mother and her children.    (c) Cultivated habits of communication, resulting in language, tend to generate commonly-participated-in thought (including numbering) behavior patterns. The name "objective relativism" has been given to the existence in a group of minds of common thought structures and processes which have been established by communication and which remain relatively stable. They have a kind of reality, i.e., existence independent of some minds, by virtue of their existing in other minds, not merely as numbers but as stable patterns of numbers which have a substantiality over and above the substantiality of particular minds participating in such communication.

Hence, although numbers exist only subjectively in the sense that without minds there would be no numbers and that no numbers exist or subsist outside of minds, nevertheless numbers are not purely subjective in the sense that they have no causes and arc not purely subjective in the sense that my feelings are private. Doubtless numbers arose, both in the history of the human race and psychogenetically in each child, as a response to experiencing apparently real things and events succeeding each other in attention. If so, then there are conditions in the real world which function causally in the production of numbering and thus of the numbers needed and used in such numbering. The invention of writing and printing and book publishing provides an additional kind of real condition sometimes facilitating the experiencing and communicating of numbers. The invention and common adoption of symbols which are printed gives to numbers an appearance of objective reality when we perceive the printed symbols intended to represent them. Yet such black marks are not numbers but only stable conditions for restimulating minds to interpret them as numbers. Numbers exist actually only in conscious interpretation. But we may think of them as existing potentially in some or all of the conditions, such as printed books and abilities of minds to recall and reperceive, which persist in existence even when not producing actual numbers in awareness.

Though all actual numbers are subjective, there are sufficient realistic aspects and conditions of number experiences to cause most of us to be Naive Realists regarding numbers most of the time. This is true of the number one.

## Individual or Social?

Does the number one exist only in one mind, in my mind, or does it exist in many minds? We have already, in the foregoing, presupposed that it can exist in many minds, and that it is communicable, i.e., can participate in communications between minds. If the number one does not exist in a mind until that mind learns about it, either from others or somehow by itself, then the quantity of the existences of the number one in different minds depends upon such learning and, in many cases, upon teaching.

Furthermore, if the existence of the number one in many minds, not merely potentially but actually, depends upon its being called to attention in minds, then differences in the numbers of persons in a classroom, or in a television audience (such as that viewing "Sesame Street" when "the number one sponsors the hour's program"), cause differences in the existence of the number one. Factors influencing the sizes of such classrooms or television audiences, and audience attentiveness, causally influence the existence of the number one.

Cultural factors influence awareness of, frequency of use of, and ways of functioning of the number one, thereby influencing its existence and nature. Problems occur concerning the nature of language and the role of words in symbolizing the number one in language. The fact that different languages have different words for one (*eka, ein, un, uno, unus*, etc.), and the number of such different languages with such differing words, influence its existence, usage, functions, and thereby something of its nature. Ease of translatability and the number of multilingual persons and of the actual occasions for translating words symbolizing the number one from one language to another affect its existence, etc.

Instruments for using numbers, such as an abacus, an adding machine, a calculating machine, an electronic computer affect the existence and usage of the number one. What is the effect on the number one of high speed computers? Given a two-valued logic, with 1 and 0 as the values, used by programmers, not only must programmers be aware of the number one myriads of times in formulating their programs, but they must intend that it functions also when they are not attending to it while the computer is operating at fantastically high speeds. The quantity of such computers in existence, their rate of production, ownership, management, repair, and usage all have bearings upon the existence and nature of the number one.

## Are There Two Ones?

On the one hand, there is only one number one. Any other number than the number one is another number, a different number, which exists and functions in its own way. If two or more people know the number one, both know the same number. It is subjective in both or all minds which know it. If those minds exist in different places, then the same number one exists in all of those various places.

On the other hand, what do we mean by "two"? The number two is another number. But the number two involves two ones. If there were only one one, then there could not be two ones and there could not be a number two. When there are two ones, is each of the ones the number one existing twice together, or are there two number ones? If there are two, is each of the two equally the number one, or is there a first number one and a second number one so that the two ones involved in constituting the number two can be distinguished from each other by some order of priority?

The number two involves two ones. But are the two ones really two different ones, or are they one one occurring twice together? If the same one can occur in different minds, why can it not also occur twice in one mind, not merely when I repeat "the number one" twice in succession but also when I mean by "two" two ones?

The problem becomes more complicated when I inquire about the number three, the number one hundred, the number one million, etc. For then I must ask are there one million number ones, for example, or is the number one such that it can exist one million times together at once in one place, i.e., in one number?

## One or Many?

We have, in effect, already asked whether the number one is one or many. On the one hand, there is only one number one. On the other hand, if there are two ones or a million ones, etc., then either there are many ones or the number one itself functions as many ones.

The number one is both one and many in different ways. As already indicated when treating it as simple or complex, as individual or social, it exists as both one and many, and, as is developed further in the following, it is both one and many, not only as a whole number but also as one which is divided, or divisible, into fractions, and which functions in multitudes of different ways.

## Same or Different?

Is the number one the same each time it recurs, as in two, in one hundred, in one million, etc.? Or is it different? Or is it both the same in some sense or senses and different in some  sense or senses? To me, it appears obvious that the number one is both.

## Positive or Negative?

On the one hand, the number one is positive. If we ask of it, "Is it, or is it not?" the answer must be, first of all, that "It is." It exists. It exists at least here and now in my awareness. The number one is nothing if not positive. Without being positive the number one cannot be. Furthermore, the number one is, or is positive, in all of the ways in which it is, including all of the different ways in which it functions. If the number one exists one million times together in the number "one million," then it is positive in so existing. In this way, it is positive a million times at least. If all other numbers involve it, then it is positive in all of them as many times as is needed by them to constitute them. Is any number more positive?

On the other hand, the number one is negative. It exists as negative in all of the ways it functions negatively. The number one is not the number two. It is not the number three, nor any other number of all the other numbers. Hence it is negative in all of these ways. If there is, as some hold, an infinity of numbers, then the number one, as not each of them, functions negatively infinitely in this way. It is not one of its fractions. It is not any of its fractions, no matter how many. And it is not all of them together as fractions. In so far as the number one: is simple, it is not complex, is complex, it is not simple; is one, is not many, and is many, is not one; is the same, is not different, and is different, is not the same; is positive, is not negative, and is not negative, is positive; etc. (See all of the following sections of this Appendix for further examples). Also, the number one is not a table, a molecule, a society, or a galaxy. Thus it is not all of the other things which exist in the universe, and so functions negatively in being not each one, and being not all of them together.

## Particular or Universal?

In so far as the number one is one number or exists as one, it is a particular. Even when the number one functions twice as two ones in the number two, each of such functioning is a particular. That is, each of the two ones in the number two is a particular, and the number two as one number is a particular number which involves two ones in a particular way. Hence, even in the number two, the number one functions particularly in at least three ways. So also, it functions multiparticularly in constituting all of the various other particular numbers. Each one is a particular. The number one is both one particular and a multiplicity of particulars when it functions as many ones.

However, if there are two ones, or many ones, then oneness, that which two or more ones have in common, is a universal. If the number one functions in multiplicities of ways, and yet remains the number one through all such functionings, then oneness, the universal, that which is common to all ones, is common to all of the ways in which the number one functions.

But does the number one, in whatever way it functions merely as one (e.g., as when an infant discovers-creates the first one that appears for it), function only as a particular or does it already involve the universal oneness? If there were only one one, universality would be only potential in it, i.e., potential in the sense that, if and when a second one would come to be, its likeness to, or commonness with, the first one would depend upon the existence of the first one as one. One alone has no potentiality merely by itself to have something in common with another one; but when a second one exists, the existence of both the first and second ones causes their existing as having something in common. So there is a sense in which one alone has potentiality for embodying and contributing to the embodiment of oneness, but this is a conditional potentiality, i.e., is dependent upon the existence of at least one other one for the coming into existence of that which is common to them.

## Potential or Actual?

The number one exists actually only in the minds which are aware of it when they are aware of it. Prior to the appearance of the number one in any mind, the number one did not exist actually. At any time when all minds are either asleep or preoccupied with other things, the number one does not exist actually. But, on the other hand, when two or more, e.g., two million television viewers, have the number one called to their attention at one time, the number one exists actually in all of those minds.

However, even though there may be times when the number one does not exist actually, once it has existed actually, can it ever cease to exist potentially? I suppose that if conditions in the universe became such that no mind could ever exist again, then the number one as mind-dependent would cease to exist even potentially. But, until then, it may be that the number one exists potentially more than actually. That is, some of the conditions needed for actualizing the number one, such as the existence of minds and of numerable objects, apparent and real, exist even though comparatively few minds are attending to the number one at any one time. Many more conditional potentialities for the actualization of the number one exist than are ever actualized. For example, the millions of books, each with a page number "1," resulting in unsalable overstock, and the millions of persons who do not have those books but who would read them if they had them, contain conditions which, in the absence of other needed conditions, remain conditional potentialities which never become actualized.

## Whole or Parts?

Is the number one a whole? Does the number one have parts? On the one hand, the number one is a whole in several senses. It is a whole in whatever sense it is a unit. Unity, wholeness, and oneness are synonyms. It is a whole in whatever sense it is simple. Being substantial, it remains the same through all changes, and in whatever sense it remains the same there is a whole of it. Each particular is a whole or has wholeness, so the number one as a particular number is or has such wholeness. Also, a universal is a whole of all that is common to different particulars, so oneness is a whole of all that is common to different ones; and that oneness (wholeness) is embodied in the number one, or the number one participates in that oneness (wholeness).

On the other hand, the number one is or has parts, several different kinds of parts. All of these may be spoken of as different kinds of functions. It functions subjectively and it functions really. It functions in one person and it functions in many persons. It functions in novel situations and it functions culturally. It functions positively, negatively, actually, potentially, particularly, universally. It functions recurrently each time it is used as the number one, and it functions recurrently each time any number involving it is used. It functions statically and dynamically, causally and as an effect, usefully and decoratively. It functions cardinally and ordinally, as a whole number and as divisible into fractions. As a whole number, it is addable, i.e., can be added to another number or have another number added to it, is subtractable, is multiplyable, and can function as a dividend from a larger number. It can be divided into fractions, and each of the different fractions (1/2, 1/59th, 1/1,000,000th, 2/7ths, 64/65ths, etc.) functions as one of its parts.

When the number one functions usefully, in enumerating things, in measuring things, in accounting, bargaining, exchanging, in building things, are not these functions to be included among its parts? Not only are there one or more goods, and bads, but many regard the number one itself as good, not merely as useful but also as a beautiful object. The number one has been deified, not only as represented in such phrases as "There is one God, and God is one," but also as "The One" of Plotinus, which is not only better than the best but also "beyond all good and evil."

Thus the number one is or has both a whole and a parts. Now whole and parts are opposed to each other. For, although a whole is always a whole of parts and a part is always the part of a whole, a whole is not one of its parts and a part is not its whole. These two kinds of negativity are also ways in which the number one is negative. But, often overlooked, is another kind of wholeness which consists in both the whole (as opposed to the parts) and the parts (as opposed to the whole) functioning together interdependently. Some call this an "organic whole" implying that both the unity and plurality, simplicity and complexity, and whole and parts function together interdependently. So conceived, the number one is an organic unity or an organic whole.

## Polarity

Involved in the foregoing interpretation of the number one as organic is something called "polarity." Polarity exists whenever two opposites (two posites which oppose each other) complement each other (involving interdependence, dimension, supplementarity, and reciprocity). Two opposites are polar, or embody polarity, when they interdepend (are partly independent of each other and partly depend upon each other) in such a way that they share something in common (called "dimension," which makes them "apposite opposites") and that each reciprocally supplies what the other lacks in constituting their polarity.

In the foregoing sections, we have surveyed some pairs of polar opposites (or apposite opposites) which together participate in constituting the number one. The number one is constituted by at least simple-complex, substance-function, subjective-real, individual-social, one-many, same-different, positive-negative, particular-universal, actual-potential, and whole-parts polarities. What other, and how many more, polarities participate in constituting the number one we do not explore here. But that many others do share in constituting it, we do not doubt.

Furthermore, these polarities interdepend and interact, for each of the polarities adds to the complexity which the number one as simple must somehow unify. Each as a persisting characteristic of the number one constitutes part of its substantiality as well as ways in which it functions. Each reveals something of the intricacies of minds attending to the number one as well as something of the apparently real world in which the number one seems to function. Each is communicable as well as individual, at least implicitly, for not everyone becomes aware of all of the potential characteristics of the number one. Each polarity contributes to the many of the one-many polarities characterizing the number one. Each polarity is a different polarity participating in the same number one. Each polarity is both positive and negative in its own way; for each is what it is and thus is something positive but also each is not any of the others and so contributes additional negativity to the nature of the number one. Each polarity is a particular polarity and the universal (polarity, polaricity, or polarness) is an additional universal embodied in the number one. Each of the polarities participates actually in the number one as actual and potentially as potential. Each of the polarities is another part of the number one as a whole.

Not only is the number one an organic whole inclusive of both poles of its whole-parts polarity, but all of the polarities, by functioning interdependently together as parts of it as a whole, contribute to constituting it as a very intricate organic unity.

## Dialectic

We must not stop exploring the nature of the number one before inquiring into its much-neglected dialectical nature. If the number one were merely a simple, static, unchangeable, wholly actual, indivisible unit, we might characterize it as undialectical. But since it does change in all of the different ways in which it functions, it can be seen to be dialectical in each of these ways.

What is dialectic? We confine treatment to three kinds: self-perpetuative, synthetic, and analytic.

Self-perpetuative dialectic is a process whereby a thing continues to exist by incorporating something other than itself into itself in such a way that it both remains the same as it was before the incorporation and also becomes somewhat different, or by losing (uncorporating or excorporating) some part of itself in such a way that it remains the same as before and also becomes somewhat different, or both.

The number one, occurring for a first time in some mind, perhaps could have disappeared and be forever forgotten without thereby being dialectical in any significant way. But when the number one recurs on a second occasion, it is both the same number one and yet it is different because it now is functioning as occurring for a second time which is a different time and a different functioning than the first. If it is first simple, then complex, first subjective, then real, first individual, then social, first particular, then universal, first positive, then negative, first actual, then potential, first a whole, then with parts, each additional way of functioning constitutes the same number one as also becoming different, or incorporating a difference into its nature and being. Once the nature of the number one grows by expanding new functions, these new functions then can participate in it as such a number when it comes to function either in still another new kind of situation or in merely another situation of the same kind.

The number one, having been used by many people for a long time in many ways, may decline in its nature and being (1) by having fewer people use it (people die, birth rates decline, other things occupy attention, some people come to prefer an antirational spiritual unity which excludes all numbers), (2) by having people use it in fewer ways (deduce it only occasionally as an optional derivative in set theory, prefer to symbolize serialization by $a$, $b$, $c$, $d$, etc., enjoy goods provided in such abundance that concern for enumeration declines), or (3) by both. Each such decline in use thereby diminishes its actual being and nature. It remains the same number one as before the decline and yet it becomes different by not functioning in each ceased way.

Synthetic dialectic is a process whereby two things perpetuate themselves growingly (or perpetuate themselves decliningly) by participating cooperatively in the emergence of a "new thesis" resulting from their joint substantial functioning. Each thing, first functioning separately, then also functions jointly through the emergence of the new thesis, thereby expanding its own way of functioning.

The number one sometimes functions by participating in the number two. The number two presupposes that there can be two ones. Despite the fact that mathematics teachers claim that "the whole is equal to the sum of its parts" ("two is two ones and nothing more"), two is itself one number which is distinguishable from other numbers such as three, ten, and forty-two. The number two can behave in ways in which the number one cannot. The number two can be divided in a way which results in whole numbers whereas the number one cannot. The number two, when multiplied by itself, results in fours, whereas one one is still only one. The number two may be used to represent pairs of things in ways which the number one cannot. Hence, the number two is a "new thesis" which has capacities and functions which the number one lacks, even though the number two continues to depend on two ones in order to exist and to function as it does. By being thus depended on, the number one not only perpetuates itself but expands growingly through participating not merely in two but additionally in all other whole numbers.

The number one functions dialectically also in a dyadic system used for programming computers. Here 1 is paired with 0. 1 and 0 are more obviously opposites functioning as antitheses. We do not have merely a simple synthesis of 1 and 0 into a 1-0 whole, but 1 and 0 as the supposed sole constituents in a system in which both recur myriads of times. On the one hand, each time 1 recurs in the system, it both remains the same number and becomes enough different to recur, thereby perpetuating itself (or being perpetuated). On the other hand, the more effectively the system works, both technically and usefully, i.e., the more 1 functions as a part of that system as a whole, and depends upon the demands for using the system because of its success as a system, the more it is perpetuated. So the number one, by participating in computer systems, dialectically perpetuates itself through its continuing service to such systems as "new theses."

Analytic dialectic, less well known then synthetic dialectic, is a process whereby new parts are generated within a whole instead of a new whole being generated by a synthesis of parts. For example, a fertilized ovum is a single cell (a whole, a thesis) which then divides itself into two cells while yet retaining a wholeness which continues not only through further division into four, eight, sixteen, etc., cells but throughout the life of a person.

The number one, as a whole number, is dialectically perpetuated through each division into fractions. A person may divide the number one into halves, each of which is also a number (i.e., a new thesis) or into quarters, tenths, thousands, etc., or into uneven fractions, such as one half, one third, and one sixth, for example. Is the number one destroyed by such division (so that the whole is equal to the sum of its parts, and nothing more; so what you have then is a sum of fractions but no number one)? Or does the number one perpetuate itself also through functioning as fractionable? In synthetic dialectic, the antitheses continue to exist and function by participating in the new thesis. In analytic dialectic, the whole continues to be embodied partially in each part or fraction. We do not say that a whole participates in the part; participating is what a part does. We say the whole is immanent in the part. For any fraction, such as a half, is always "a half of a whole." If the whole does not continue to function (i.e., to perpetuate itself through functioning) in each part, then the part must also cease to be a part of that whole. Hence, each fraction of the number one dialectically embodies it even if only partially (analytically) rather than as a part (synthetically).

# NOTES

## NOTES TO INTRODUCTION

1. Work on this book was begun in earnest in 1975. It had antecedents: My doctoral dissertation dealt with problems of intuition: *An Interpretation of the Nature of Presence and Some Implications of the Interpretation*, 1933. "Organicism," Chapter 20, *Philosophy: An Introduction*, New York: Wiley, 1953. "Organicism: The Philosophy of Interdependence," *International Philosophical Quarterly* 7 (June, 1967): 251-284. *Polarity, Dialectic, and Organicity*, Springfield, Illinois: Charles C Thomas, 1970. Chapter 2, "Intuition," was published in *Darshana International* 26: 4 (Oct., 1986): 23-36.

Influences from Chinese thinking about yin-yang opposites as polarities involving mutual immanence now requires some additions to my understanding of how knowledge, including intuition, inference, generalization, mind, mind-body, other minds, reasoning, and experience, is understood.

Although I have consistently named my philosophy "Organicism: The Philosophy of Interdependence" for a long time, I am now inclined to rename it, "Organicism: A Philosophy of Mutual Immanence." I have not had time to rework other problems, but I intend to introduce some new language within this text.

## NOTES TO CHAPTER 1: INTUITION

1. Awareness and appearance are such that the nature of each involves the nature of the other, since neither can exist without the

other. This involving is mutual. So the relations between awareness
and appearance are more adequately stated by saying that the nature
of each is immanent in the other because the nature of each depends
upon the nature of the other for its existing since it cannot exist
without the other and its nature.

2. Intuiting and intuiter involve each other naturally. The nature of
each involves the nature of the other. Thus the existence and natures
of both are mutually immanent. Knowing and intuiting are mutually
immanent because the nature of each involves the nature of the other.
Neither exists without the other.

3. Every intuition depends for its existence and nature on its
conditions and causes. Although the conditions and causes of each
intuition may also function as conditions and causes of other things,
to the extent that they do have natures  actually contributing to its
existence and nature, their natures are such as to so contribute to it,
and thus have the nature of the intuition immanent in them as so
contributing. Each intuition exists as a result of its conditions and
causes and so has a nature that embodies what they contribute to it.
What they contribute to it is embodied in it and thus is immanent in
it.

4. My interpretation of the mind-brain problem is explained in
Chapter 5. I mention here that the natures of mind and brain are
mutually immanent in many ways, and that any adequate account of
the nature of intuition involves how intuition, as an omnipresent
condition of actual knowing, has its nature inherently involved in the
mutual immanences of mind and brain. Both the potentialities and
limitations of intuition are conditioned by the potentialities and
limitations of mind and of brain and of their varieties of mutual
immanence, as well as mutual immanences with other conditions of
the existence of persons.

5. And mutual immanence of complementary poles.

6. Although any theory of the mutual immanence of multiplicities of kinds, complexities, and levels of organic conditions of the existence and nature of persons, and thus of knowing and intuiting, may provide assurance of the stable nature of presences, I do not anticipate that the absence of uncertainty inherent in the nature of intuition can be relied upon to provide certainty after doubt because absence of awareness of gaps in awareness provides illusory continuity. Although the human, and my, quest for certainty may achieve sufficient theoretical understanding of the nature of existence to warrant practical, or pragmatic, confidence in the reliability of principles regarding the nature of knowledge to warrant ignoring this problem as insignificant, for me it remains an Achilles heel in any claim that absolute certainty can be achieved. This is part of the reason why I insist on a principle of tentativity in stating my theory of knowledge as "Tentative Realism."

# NOTES TO CHAPTER 2: INFERENCE

1. See my *Metaphysics: An Introduction*, Chapters 10, 24. New York: Harper and Row, 1974. "Organic Logic: An Introductory Essay," *Dialogos* 40 (1982): 107-122. "Wholes and Parts of Things," *Contextos* 11:4 (1984) 7-26. "Holons: Three Conceptions," *Systems Research* 1:2 (1984): 145-150. *Polarity, Dialectic, and Organicity.* Springfield, Illinois: Charles C Thomas, 1970.

2. I am trying here, as elsewhere, to locate, if possible, any bases for certainty (or at least bases for prior absence of uncertainty that may serve as bases for some kind or degree of certainty at least analogically). Failure continues to be in prospect, but I must keep trying.

3. Roy Wood Sellars, *The Principles and Problems of Philosophy*, Chapters 3, 9. New York: The Macmillan Company, 1926.

4. William James, *The Meaning of Truth*, p. 218. New York: Longmans, Green and Company, 1909.

5. Archie J. Bahm, *Philosophy: An Introduction*, p. 155. New York: John Wiley and Sons, 1953.

6. *The Personalist* 28 (1947): 370-374.

7. Aristotle, *Metaphysics*, tr. by W. Ross, Second Edition, 1011b. Oxford: The Clarendon Press, 1928.

8. *The Southwestern Journal of Philosophy* 6:3 (Fall, 1975): 201.

9. Further criticisms of Naive Realism can be found in my *Philosophy: An Introduction*, pp. 38-49.

10. Roy Wood Sellars, *Critical Realism*. New York: Rand McNally & Company, 1916. See my *Philosophy: An Introduction*, Chapter 10, for a summary of Sellar's explanation of perceptual inference.

11. For details, see my *Metaphysics: An Introduction* and *Polarity, Dialectic, and Organicity*.

12. For example, John Dewey, *How We Think*, pp. 161-166. Boston: D.C. Heath & Co., 1910. John Dewey, *Essays in Experimental Logic*, pp. 137-142. Chicago: University of Chicago Press, 1916. John Dewey, *Experience and Nature*, pp. 218-222. Chicago: Open Court, 1925.

13. See my "Dialectics of Communication." *Contemporary Philosophy* 8:3 (1990): 1-4.

14. See my *The World's Living Religions*, Chapter 2. New York: Dell, 1964; and Joseph Campbell, *The Hero With a Thousand Faces*. New York: Bollingen Foundation, 1949.

15. See "The Cycle of Institutional Development," Charles Horton Cooley, Robert Cooley Angell, and Lowell Juliard Carr, *Introductory Sociology*, pp. 406-415. New York: Charles Scribner's Sons, 1933. Also my *Why Be Moral?*, pp. 376-479. Albuquerque: World Books, 1992; or *Ethics: The Science of Oughtness*, pp. 146-148. Amsterdam: Editions Rodopi, 1994.

16. See my: *Philosophy: An Introduction*, Chapter 20. New York: John Wiley, 1953. *Metaphysics: An Introduction*. New York: Harper and Row, 1974. *Polarity, Dialectic, and Organicity*, Springfield, Illinois: Charles C Thomas, 1970. "Wholes and Parts of Things," *Contextos* 2:4 (1984): 7-26. "The Nature of Existing Systems," *Systems Research* 3:3 (1986): 177-184. *The Philosopher's World Model*, pp. 118-146. Westport, Conn.: Greenwood Press, 1979.

17. See *Philosophy: An Introduction*, pp. 237-239.

18. *Science*, an official publication of the American Association for the Advancement of Science, of which I have been a reader since its beginning, is replete with articles reporting on current research.

19. *Philosophy: An Introduction*, p. 45.

20. *Polarity, Dialectic, and Organicity*, p. 280.

21. See *Philosophy: An Introduction*, pp. 4-417.

22. For my exposition of Asian philosophies, see my *The World's Living Religions*, Chapters 3-10. New York: Dell, 1964.

23. See also Robert S. Brumbaugh, *Unreality and Time*, Albany: SUNY Press, 1984, and my review of it in *International Studies in Philosophy* 19:3 (1987): 68-70.

24. See also *Polarity, Dialectic, and Organicity*, Chapters 2, 13-17, 19 and 20.

25. "What is Self? The Organicist Answer," *Darshana International* 2:1 (January: 1972): 9-35. *Why Be Moral?* Parts I and III (especially Chapters 2 and 3). *Ethics as a Behavioral Science*, Chapter 8. *Ethics: The Science of Oughtness*, Chapter 3. "Reflections by a Philosopher on Organicistic Psychology." *Genetic, Social, and General Psychology Monographs* 119:4 (November, 1993): 419-435.

26. See my *The Specialist: His Philosophy, His Disease, His Cure*. New Delhi: Macmillan of India, and Albuquerque: World Books, 1977.

27. Robert S. Woodworth, *Psychology: A Study of Mental Life*. New York: Henry Holt, 1921.

28. H. H. Price, *Perception*, London: Methuen and Co., 1932, Revised, 1950.

29. S. Howard Bartley, *Principles of Perception*, Second Edition, p. 15. New York: Harper and Row, 1958.

30. See my "Interdisciplinology: The Science of Interdisciplinary Research," *Nature and System* 2 (1980): 29-35, for a challenge to overcome this unnecessary kind of ignorance.

31. George O. Abel, David Morrison, and Sidney C. Wolff, *Exploration of the Universe, Sixth Edition*, p. 534. Philadelphia:

Saunders College Publishing (division of Holt, Rinehart and Winston), 1991.

32. Chicago: University Chicago Press, 1962.

33. I am indebted to an at-first-unbelievable theory expressed in *The Triple Key: A Primer of Basic Philosophy* by Rev. K. Sebastian (Jafna, Ceylon: Tritumakal Press, Chinakam, 1950), handed to me by a stranger on the streets of Banaras. The evidences that the author had assembled and used in his theory of language seem to me to provide considerable corroboration of the grunt theory of the origin of language, which I accept.

34. Albuquerque: University of New Mexico Press, 1945.

35. Princeton: D. Van Nostrand Company, 1967.

36. Glenview, Illinois: Scott Foresman and Co., 1969.

37. For further complications, see my "Dialectics of Communication," *Contemporary Philosophy* 13:3 (1990): 1-4.

38. See my *Why Be Moral?* which persistently explores the presence of organic unities in personal, social, and cosmic quests for ethical understanding.

39. See E. B. McGilvary, *Toward a Perspective Realism.* LaSalle, Illinois: Open Court Publishing Company, 1956, and A. E. Murphy, "Objective Relativism in Dewey and Whitehead," *Philosophical Review* 37 (1927): 121-144.

40. See Note 15.

41. I have offered some organistic suggestions in *Why Be Moral?*, Part 3.

42. Ranges of inference: Given the distinction between immediate, intermediate and mediate inferences, I recognize that variations in the ways that these kinds of inference shade into each other involve not only uncertainties regarding such shading but also that when persons become more familiar with inferences of one kind they tend to shift their intention more from intermediacy to immediacy and from mediacy to intermediacy.

Given the distinction between immediate and mediate inferences, one may regard the nature of inferences as ranging not only from immediate to mediate but also as ranging between two opposite poles, extreme immediacy and extreme mediacy.

If an extremely immediate inference occurs, e.g., "Nothing appears," while falling asleep or practicing yoga, and then disappears so that only awareness of appearance without any content (pure intuition) is in presence, knowledge ceases. Knowledge involves intuition as a universal condition, but pure intuition is not knowledge.

If an extremely mediate inference intends that the inferred object appears to be completely unlike any immediately intuited object, it exemplifies extreme mediacy. If an inference intends that the thing is so completely different that it cannot even appear, then knowledge ceases. Knowledge involves appearance as a universal condition, but intending non-appearance (inability to appear) (ignorance) is not knowledge.

# NOTES TO CHAPTER 3: GENERALIZATION

1. Charles F. Walraff, *Philosophical Theory and Psychological Fact*, p. 29. Tucson: The University of Arizona Press, 1961.

2. D. W. Gotschalk, *The Structure of Awareness*, p. 18. Urbana, Illinois: University of Illinois Press, 1969.

3. See Chapter 2, Note 25.

4. See Chapter 2, Note 14.

5. See my *The World's Living Religions*, Chapter 3. New York: Dell Publishing Co., 1964.

6. Bertrand Russell, *The Analysis of Matter*. p. 402. New York: Harcourt, Brace and Co., 1927.

7. See Chapter 11, "Time," in my *Metaphysics: An Introduction*.

8. *Science News Letter* 140:3 (July 20, 1991): 39.

9. *Science* 243: 4893 (February 17, 1989): 893.

10. *Physics Today* 19:3 (March, 1966): 23-31.

11. *Discover* 10:12 (November, 1989): 63.

12. Isaac Asimov, *The History of Physics*, p. 737. New York: Walker and Co., 1920, 1984.

13. See Appendix I.

# NOTES TO CHAPTER 4: MIND

1. Although this statement may seem to quote John Dewey's conception of functional behaviorism, I revise his conception by claiming that substance and function interdepend, so that whatever

exists functions as existing and whatever functions exists as functioning. Substance is not something "standing by itself" (the traditional definition which caused Dewey to reject it) but is anything that remains through change (something Dewey failed to recognize when he rejected the traditional definition). My view is that mind exists, and is substantial in whatever ways it remains through change. In this sense, each mind is a substance. Each of a mind's functions that remains through change is also substantial, and, in this sense, a substance.

2. "Mind" or "mindness" is something common to all minds. References to minds and mind in this chapter are intended to be limited to human minds, i.e., normal human minds. How much human minds are like or different from the minds of other animals or animate beings remains open for discussion.

3. See my *Metaphysics: an Introduction, Polarity, Dialectic and Organicity*, especially Chapter 2, and *Philosophy: An Introduction*, Part II, for evidence of its historical origin and development; "The Nature of Existing Systems," in *Systems Research* 3:3 (1986): 177-184; and "Holons: Three Conceptions," *Systems Research* 1:2 (1984): 145-150.

4. Ralph Barton Perry has generalized his definition of value as "any object of any interest." *General Theory of Value*, Chapter 5. New York: Longmans, Green and Co., 1926.

5. Dialectical interactions of a mind with its brain will receive consideration later, at least in the chapter on Mind-Body.

6. John Dewey, *How We Think*. Boston: D. C. Heath and Co., 1910.

7. *Axiology: The Science of Values*, pp. 14-49. Albuquerque: World Books, 1980.

8. Archie J. Bahm, "The Organicist Theory of Truth," *The Southwestern Journal of Philosophy* 6:3 (Fall, 1975): 198.

9. See my *Comparative Philosophy: Western, Indian and Chinese Philosophy Compared*, Chapter 3, for culturally inherited ideals regarding willfulness, will-lessness and willingness. Albuquerque: World Books, 1977.

10. For more on goodness and oughtness, see my *Axiology: The Science of Values.* Albuquerque: World Books, 1980, 1984; *Ethics: The Science of Oughtness.* Albuquerque: World Books 1980, 1984; *Ethics as a Behavioral Science*, Chapters 3, 6. Springfield, Ill.: Charles C Thomas, 1974; *Why Be Moral?* pp. 66-96, 107-124. New Delhi: Munshiram Manoharlal Publishers, 1980.

11. For further suggestions about how minds organize, see "General Characteristics of the Executive System," Chapter 5 in *Cognitive Psychology* by Barry E. Anderson. New York: Academic Press, 1975.

12. For my exposition of the philosophy of Gotama, see my *Philosophy of the Buddha.* New York: Harper & Brothers, 1958; and *The World's Living Religions*, pp. 97-104. New York: Dell Publishing Co., 1964.

13. Archie J. Bahm, *The Philosopher's World Model*, p. 189. Westport, Connecticut: Greenwood Press, 1979.

14. Newly-coined term.

# NOTES TO CHAPTER 5: MIND-BODY

1. Since this is so, the term "mind-body problem" serves to name this problem better than the phrase "mind and body problem" in which "and" connects two separate beings and "mind-body" connotes a single being having two interdepending and mutually-immanent parts.

2. Stephen Jay Gould, *Ontogeny and Phylogeny*, pp. 135-36, 146. Cambridge, Massachusetts: The Belnap Press of Harvard University Press, 1977.

3. See A. J. Bahm, *Metaphysics: An Introduction*, New York: Harper and Row, 1974; and *Polarity, Dialectic, and Organicity*, Springfield, Illinois: Charles C Thomas, 1970. Also "The Nature of Existing Systems," *Systems Research* 3:3 (1986): 177-184.

4. R.W. Sperry, "Mental Phenomena as Causal Determinants in Brain Function," in *Consciousness and the Brain: A Scientific Inquiry*, edited by Gordon C. Globus, Grover Maxwell, and Irwin Savodnik, pp. 170, 172. London: Plenum Press, 1976.

5. Alan E. Nourse, *The Body*, p. 147. New York: Time, Life Science Library, 1964.

6. Sperry, *ibid.*, 173, 174.

7. *Ibid.*, 175.

8. For more on relations, see *Metaphysics: An Introduction*, Chapter 13.

9. "Hol" means "whole" and "on" means "part."

10. See A. J. Bahm, "Holons: Three Conceptions," *Systems Research* 1:2 (1984): 145-150; and "The Nature of Existing Systems," *Systems Research* 3:3 (1986): 177-184. Also *Philosophy: An Introduction*, 237-238. New York: John Wiley, 1953.

11. For more on causation, see *Metaphysics: An Introduction*, Part 2.

12. Attention needs to be called to the commonly mistaken identification of freedom with determinism. Regarding freedom of will, a person is free whenever one is able to do what one wants to do. Since both what one wants to do and what one is able to do are caused (determined), one is free whenever what causes one to want and what causes one to be able are fitted to each other, freedom is naturally completely caused or determined. See "Freedom is Fitness," *The Scientific Monthly* 63 (August 1946): 135-136.

13. See A. J. Bahm, *Tao Teh King by Lao Tzu: Interpreted as Nature and Intelligence*, p. 42. New York: Unger Publishing Co., 1958.

14. For more dialectic, see *Metaphysics: An Introduction*, Chapters 34-37, and *Polarity, Dialectic, and Organicity*.

## NOTES TO CHAPTER 6: REASONING

1. William Sacksteter, "The Logic of Analogy," in *Philosophy and Rhetoric* 7:4 (Fall, 1974): 252.

2. Edwin A. Burtt, *Principles and Problems of Right Thinking*, p. 108. New York: Harper and Brothers, 1931, p. 108.

3. Alfred North Whitehead and Bertrand Russell, *Principia Mathematica*, Vol. 1, Second Edition, 1925, p. 217. London: Cambridge University Press.

4. L. S. Stebbing, *A Modern Introduction to Logic*, p. 253. New York: Thomas Y. Crowell, 1930.

5. "Organicism: The Philosophy of Interdependence," *International Philosophical Quarterly* 7:2 (June, 1967): 251-284.

6. See Appendix II.

7. *Polarity, Dialectic, and Organicity*, pp. 5-7.

8. *Ibid.*, p. 8.

9. *Ibid.*, pp. 9-10.

10. *Ibid.*, p. 11.

11. See my "Holons: Three Conceptions," *Systems Research* 1:2 (1984): 145-150.

12. *Metaphysics: An Introduction*, p. 164.

13. *Ibid.*, pp. 170-173.

14. *Ibid.*, pp. 50-51.

15. John Dewey, *How We Think*. Boston: D. C. Heath, 1910.

# NOTES TO CHAPTER 7: CONCLUSION

1. See my "Reflections by a Philosopher on Organicistic Psychology." *Genetic, Social, and General Psychology Monographs* 119:4 (November, 1993): 417-435.

2. See my *Metaphysics: An Introduction*. New York: Harper and Row, 1974.

# NOTES TO APPENDICES

### Appendix I. Subject-Object Theories

1. "Subject-Object Theories." Pre-printed in *Journal of Indian Council of Philosophical Research* 6:1 (September-December, 1988): 87-94. The second purpose of the appendix was not included. Omission of lines from charts made the article unintelligible.

### Appendix II. The Number One.

1. Pre-printed as "The Number One: More Than a Sum of Parts," *Contemporary Philosophy* 11:5 (September, 1986): 4-6.

# INDEX OF PERSONS